A MOST
UNGENTLEMANLY
WAY OF
WAR

A MOST UNGENTLEMANLY WAY OF WAR

The SOE and the Canadian Connection

Colonel Bernd Horn

Foreword by Lynn Philip Hodgson

DUNDURN
TORONTO

Design: Jennifer Gallinger
Cover design: Laura Boyle
Printer: Webcom

Library and Archives Canada Cataloguing in Publication

Horn, Bernd, 1959-, author
        A most ungentlemanly way of war : the SOE and the Canadian connection / by Colonel Bernd Horn ; with a foreword by Lynn Philip Hodgson.

Includes bibliographical references and index.
Issued in print and electronic formats.
ISBN 978-1-4597-3279-7 (paperback).--ISBN 978-1-4597-3280-3 (pdf).--
ISBN 978-1-4597-3281-0 (epub)

        1. Great Britain. Special Operations Executive. 2. World War, 1939-1945--
Secret service--Great Britain. 3. World War, 1939-1945--Secret service--Canada.
I. Title.

D810.S7H65 2015   940.54'8641   C2015-906081-8
                                                                  C2015-906082-6

1 2 3 4 5   20 19 18 17 16

Conseil des Arts du Canada   Canada Council for the Arts

ONTARIO ARTS COUNCIL
CONSEIL DES ARTS DE L'ONTARIO
an Ontario government agency
un organisme du gouvernement de l'Ontario

We acknowledge the support of the Canada Council for the Arts and the Ontario Arts Council for our publishing program. We also acknowledge the financial support of the Government of Canada through the Canada Book Fund and Livres Canada Books, and the Government of Ontario through the Ontario Book Publishing Tax Credit and the Ontario Media Development Corporation.

VISIT US AT
Dundurn.com | @dundurnpress | Facebook.com/dundurnpress | Pinterest.com/dundurnpress

Dundurn
3 Church Street, Suite 500
Toronto, Ontario, Canada
M5E 1M2

TABLE OF CONTENTS

Foreword   7
Introduction   9

1   With Backs to the Wall: Taking Back the Initiative   15
2   "Setting Europe Ablaze": The Creation of the SOE   25
3   A Man Called Intrepid: The Beginning of the   42
    Canadian Connection
4   Out of Europe: BSC and SOE Operations in the Americas   51
5   Killing Two Birds with One Stone: The Creation of Camp X   72
6   Shrouded in Secrecy: Training and the Introduction of   84
    Hydra at Camp X
7   Down to Business: Operations in Europe   95
8   "The Simplest Things in War ...": Clausewitzian Friction   117
9   Turning Theory to Reality: Canadians on SOE Operations   132
10 Reckoning: The Value of the SOE in the Second World War   154
11 Settling Accounts: The SOE at War's End   168

Acknowledgements   183
List of Abbreviations   185
Notes   188
Index   230
About the Author   239

FOREWORD

I am delighted to introduce *A Most Ungentlemanly Way of War: The SOE and the Canadian Connection*, particularly since some say I am the catalyst for the book. Having written, lectured, and given tours — including to audiences within the special operations community — on Camp X for over thirty years, I decided to float the idea of a larger history being written, one that would capture the Canadian SOE experience as part of the greater Canadian Special Operations Forces (CANSOF) legacy. I opened my archives and experience to the CANSOF historian, Colonel Bernd Horn, and he ably followed through.

The Canadian SOE experience, especially regarding Camp X (also known as Special Training School 103), is an important component of Canadian military history. Camp X and the Canadians who trained there as agents, as well as those individuals in key leadership roles such as the man called "Intrepid," namely Sir William Stephenson, played a critical role in destroying Hitler's Nazi regime. Cloaked in secrecy for decades, the full story of the SOE is only now beginning to see the full light of day. *A Most Ungentlemanly Way of War* is an important part of this disclosure, as it puts the entire Canadian effort and participation in the SOE into one volume.

I believe you will find the story in the following pages both enlightening and fascinating. Having immersed myself in the Camp X story for all these years, I am heartened to see the full story of Canada's contribution to the SOE captured in this book. I believe all Canadians will feel, as I do, proud once again of our national military legacy.

Lynn Philip Hodgson

INTRODUCTION

The loud, monotonous drone of the Whitley bomber's engines filled the darkened fuselage of the aircraft. Three shadowy forms sat astride the round belly hatch located in the centre of the plane. Their feet dangled in the hatch. It was virtually impossible to see anything to guess their altitude or location.

For the crew of the Whitley, it was just another mission to drop agents into occupied France. As the bomber flew low over the English Channel, the crew in the cockpit could easily make out the white tips of the waves breaking over the rough waters. As they neared the coast, all parties involuntarily tensed, realizing that enemy anti-aircraft guns or marauding Luftwaffe fighters on patrol could easily end their mission.

Safely over the coastal belt, the navigator indicated they were nearing their drop zone (DZ). The crew strained to see the bonfires arranged in a "T" that indicated the field where French Resistance fighters waited anxiously for the arrival of the agents and the canisters of supplies. As the plane flew further inland, the co-pilot flipped the toggle that triggered a light in the back of the airplane close to the belly hatch. As the red light came on, the flight engineer clamped his hand on Lieutenant Charles Gabriel's shoulder to get his attention. Gabriel nodded acknowledgement and immediately struck the thighs of his comrades sitting on either side of him. They all prepared to jump. All three agents now squirmed in place, room being too cramped to fully flex muscles to ensure no appendages had gone to sleep during the flight from England. Lieutenant

Gabriel, known to the Resistance fighters awaiting him below by his *nom de guerre*, Henri Moulin, steeled himself for the next phase. Once he propelled himself through the three-foot-deep hatch, he and his team would be on their own. Their year of preparation and training would be all they had to rely on.

Suddenly, the fuselage was illuminated by the dull green light that indicated it was time to go. Gabriel gave a thumbs-up to his colleagues and then pushed off with his two hands, propelling himself into the centre of the hatch, where he maintained a rigid, ramrod-straight posture to ensure he did not slam his face on the way out. He dropped to the ground below. The freefall seemed to be forever, but was really only mere seconds. The canopy of Gabriel's parachute opened fully and arrested his fall.

Where minutes earlier there was only the loud drone of engines, now Lieutenant Gabriel found himself in a tranquil solitude with only the soft wind whistling through the risers of his parachute breaking the silence. Down below, although bathed in darkness, Gabriel could make out the red glow of the bonfires. Unfortunately, they were somewhat distant. Gabriel realized immediately that the signal to jump had been too early; he would drop outside the DZ. Nonetheless, he figured his colleagues should make the DZ, or at least be right on its edge.

As he neared the earth, Gabriel felt the ground rushing up to him and he stretched his feet to meet it. The dark caused him to misjudge the distance and Gabriel hit hard and crumpled into the ground. He felt a sudden pain in his foot as he tried to get up and orient himself. He collapsed and rubbed his injured ankle. As he lay there he heard a crashing in the trees followed by a bang as some of the supply containers landed close by.

Gabriel got up and limped towards the noise, which was in the direction of the DZ. In the tranquility of the dark French countryside, Gabriel paradoxically felt as if he had all the time in the world. Then, as he began to tug at a container that was dangling a few feet from the ground, suspended from a tree by its parachute lines, the night erupted in a violent, angry outburst of noise. Several small explosions were followed by the distinctive retort of small arms, German, as well as British. The smooth, rhythmic staccato of a German MG 42 machine gun cut through the darkness, accentuated by its tracer as it stitched through the air. Clearly, a battle was underway.

For a moment Gabriel froze, thanking his luck for having missed the DZ. His thoughts were interrupted as he heard the banging and thrashing of brush directly to his front. In a panic he groped for his pistol, only to remember he had placed it on a suitcase to give him more flexibility for retrieving one of the canisters. Before he could find it, two silhouettes appeared before him.

"Henri," whispered Sergeant Guy Chartrand, using Gabriel's code name, "is that you?"

Gabriel breathed a sigh of relief. "Yes, Gilbert, it's me," he replied using Guy's code name, Gilbert Roulier. "What happened?"

"We were betrayed!" hissed the other apparition, Yves LeRoux, the local Resistance leader. "The bastards have infiltrated a number of our cells because of traitors in our ranks and the Boche have begun to roll up one cell after another." Anger and hatred radiated from LeRoux's face, even in the dark. "We must go, there is car nearby."

Despite the urgency, Gabriel hesitated.

LeRoux stopped, sensing Gabriel's dilemma. "There is nothing we can do for your friend, or my men," LeRoux stated emotionlessly. "They are either dead or on their way to 3 bis."

Three bis, Place des Etats-Unis, in Paris, was an infamous Gestapo prison. The agents had all been briefed on the Gestapo and their methodologies for extracting information. No one had pulled any punches. If they were caught, they could expect to be tortured — extensively and without mercy. Those who volunteered to serve with the Special Operations Executive (SOE) to conduct sabotage and subversion behind German lines in occupied Europe knew the risks and the consequences of being captured.

This drama played out for many SOE agents located in many different Axis-occupied countries. In the early days of the war, with Britain reeling from the German victory in France and the desperate British evacuation from the beaches of Dunkirk, Britain, and to a lesser degree its allies, found themselves in a position of extreme vulnerability. British heavy equipment was smoldering on the French coast and the way ahead looked bleak. Britain had to rebuild, re-equip, and retrain its army, all the while preparing for what was considered the inevitable invasion of England by Hitler.

Unfortunately, with the exception of economic blockade and strategic bombing, Britain had no apparent means of striking back. Nonetheless, the new prime minister, Winston Churchill, refused to accept a defensive mentality. Instead, he insisted on lashing out at the Germans and forcing them to relinquish at least some of the initiative. One means he actively pressed for was the ability to sabotage and subvert the German war effort and industry. He understood that the vast occupied territories and populations the Germans controlled represented their Achilles heel. Churchill believed if he could create an organization that could conduct sabotage, subversion, and assemble secret armies in the German-controlled areas, he could cut into the effectiveness of the enemy's war effort and force them to redirect military personnel and resources to the internal threat.

Despite the conventional military's long-standing philosophical aversion to guerrilla warfare and sabotage, a methodology they tended to view as a most ungentlemanly way of war, Churchill forced the change, and the SOE was born. The Canadian connection was not long in coming. Very quickly, it became evident that there was a lack of British personnel who were not only thoroughly acquainted with the target countries to which they were to be sent, but who also possessed the necessary cultural and linguistic skills. Moreover, those who would serve in the SOE would also need extreme levels of courage and tenacity as they were required to live the lives of fugitives, constantly on the alert, always hunted, and with the threat of torture and death always at their shoulder.

As a result, British recruiters tapped into the multicultural mosaic that was Canada. In fact, Canadians became the first non-British personnel to be selected for the highly secret SOE operations in the war. Canadians of Yugoslav, Italian, Hungarian, Romanian, and Bulgarian heritage were actively sought. French Canadians were recruited for their language proficiency, as were Chinese and Japanese Canadians. With the racial, linguistic, and cultural attributes and skills in place, it was only a matter of training the techniques of sabotage, subversion, and, ultimately, killing.

The recruitment of agents was not the only link between the SOE and Canada. A Canadian, Sir William Stephenson — known by many as the "Man Called Intrepid" — and his North American network became a key SOE asset, responsible for operations in North and South America. His link to the Americans, particularly J. Edgar Hoover, the head of the Federal Bureau of Investigation (FBI), and Colonel Bill Donovan, the director of the Office of Strategic Services (OSS), made him invaluable to British/American relations with regard to SOE operations.

Additionally, Canada became the home of SOE Special Training School (STS) 103, commonly known as Camp X, where agents underwent their first phase of training. The school also covertly opened its doors to American FBI and OSS agents prior to the US entry into the war. The neophyte Americans had their first taste of the shadow war in Canada, and would later take what they had learned to their own schools back home.

Finally, located in Camp X was Hydra, the top secret British communications facility that encrypted and decrypted all secret messages between Britain and stations in the Western Hemisphere. It was also the only means by which to send Ultra traffic (top secret intercepted German coded messages) from London to North America.

Remarkably, the SOE's contribution to the Allied war effort is still debated. Some of its files remain classified to this day, which speaks to the sensitivity of its actions during the war and, arguably, to its accomplishments. Undisputedly, the SOE was a unique wartime creation that represented innovation, adventure, and a fanaticism by its personnel to the Allied cause. With extreme courage, tenacity, and guile, and an underlying "end justifies the means" approach to war, the SOE, in consonance with Churchill's directive and with an ever-present Canadian nexus, set Europe ablaze.

1

WITH BACKS TO THE WALL: TAKING BACK THE INITIATIVE

The high-pitched wail of the JU 87 Stuka dive-bombers as they streaked toward the ground to deliver their lethal payload filled the air and instilled near panic in the French defenders guarding the Meuse River defensive line. No sooner had the sound of the aircraft stopped than the roar of German artillery began. The sound of explosions throwing earth and human debris into the air reached a crescendo just as the lead elements of the German assault formations advanced. Soon the throaty roar of powerful twelve-cylinder Maybach engines reverberated through the Ardennes forests as the clanking and creaking of the Mark IV tanks thread their way forward through what most had discounted as a probable approach for an armoured thrust.

The Allies were in disarray. Arguably, they had been for a long time. By 1939, despite Hitler's provocative moves (the rearmament of Germany, the annexation of Austria, the occupation of the Sudetenland, and annexation of parts of Czechoslovakia), the Allies were hesitant, if not reluctant, to go to war. However, Germany's invasion of Poland forced the issue, largely due to alliance guarantees. Nonetheless, it appeared that there was little Britain and France could do. On September 1, 1939, the German Army, consisting of 1,250,000 men in 60 divisions, 9 of which were armoured, cut a swath of destruction through Poland. The country fell in less than a month. The use of the aptly titled *Blitzkrieg* (lightning war) tactic, which combined tanks, armoured vehicles, and close support aircraft, created an impressive offensive capability empowered by surprise, speed, mobility, and destructive power. It appeared to be the perfect marriage of fire and movement.

In the aftermath of the victory over Poland, Hitler halted his war machine. Hitler had gambled that the Allies would not act. As such, he left his western frontier practically undefended, utilizing second-rate frontier troops to guard the border. He allocated his best forces for the attack on Poland. Once his new prize was secured, Hitler halted further offensive action, which led to a stalemate on the western front as Germany faced down Britain and France along the French border. Belgium and Holland maintained strict neutrality in the naive hope that they would be spared the impending showdown. Through the lens of history, it appears as though the Allies gave up a golden opportunity to strike at — and perhaps defeat — Germany early on.

The "Phoney War" dragged on through the winter months. Then, in April of 1940, German forces seized Norway and Denmark. Few doubted that France and the Low Countries would be next.

The Allies had apparently learned nothing in the period after the First World War, or from the German invasion of Poland and the Scandinavian countries. They still clung to their First World War experience and doctrine as they prepared for a replay of the Great War. The majority of the British Expeditionary Force (BEF), approximately four hundred thousand strong, along with their French allies, stuck to the "Dyle Plan" and waited for what seemed the inevitable German sweep through northern Belgium and Holland. Their plan was to counterattack the enemy and halt them as they had done in the First World War.[1]

The Germans, however, had not spent the two decades since the end of the First World War idly. They evolved their tactics. They focused on speed, mobility, and combat power at the main point of effort, or *schwerpunkt*, of their attack.

On May 10, 1940, Germany struck. In total, 2.5 million German soldiers, divided in 104 infantry divisions, 9 motorized divisions and 10 armoured divisions, supported by 3,500 combat aircraft, smashed into France and the Low Countries.[2]

German Major-General F.W. von Mellenthin later revealed:

> In November 1939, the German plan of attack in the West was very similar to the famous Schlieffen Plan of World War I, i.e. the schwerpunkt was to be the right wing, but swinging a little wider than in 1914 and including Holland....[3] All ten of Germany's panzer divisions, grouped under Army Group B, were assigned to this mission. Meanwhile, Army Group A was responsible for penetrating the Ardennes and advancing up the line of the Meuse River with infantry, while Army Group C fought a defensive battle facing the Allied Maginot line.[4]

Nonetheless, an unfortunate blunder by a German courier changed the fate of the Allies. A Luftwaffe officer, who, contrary to standing orders, flew at night with important papers containing references to the planned invasion, inadvertently crossed the Belgian frontier and was compelled to make a forced landing on Belgian soil. As Hitler and the German high command were unsure whether the plan was compromised or not, an alternate scheme was required. The Manstein Plan now captured Hitler's imagination, even though the majority of the old German high command insisted it was too risky, if not reckless.[5]

The Manstein Plan, devised by Major-General Erich von Manstein, and favoured by most of the new breed of German generals who believed in the power of mobility and speed, still centred on the concept of three army groups sweeping through the Low Countries and France. The difference, however, lay in the emphasis of the main point of effort. The Manstein Plan put the focus on Army Group A. In a risky gambit, Manstein proposed that the bulk of the panzer forces be sent through the confining Ardennes forests in a bold thrust that would hopefully catch the Allies by surprise and cut off their forces in the North, in Belgium and Holland. Army Group B would swing through Belgium and Holland (much like the Schlieffen Plan of the First World War) and draw the Allied forces away from the main blow in the Ardennes. The Allied forces rushing to block what they believed to be the German main effort in the North would then be cut off once Army Group A sliced through the Ardennes and reached the coast. Army Group C would continue to fight a defensive holding action facing the vaunted, impregnable Maginot line.[6] Major-General (later Field Marshal) Manstein was convinced that the real chance lay with Army Group A, and consisted in launching a surprise attack through the Ardennes — where the enemy would certainly not be expecting any armor because of the terrain. He realized this was the only way "of destroying the enemy's entire northern wing in Belgium preparatory to winning a final victory in France."[7]

Manstein's belief in mobility and armoured force proved to be right. "The whole campaign," Major-General von Mellenthin concluded, "hinged on the employment of armor, and was essentially a clash of principles between two rival schools." He insisted, "The Battle of France was won by the German Wehrmacht because it reintroduced in warfare the decisive factor of mobility. It achieved mobility by the combination of firepower, concentration, and surprise, together with expert handling of the latest modern arms — Luftwaffe, parachutists and armor."[8]

General, the Viscount Gort, the BEF commander-in-chief, agreed. He observed, "So ended a campaign of 22 days which has proved that the offensive has once more gained ascendency in modern war when undertaken with an army equipped with greatly superior material power in the shape of air forces and armoured fighting vehicles." He added:

> The speed with which the enemy exploited his penetration of the French front, his willingness to accept risks to further his aim, and his exploitation of every success to the uttermost limits emphasized, even more fully than in the campaigns of the past, the advantage which accrues to the commander who knows how best to use time to make time his servant and not his master.
>
> Again, the pace of operations has been so accelerated by the partnership between offensive aircraft and modern mechanised forces that the reserves available for the defence are of little use unless they are fully mobile or already in occupation of some reserve position.[9]

In the end, the enemy's speed and nature of the multi-dimensional battlefield simply paralyzed the Allied forces deployed to defeat the enemy offensive. The German success, as already noted, was due to mobility, which was achieved by a combination of concentration, firepower, surprise, and combined-arms co-operation. The destruction of the West took forty-six days, but it was decided in only ten.[10] As such, on the night of June 2, 1940, the last of the British and French soldiers were evacuated from the beaches of Dunkirk, France. The desperate withdrawal resulted in the loss of virtually all their heavy equipment, weapons, and vehicles.[11] Moreover, Britain now braced for what seemed to be the inevitable conclusion to the German master plan — the invasion of England.

Devoid of any major equipment or weapons and encumbered by a doctrine and war-making methodology that was now clearly defunct, England was on the precipice of disaster. Simultaneously, it had to re-equip, rebuild, and retrain its armed forces, and also prepare the island for defence. It seemed that Britain had no other choice but to surrender the initiative and dig in and wait for the inescapable onslaught.

This logic represented the thinking of most of the British military high command. Overwhelmed by the task ahead of them, they saw only a defensive battle — at least in the short term. The only two forms of offensive action they considered were the traditional economic blockade, utilizing the superiority of the Royal Navy on the high seas, and strategic bombing. One lesson taken from the First World War was the importance of long-range bombers. The lingering psychological effect of the 1917 Zeppelin bombing raids on London had struck home, and Britain invested heavily in strategic bombers during the interwar years. As such, after the debacle in France, the bombing fleet was one of the only offensive tools capable of physically striking back at Nazi Germany.[12]

Not all the top decision makers in Britain were satisfied with a defensive strategy. Even though British equipment was still smouldering on the beaches of Dunkirk, the combative new prime minister, Winston Churchill, declared in the House of Commons on June 4, 1940, that "we shall not be content with a defensive war."[13] He was well aware that to win a war meant, ultimately, offensive action. Moreover, only through offensive action could an army provide the needed confidence and battle experience to its soldiers and leaders. Furthermore, he strongly believed that only offensive action could sustain public and military morale — offensive action represented a shift in initiative. By striking at the enemy, an opponent is forced to take defensive measures that represent a diversion of scarce resources. The more an antagonist is required to allocate forces and energy on defending his territory, the weaker becomes his ability to launch expeditionary initiatives.

For that reason, Churchill directed General Hastings Ismay, his principal military adviser, to liaise with the Joint Chiefs of Staff Committee to develop a more offensive approach. Churchill railed, "We are greatly concerned ... with the dangers of the German landing in England.... Why should it be thought impossible for us to do anything of the same kind to them? We should immediately set to work to organize self-contained, thoroughly-equipped raiding units."[14]

For Churchill, it was about the initiative. He insisted that the Germans should not be left to focus their attention on concentrating their forces for the attack. He also wanted them to suffer the insecurity of postulating where the next attack would occur. Specifically, the prime minister was adamant that the Germans would not force the British "to wall in the island and roof it over!"[15] Churchill's close ally, Vice-Admiral Lord Louis Mountbatten, agreed. "We cannot win this war," Mountbatten proclaimed, "by bombing and blockade alone."[16]

Churchill was relentless. Two days later he sent yet another missive to Ismay. "Enterprises must be prepared," he directed, "with specially trained troops of the hunter class who can develop a reign of terror down these coasts, first of all on the butcher and bolt policy; but later on, or perhaps as soon as we are organized, we should surprise Calais or Boulogne, kill and capture the Hun garrison and hold the place until all the preparations to reduce it by siege or heavy storm have been made, and then away." However, his direction to Ismay was not enough. Churchill next targeted the Joint Chiefs of Staff Committee: "Propose [to] me measures for a vigorous, enterprising, and ceaseless offensive against the whole German-occupied coastline," he ordered. Churchill also demanded plans for deep inland raids that left "a trail of German corpses behind."[17]

Churchill's detailed instructions were also passed to the Chief of the Imperial General Staff (CIGS), General Sir John Dill. Knowing Churchill's impatience, the CIGS quickly passed the issue to one of his general staff officers, Lieutenant-Colonel Dudley W. Clarke. Clarke was now responsible for determining methods by which the British Army could nurture an offensive spirit until it was in a position to resume the offensive. Clarke fully understood the challenge. "The mind of the entire nation — and above all of the Army," Clarke observed, "had been turned violently to Defence to the exclusion of all else." Clarke, much like Churchill, however, understood that "even the lightest threats, if only they could be produced, must compel the Germans to turn in the midst of their feverish invasion preparations to organize defence and divert troops to guard this enormous front line [occupied Europe]."[18]

For Clarke, who grew up in the Transvaal and was raised on stories of how the outnumbered Boer commandos had defied Britain and tied down thousands of troops for years, the solution came quickly: guerrilla operations. His childhood stories were reinforced by his study of military history, as well as his own experience in Palestine in 1936 during the Arab Rebellion, where armed Arab bands tied down an entire British Army corps and their auxiliaries.[19] Not surprisingly, he proposed guerrilla warfare as the best model for the British Army to adopt under the circumstances.

As such, Lieutenant-Colonel Clarke recommended that "commandos" — the term taken directly from the Boer War experience — be established to create a threat to divert German resources and restore the offensive spirit to the British Army.[20] Churchill leapt on the idea immediately. After all, it appealed to his character and love of the offensive.

Winston Churchill, himself an accomplished adventurer, journalist, and soldier, held a heroic and romantic image of war. Moreover, he maintained "an almost abstract attachment to the offensive."[21] He believed that audacity and willpower constituted the only sound approach to the conduct of war.[22] In fact, Churchill confided to President Franklin D. Roosevelt, "[The] essence of defence is to attack the enemy upon us — leap at his throat and keep the grip until the life is out of him."[23]

His overpowering ardour for the offensive, however, caused great consternation amongst his generals. General Archibald Wavell grumbled that Churchill "always accused commanders of organizing 'all tail and no teeth.'"[24] Similarly, General Sir Alan Brooke lamented that the prime minister was "like a child that has set its mind on some forbidden toy." He elaborated that "It is no good explaining that it will cut his fingers or burn him. The more you explain, the more fixed he becomes in his idea."[25] The resistance of many of Churchill's senior generals, who felt that valuable resources were being frittered away for no valuable return at a time when the nation faced invasion, was to no avail. Churchill pressed on.[26]

In a remarkable display of military efficiency, by June 8, 1940, General Dill received approval for the creation of the commandos, and that same afternoon Section MO9 of the War Office was established. Four days later, Churchill appointed Lieutenant-General Sir Alan Bourne, the adjutant-general of the Royal Marines as "Commander of Raiding Operations on Coasts in Enemy Occupation and Advisor to the Chiefs of Staff on Combined Operations."[27]

The commandos became only one of many Allied Special Operations Forces (SOF) organizations (others included the Long Range Desert Group (LRDG), Special Air Service (SAS), Special Boat Service (SBS), and the First Special Service Force (FSSF)) that would be created in the early years of the war to take the fight to the Germans until the conventional forces were built up enough to renew the offensive. Although they proved to be effective, their ability to blunt German military capability was extremely limited. For example, when special troops were used in a SOF capacity by the Germans, the BEF commander reported, parachute troops, "though effectively employed in Holland, were less used against the BEF; however, the nuisance value of those which were employed, by their interference with railway, telephone and telegraph communications in rearward zones, was altogether out of proportion to their numbers."[28]

The entire premise of guerrilla warfare, or creating chaos behind an opponent's front line, was not a totally new concept. As early as March 1938, British planners in MI6, which was also known as the Secret Intelligence Service (SIS), had already established a new department "to plan, prepare and, when necessary, carry out sabotage and other clandestine operations, as opposed to the gathering of intelligence."[29] The new organization was titled Section "D," the "D" referring to destruction. The cell was also commonly referred to as Section IX. By May 31, 1938, they had gone so far as to conduct a preliminary survey of possible targets for sabotage, mainly in Germany, which included the electrical supply system, telephone communications, railways, and defilement of food supplies and agriculture through the dissemination of pests to crops or diseases to animals. The head of the SIS was convinced of the need to use both propaganda and terrorism against Germany and Italy, to the point that by February 1939, he was trying to convince his counterparts in Allied countries of the necessity. Section D (IX) had gone so far that by 1939, they had established a presence at Bletchley Park to develop sabotage material that included incendiaries, plastic explosives, and fuses.[30]

Concurrently, the General Staff (Research) (GS(R)), later renamed Military Intelligence (Research) (MI(R)) department of the British War Office, was examining the potential employment of guerrilla warfare. Not surprisingly, both GS(R) and Section "D" developed plans during the pre-war period in anticipation of German aggression. As such, they discussed creating small sabotage parties that would be stationed in countries that were threatened by potential German invasion. At the same time, MI(R) examined the feasibility of creating "secret armies" of guerrilla fighters who could resist German occupation and assist the Allied cause. They too looked at German targets to sabotage.[31]

There was yet a third organization during the pre-war period that was created to fight in the shadows. The Foreign Office established a Department of Propaganda. Its headquarters was located at 84 Moorgate Road in the Electra House Building. As a result, it was commonly referred to as Department EH (Electra House). This department was responsible for "black," or unattributable, propaganda.[32]

British planners clearly understood the value of sabotage and guerrilla operations. They also realized that German victories would leave the conquerors with a critical weakness. Namely, as the Germans occupied more territory they would become overextended. Moreover, the Allies could exploit national resistance as a weapon. And as the Germans became more repressive to stamp out the Resistance, the greater was the opportunity for recruitment of more insurgents.[33]

The scene had already been set psychologically for an approach to the war that would take the fight more directly to the Germans despite the dilemma that faced the Allies. Churchill was not mentally prepared to allow the Germans free reign, to control the initiative, and decide when and where to focus British military forces. He was intent on taking back the initiative and forcing the Germans to dissipate their resources by continually looking over their shoulder, wondering, preparing for the next Allied strike by whatever means possible.

2

"SETTING EUROPE ABLAZE": THE CREATION OF THE SOE

Over time, commando and SOF actions proved to be extremely effective. They fed an offensive attitude, provided combat experience, and forced the Germans to place more emphasis on defending the occupied coastlines. Furthermore, the actions destroyed German war materials and economic capacity and delivered a number of important tactical and strategic victories, particularly the capture of German Enigma coding equipment and radar technology. Nonetheless, in the early days of the war as one country after another fell to Hitler's onslaught, not many senior Allied leaders believed raiding actions, even when combined with the strategic bombing of enemy cities, could wear down or attrite German military capability quickly enough to slow its relentless progress. Clearly, until Allied military power could be rebuilt, additional measures were required.

Somewhat surprising was that even the conservative, conventionally minded senior political and military decision makers desperately grasped at the concept of irregular warfare to strike back at the Germans. After all, the dire situation called for desperate action. If that meant supporting what many perceived as left wing, insurrectionist revolutionaries on the Continent, so be it. After all, in the immediate aftermath of the drubbing of the Allied armies in Europe, rumour spread quickly that the defeat was assisted by German fifth columnist working behind Allied lines. Although the rumours were later proved false, at the time, the perception remained. If it worked for the Germans, why not for Britain?

As such, focus on Section D, MI(R), and Department EH suddenly increased.[1] The idea of bolstering the strength of these entities began in March 1940, when the Joint Intelligence Committee (JIC) drafted a proposal for an Inter-Service Projects Board to coordinate irregular activities. The British Chiefs of Staff Committee informally accepted the concept, and the board met often over the next two months; however, little concrete action came of it.[2] Events in Europe quickly changed the attitudes of those involved, however. On May 19, 1940, the Chiefs of Staff Committee began to look at irregular warfare in a more serious light and began to consider the requirement for a special organization. In the chaos of the time they concluded:

> The only other method [aside from economic block-ade and bombing] of bringing about the downfall of Germany is by stimulating the seeds of revolt within the conquered territories. The occupied countries are likely to prove a fruitful ground for these operations, partic-ularly when economic conditions begin to deteriorate.
>
> In the circumstances envisaged, we regard this form of activity as of the highest importance. A special organ-isation will be required and plans to put these operations into effect should be prepared, and all the necessary preparations and training should be proceeded with as a matter of urgency.[3]

Six days later, on May 25, the Chiefs of Staff submitted a report to the War Cabinet that stated, "Germany might still be defeated by economic pressure, by a combination of air attack on economic objectives in Germany and on German morale, and the creation of widespread revolt in her conquered territories." Later in the report, they went on to say that "the only method of bringing about the downfall of Germany is by stimulating the seeds of revolt within the conquered territories." The

Chiefs of Staff asserted once again that they considered "this form of activity as of the highest importance."[4]

Over the next several weeks a myriad of discussions between the War Office, SIS, and various ministers transpired in an attempt to find a solution to how best create the necessary organization. By June 29, 1940, a report from a meeting held by the foreign secretary recommended concentrating the various secret services (Section D, EH, and MI(R)) under one organization. It went as far as to recommend divorcing Section D entirely from SIS, which was more concerned with intelligence. Of importance was the continuing debate on the nature of the organization, whether it would be under military authority, or whether it should be a separate ministry such as a Ministry of Political Warfare.

Dr. Hugh Dalton, an outspoken, ambitious, socialist-leaning, Labour minister, was insistent the new organization not fall under military control. He believed, "Regular soldiers are not fit to stir up revolution, to create social chaos, or to use all those ungentlemanly means of winning the war which come so easily to the Nazis."[5] Dalton, who was a member of the wartime coalition government and in charge of the Ministry of Economic Warfare, which included "black" propaganda — namely lies and misinformation — insisted that the new organization responsible for creating these movements in the Nazi-occupied territories must operate "entirely independent" of ordinary governmental, departmental, or Cabinet rules and supervision. He even included the War Office in the exclusion of a supervisory role. Demonstrating an apparent understanding of what was required, he explained that the key to success was not only the exemption from oversight, but also "a certain fanatical enthusiasm" by those in the secret special organization.[6] He stated:

> We must organise movements in every occupied territory comparable to the Sinn Fein movement in Ireland, to the Chinese guerrillas now operating against Japan, to the Spanish Irregulars who played a notable part in Wellington's campaign or — one might as well admit it — to the organisations which the Nazis themselves have developed so remarkably in almost every country of the

world. We must use many different methods, including industrial and military sabotage, labour agitations and strikes, continuous propaganda, terrorist acts against traitors and German leaders, boycotts and riots.[7]

By July 8, Winston Churchill, the eternal proponent of audacious offensive action and an individual always willing to entertain new ideas, pressed Neville Chamberlain, now the lord president of the War Cabinet committee, to ascertain what progress had been made on development of the new organization responsible for irregular warfare. Momentum now propelled the initiative forward.

Churchill, like Dalton, supported the need for a single organization to coordinate irregular warfare activities. As he was apt to do, Churchill invited Dalton to dinner and drinks late one evening in order to further explore the concept. Later that night, the prime minister offered Dalton the job of heading up a "new instrument of war," officially called the Special Operations Executive (SOE) or, unofficially, as Churchill preferred, the "Ministry of Ungentlemanly Warfare." Prior to dismissing Dalton for the evening, Churchill commanded the new SOE head, "now, set Europe ablaze!"[8]

Churchill was quick to announce the creation of SOE to his War Cabinet. On July 19, Chamberlain penned, "The Prime Minister has further decided, after consultation with the Ministers concerned, that a new organization shall be established forthwith to co-ordinate all action, by way of subversion and sabotage, against the enemy overseas."[9] The War Cabinet subsequently approved the new SOE and its charter on July 22, 1940.

With Churchill's directive, Section D was cut and turned into the new SOE. The change happened so quickly that the head of the SIS was only notified after the fact. SOE also absorbed EH and MI(R). Although the amalgamation was executed swiftly, there was agreement by the two heads of the separate organizations that encrypted signals traffic would be passed through SIS. Furthermore, they agreed that any information of potential intelligence value that the SOE collected would also be shared with the SIS. Finally, key to the agreement was the understanding that the SOE would not approach SIS agents without first seeking approval from SIS headquarters.[10]

The mandate and objectives given to Dalton and the SOE were almost unlimited. The prime minister's charter to the SOE instructed them "to undertake subversive action of every sort and description against the enemy." It had a twofold objective. The first was to exploit "every present means of harassing the enemy and damaging his war effort." The second was to assist in the organization of secret armies "by arranging for the supply of personnel, communications, arms and explosives etc., and by strengthening any underground propaganda that may be necessary to the ultimate objective of embarking on large-scale operations."[11]

The SOE was given both short- and long-term objectives. The short-term policy of SOE was to create as much administrative difficulty as possible for the Axis powers. Planned measures varied "from the encouragement of venality amongst officials and of 'go slow' movements in industry, to active sabotage of shipping, factories and transportation facilities. The SOE also attempted to create a 5th Column organisation with the object of assisting eventual military re-occupation."[12]

The long-term objective of the SOE was aimed at organizing a concerted rising amongst the peoples of the occupied territories. This objective entailed maintaining pro-Allied sentiment in the occupied territories, as well as fostering active anti-Axis movements. Specific instruction detailed the requirement. The SOE policy stated:

> In all countries now occupied or likely to be occupied by the Axis powers we must establish:
>
> a. An organisation to carry out skilled sabotage and raids which, combined with air and seaborne raids from overseas, will reduce the vital resources of the Axis. This sabotage organisation, assisted by propaganda from overseas, will also be responsible for fostering a campaign of passive resistance and

minor sabotage amongst the population with the object of reducing Axis morale.

b. An organisation of secret armed forces that can co-operate in any military offensive we may be able to take in the future and so compensate for our lack of trained troops.[13]

To achieve the necessary effect, Dalton was given sweeping powers. By a clear War Cabinet ruling, the SOE was not to be the subject of Parliamentary discussion.[14] But Dalton was expected to receive directives from the Chiefs of Staff Committee; guidance from the Foreign Office regarding objectives for underground political activity in enemy-occupied countries, as well as control and direction with regards to neutral countries; and guidance from the Dominions Office, Colonial Office, and India Office regarding activities in their respective spheres of administration. On top of that, the SOE was also to be open to requests for certain special activities to be undertaken on behalf of Government Departments, such as the Treasury, the Foreign Office, Ministry of Economic Warfare, the Ministry of Supply, the India Office, the Dominions Office, the Colonial Office, and the Admiralty.

Attempting to serve so many masters can only create difficulty and frustration for an organization. Nonetheless, Dalton organized the SOE to maximize its effectiveness. Of great significance was the fact that the SOE, as an organization and concept, was completely new. Very few had given much thought to, and most were still suspicious of, irregular war activities. As such, the SOE was an "enormous experiment." All of the SOE's participants were playing with elements and situations of which they had little to no previous experience. The system was constantly evolving, with few precedents to guide it. As one noted historian remarked, "Costly mistakes were inevitable."[15]

Despite the lack of institutional experience, the SOE was initially organized into three functional branches that reflected its originating elements — EH was rechristened SO 1 (propaganda), and Section D was recast as SO 2 (operations). A third entity called SO 3, which became responsible for planning and intelligence, was also created; however, it was disintegrated by September 1940 and its elements were absorbed into SO 2. For SO 1 operations there were two forms of propaganda. One was titled "preparational," intending to produce merely a sympathetic frame of mind to Allied causes. The other was "operational," which intended to persuade people to take action on behalf of the Allies.[16]

For the War Cabinet and the Chiefs of Staff Committee, the presentation of news was an important weapon in the conduct of political warfare. For example, as early as November 25, 1940, the Chiefs of Staff ordered that "subversive activities should be given preference over the [organization of] secret armies in occupied territories." As a result, broadcasting stations, or Research Units (RU) as they were called, with content aimed specifically to shape audiences in Germany, Italy, and occupied Europe began to broadcast starting in November 1940. "We want to spread disruptive and disturbing news among the Germans which will induce them to distrust their government and disobey," Sefton Delmer, the head of SO 1 revealed. He clarified, "Not so much from high-minded political motives as from ordinary human weakness.... [The listener] finds that we are anti-communists who once thought Hitler pretty good, fought alongside him in fact, but are now appalled at the corruption, godlessness, profiteering, place-hunting, selfishness, clique rivalries and Party-above-the-law system which the Party has."[17]

Despite the importance of SO 1, or perhaps because it, on August 27, 1941, the continuing rivalry and struggle between the Ministry of Economic Warfare (responsible for SO 1) and the Ministry of Information over their relative responsibilities for propaganda and the dissemination of information resulted in the merging of SO 1 with the Ministry of Information, as well as the propaganda wing of the British Broadcasting Corporation (BBC). They formed a new independent organization entitled the Political Warfare Executive (PWE). From this point on, the SOE consisted solely of SO 2.

SO 2 (operations) was now renamed simply SOE. It was broken into country directorates, with each respective country directorate divided into one or more sections. For example, France had six distinct sections within its directorate. The official SOE policy articulated:

The activities of SO 2[SOE] may be divided as follows:

a. <u>Direct Action</u> which embraces all operations requiring some degree of force, such as Savanna,[18] or projected attacks on certain power stations in France. Direct action is limited to countries now occupied by Germany.

b. <u>Indirect Action</u> covers every means from clandestine sabotage to moral disintegration and may take place in any country where the Germans are undertaking activities in support of their war effort.[19]

As such, the SOE was engaged in training agents and organizers, as well as deploying them into the various target countries with the object of establishing basic subversive organizations that could be expanded as required and as the situation allowed. The main functions of the subversive organizations were explained as:

a. <u>Political Subversion and Propaganda</u>: to encourage the population of the occupied countries against the forces of occupation and to undermine the morale of the latter.

b. <u>Sabotage</u>: to build up a sabotage organization wherever the Axis can be effectively attacked, which is mainly in the occupied territories. The object of this activity is to wear down the Axis morally and economically and so hasten the date by which our military forces can take the offensive. Sabotage efforts must be correlated with those of the fighting services especially the bomber forces, and our present short term policy is, therefore, based on the instructions recently given to Bomber Command whose efforts we intend to supplement by attacking rail, sea, canal and road transport. The sabotage organization must also be prepared to harass the Axis lines of communication, should Great Britain be invaded, and to intensify its activities in close co-operation with any allied invasion of the continent.

c.   The Organization of Secret Armies: To build up and equip secret armies in occupied territories. These armies, in co-operation with the sabotage organizations, will be prepared to assist our military forces when they take the offensive, either directly in the theatre of operations or indirectly elsewhere, by attacks on communications, whether telegraphic or transport, by neutralization of seizure of aerodromes, by a general attack on enemy aircraft and personnel, and by producing disorder in the enemy's rearward services.[20]

In essence, the SOE was charged with carrying out subversive warfare against the Axis by any method that suited the circumstances, albeit in accordance with the overriding policy expressed by the War Cabinet and to the interests of other Departments of State.[21]

Key to the SOE's initial success was the November 1940 arrival of Colonel Colin Gubbins, who had been released from the Auxiliary Units, an organization for guerrilla warfare in England. He brought with him many credentials. Of note, he had been a key component of MI(R) from the beginning, had commanded the independent guerrilla companies in Norway during the German invasion, and was the author of a series of pamphlets for the War Office on the principles of guerrilla warfare and sabotage. Gubbins, who would later head the SOE, was first responsible for training and the conduct of operations planned and executed by the respective country sections.[22] His experience and leadership helped the burgeoning organization move forward and prosecute missions.

And move forward it did. However, although Dalton had secured autonomous control over the SOE, there was still a degree of oversight and coordination. Integral to this was the SO 2 Executive Committee, later named the SOE Council, which consisted of the heads of the various government and military branches. It met once or twice a week for the lifespan of SOE.

Getting the organization up and running was only one of the challenges. Although initially there was a desperate appeal to the idea of subversion, sabotage, and guerrilla warfare as a means to defeat Germany, once the initial shock of the fall of France dissipated and the looming spectre of an invasion drifted away, senior military commanders quickly distanced themselves from the idea that irregular warfare would win the day. Instead, they withdrew to their previous perspective of disdain. By September 4, 1940, the Chiefs of Staff forwarded a report to the War Cabinet that declared, "Subversive operations must be regarded as a strictly supplementary course of action, and must conform with regular operations undertaken as part of our strategic plans." Objectives for the SOE were clearly set out:

    a. Sabotage of key plants, commodities and communications, to supplement the effects of the blockade and air attack;

    b. the containing and extending of as many of the enemy's forces as possible, thus forcing him to expend his military resources; and

    c. the preparation of the requisite conditions for a general rising of subject populations to synchronize with the final military pressure we exert on Germany and Italy or to coincide with land operation in any particular theatre.[23]

Dalton and his staff had to quickly sort out not only what was required but how to do it. SOE documents capture the early philosophical and practical complexity. For example, one SOE memorandum noted, "It is, therefore, an appropriate moment to-day to take stock of the revolutionary potential in Europe at the present time in order to determine how SOE, recently constituted the official midwife of revolutions, may ease the birth pangs and minimize the danger of stillbirth." It went on to reveal, "It is, nevertheless, SOE's task in the present struggle to harness such revolutionary potential as exists in Europe to-day and to direct it to the best advantage of the Allied war effort."[24] As the growing pains were worked out, specific lines of operation slowly fell out for the SOE. These were subversion, sabotage, the raising of secret armies, and the conduct of guerrilla warfare.

SOE planners made a deliberate decision early on to separate the sabotage cells from any creation of a secret army. Although both could be controlled from the United Kingdom, separation would ensure that if one component was compromised, the other would not be affected. This separation was critical since both activities called for completely different qualities and characteristics in both the personnel selected to organize and lead the respective organizations. Sabotage cells would be expected to conduct operations immediately, while the secret armies would only be mobilized once Allied ground force operations were ready to strike at Germany in the occupied territories.[25]

Initially, the primary focus was sabotage to lessen the economic contribution of the conquered countries to the German war effort. However, these actions had to be tempered by the concern that trivial provocations early in the war would do irreparable, perhaps fatal harm to potential resistance movements. If a minor sabotage act induced savage enemy reprisals, the first shoots of resistance would be damaged. One successful SOE agent observed, "In partisan warfare it is better to do a really big job or none at all. The small ones make for more backlash than they're worth."[26]

Concomitant with the "pointy end" operations conducted in the field, the SOE was also responsible for the unenviable task of coordinating and dealing with the General Staffs of the Allied Governments whose territories were occupied and with the Free French General Staff. In short, the SOE was the organization to whom these General Staffs referred to "all matters in connection with sabotage and the organisation of resistance and secret armies."[27] This task proved to be taxing.

Faced with such a daunting mandate, one of Dalton's first challenges was actually recruiting the necessary qualified personnel. Due to the secrecy of the SOE, a general advertising campaign was out of the question. As such, recruitment was done individually, normally by the country sections. Discrete inquiries were made to find service personnel with specific language and country profiles. More often than not, it was individuals tapping into their own networks of friends and acquaintances. One agent recalled, "It was [as his recruiters told him] a kind of club; you were invited to join. There were academics ... oil men, bankers and regimental soldiers; all had to be ready to collaborate with civilians, opposition leaders, monarchists, anarchists, Communists, anyone who could harass the Germans, and be ready by any means to blow up bridges, derail trains and help create civil disobedience."[28]

Initially, the ad hoc recruitment and lack of any form of rigorous selection process, due as much to the need for haste in standing up the SOE as it was the absence of the art and science of SOF selection, created a lack of credibility in the new organization. The initial philosophy of seemingly "anything goes" also strained acceptance to many outsiders. Moreover, Dalton's view that a "fanatical enthusiasm" was required quickly galvanized into an "ends justify the means" approach. One SOE report clearly acknowledged this, "We do not really 'ex officio' care whether anti-Axis elements which we support are cannibals, anarchists, atheists, or thugs; our role is to cause embarrassment to the Axis by fostering and supporting any movements which may be inimical to the Axis, but we take no responsibility for the beliefs held by our protégés."[29]

There was initially a seemingly complete absence of moral conscience or conduct. One SOE report noted, "Blackmailing responsible personnel connected with targets and threats of a 'dim' future that awaits them on our arrival should they not cooperate with us achieved results. The kidnapping and temporary restoration of wives and mistresses has also been successful."[30] In another example, a letter detailing SOE operations revealed, "We know of a certain rather famous brothel keeper in Rhodes. Overtures are to be made to him regarding the acceptance of certain highly attractive and desirable ladies who are at present interned in Cyprus, and who are willing to work for us. These ladies can be sent in by the ordinary white slave traffic smuggling process, which has been going on between Turkey and Rhodes continually. This particular brothel caters for the amusement of many highly placed officials in the Island,

and we hope it may prove firstly a source of information and secondly a means of contacting these officials."[31]

Not surprisingly, one of SOE's most invaluable sources for personnel was the underworld. In addition to the brothel owner, the SOE relied on professional forgers to manufacture the right papers since it had difficulty getting support from MI6. A retired burglar ran the SOE's lock-picking course. In one case, a general who was fired by Eisenhower was immediately recruited by SOE.[32] With this type of "human resources" policy, it is not hard to understand why the SOE, to conventional military minds, was considered highly disreputable. Dalton himself quipped of one his new recruits, "a thug with good commercial contacts," while a colleague rejoined, "Not exactly the person to be trusted with the private means of a widow or orphan." Yet, the individual was deemed perfect for the SOE. He was used to smuggle out raw materials and deal in black market currency to subvert the Japanese war effort.[33]

The SOE did themselves no favours by highlighting the type of characters they were recruiting; their philosophical approach was not a closely guarded secret. One government official noted, "Valuable work is, I am informed, being done by SOE personnel in maintaining and developing useful contacts amongst certain categories of persons not readily accessible to Government officials; but here again it is for consideration how far this work is vitally necessary and how much of it ought not to be done."[34]

The anything goes mindset was pervasive within the SOE. One instructor regularly told recruits, "[We] don't pull our punches in this kind of work."[35] In the end, contemporary values were quite starkly absent during the war. In what was arguably the last "pure" struggle of good versus evil, decision makers were not afraid to acknowledge the simple premise that "the end justifies the means."[36]

Throughout many documents pertaining to the SOE, this mentality was clearly articulated. The question of incentives to attract subversives and guerrilla fighters reveals the unlimited scope with regard to recruitment. One report asserted:

> However, it is not enough to dangle the bait of the removal
> of German oppression before prospective revolutionaries.

They must be offered some golden prize as a reward for their active collaboration, which will elevate them as far above their pre-war standards as the Germans have depressed them below it, and these rewards must be very tangible, and to be such as would interest all classes and types. They should, therefore, include the following categories:

(a) Satisfaction of their desire for revenge.
(b) A personal share in the looting of Germany.
(c) Wherever feasible, territorial aggrandise-ment.
(d) Promises of future support of the retention of these gains.
(e) As far as possible no participation in these benefits to be given to those who made no effort to achieve them.[37]

Throughout its existence, the SOE, as well as its political masters, were continually pressured to consider the option of executing expatriate Germans in North and South America as a means to curtail German mass executions in Poland. Although these actions never came to pass, the SOE did regularly turn a blind eye to the killing of prisoners.[38] In an October 1943 debriefing of a general officer on the conditions under which guerrilla warfare was being waged, the SOE planning staff noted in a "Most Secret" document with regard to prisoners that, "Disposal of prisoners after capture is a very difficult problem." Almost seventy years later, the details of the rather lengthy paragraph remain classified.[39] Numerous SOE reports by agents reveal that prisoners were regularly killed by partisans and guerrilla bands and there was little they could have done, even if they had wanted to, to prevent it. At one point, SOE supported partisans were told to issue "passes" to Italian troops that would provide safe conduct. The SOE operatives readily admitted "we don't know whether the partisans would honour that pass, but we didn't give a damn; the idea was to make the Italians completely useless to the Germans."[40]

In the end, it was a question of Clausewitzian *realpolitik*. The SOE was tasked with achieving results, any way possible. And, they were determined to succeed. As one SOE memorandum made clear:

> Brutal and cynical as these postulates may seem, it is doubtful whether, except in the case of Poland, any wide spread popular support of our movements can be expected, for by doing nothing it is obvious that the conquered countries would extract the utmost benefit of the situation. "Good intentions butter no bread," and however fervently the whole of occupied Europe may pray for an Allied victory it is our business to see that we reward those who have helped us, and punish those who have hindered, and to give nothing to those who have done nothing, and this should be clearly understood.[41]

Not all embraced the SOE's fanatical approach to subversion and sabotage. As previously noted, once the immediate shock of the fall of France disappeared and the threat of a German invasion of Britain waned, the deep-rooted, long-standing disdain for irregular warfare crept to the forefront once again. Adding to its virility was the perceived lack of credibility and competence of SOE leaders and personnel, and their apparent absence of a moral compass.[42] A large degree of organizational and philosophical competition and rivalry underscored the personal biases.

Whatever the reason, in no time the SOE had internal enemies. Professor M.R.D. Foot, the official historian of the SOE, observed, "SOE was never a popular department. It was created in a tearing hurry, during the appalling summer crisis of 1940 when it felt as though the heavens were falling."[43] He assessed its newness was a key reason for the enmity of others. "Like haste," he wrote, "[newness is] always a point of offence to the set-minded." Foot asserted that the SOE, from the very beginning, consciously set out to be original and different from what others were used to. He assessed, "therefore, it [the SOE] collected enemies in Whitehall [British Government]." Foot also revealed that the SOE also suffered as a result of its first head, Dr. Hugh Dalton, who was abrasive and normally rubbed people the wrong way.[44]

What is clear is that critics abounded. A writer for the *Times Literary Supplement* assessed, "among whose [SOE] higher executives many displayed an enthusiasm quite unrestrained by experience, some [of whom] had political backgrounds which deserved a rather closer scrutiny than they ever got, and a few [who] could only charitably be described as nutcases"[45] Additionally, Churchill was regularly met with comments that the SOE was "infested with crackpots, communists, and homosexuals."[46] Colin Gubbins recalled, "at the best SOE was looked upon as an organization of harmless backroom lunatics which, it was hoped, would not develop into an active nuisance."[47] Both General Sir Claude Auchinleck and Air Chief Marshal Charles Portal complained to Churchill that parts of the SOE were "a bogus, irresponsible, corrupt show."[48]

In fact, Air Chief Marshal Portal regularly attacked SOE effectiveness. He carped, "It [the SOE's effect] is anybody's guess. My bombing offensive is not a gamble. Its dividend is certain; it is a gilt-edged investment. I cannot divest aircraft from a certainty to a gamble which may be a goldmine or may be completely worthless."[49] Portal also had issues with the morality of dropping agents who would then assassinate enemy personnel. For him there was a clear difference between dropping a spy and encouraging assassins, one he was not so sure the SOE could distinguish.[50]

Anthony Eden, the minister responsible for the Foreign Office, which included stewardship over the SIS, was another major adversary. A Foreign Office senior officer sent a letter that captured the sentiments at the time: "You [Eden] know that you have always had my sympathy in your dealings with SOE and your endeavours to control them.... All along I have had the impression that S.O.2 [SOE] rather stank in your nostrils."[51]

Eden's head of the SIS, Stewart Menzies, was no less an opponent to the SOE. At first the SIS saw the SOE as a "rather ineffective and ridiculous collection of amateurs who might endanger SIS if not kept quiet." However, this view soon changed and the SIS came "to regard SOE as dangerous rivals, who if not squashed quickly, would eventually squash them."[52] As one observer noted, there was always the looming threat of "C's [Menzies's] determination to expunge SOE from the Intelligence alphabet."[53]

To a point, the animosity between SIS and SOE is not hard to understand. Any spectacular act of sabotage would provoke an intense security response from the enemy, which, in turn, would threaten agents responsible for acquiring secret information. In fact, the SIS second-in-command counselled his senior:

> We have to face the fact that S.O.2 [SOE] lives and grows — at an astonishing rate — seemingly without any governing factor as far as finance goes, and that whether we like it or not they do become in a sense competitors. If we cannot kill [it], and I do not think we can let us for [the] sake of work and war effort try to live on & work on friendly terms. I for one counsel Collaboration.[54]

Aside from the philosophical differences and the rivalries, another irritant that created animosity and enmity was the heavy cloak of secrecy that the SOE adopted. Professor Foot noted, "The haste of SOE's begetting was one reason for its unpopularity; another was the density of the veil of secrecy in which shrouded itself. This was sometimes overdone."[55] As many SOF organizations have recognized only too late, excessive secrecy actually harms an organization. People tend not to accept or trust what they do not understand. Senior political and military decision makers and commanders resent, and often take as personal insult, the inference that they are not important enough to be included in the secret circle of information. This makes for bad relations.

In the end, despite the challenges of mandate, manning, and critics, the SOE was stood up and provided the necessary resources to undertake its devious tasks. It did so with the full support of Prime Minister Churchill. As a result, and not surprisingly, it grew at a rapid rate and its tentacles were soon far-reaching. In fact, a Canadian connection was not far off.

3

A MAN CALLED INTREPID:
THE BEGINNING OF THE CANADIAN CONNECTION

Despite the resistance within the British government and the military, or perhaps because of it, the SOE quickly scrambled to get itself up and running in the early years of the war. Its mandate was daunting and the SOE required a wide range of talented individuals. Luckily for them, some of its work recruiting these individuals was being done for them, albeit unknowingly. As Churchill and Stewart Menzies, the head of SIS, went about recruiting gifted, influential, and trusted agents who could be counted on to push Churchill's objectives in support of the British war effort, they also unwittingly provided the SOE with opportunity. The most celebrated case was that of Sir William Stephenson, a Canadian who went on to run Britain's security apparatus in the Americas. In many ways, he personified the Canadian nexus to the SOE.

Stephenson was a forty-five-year-old businessman who many who knew him often called the "Quiet Canadian." Born in Winnipeg, Stephenson came from humble beginnings.[1] Leaving his employment as a telegraph delivery boy, he enlisted in the 101st Battalion, Winnipeg Light Infantry, on January 12, 1916. In England, he was transferred to the 17th Battalion and sent to France in July 1916, where he was gassed during a German attack the following week. Less than a year later, in April 1917, he was a full sergeant and he joined the Royal Flying Corps. He deployed to France once again in February 1918. As a fighter pilot he crashed behind enemy lines, was wounded, captured, and later escaped. He won both the Distinguished Flying Cross (DFC) and the Military Cross (MC). During the war he also took up amateur boxing.

After the war, Stephenson transitioned into a career as a successful entrepreneur and businessman. He also devoted much of his time to studying the application of radio. As a result, he invented a means of publishing photographs for newspapers by transmitting the images through radio waves. The first image appeared in the *Daily Mail* in December 1922.[2] He patented the wireless photography process, which was rumoured to have made him a millionaire before he was thirty years old.[3] He soon acquired an interest in two radio companies and in short order owned Sound City Films, which encompassed the largest film and recording studios outside of Hollywood. He extended his portfolio to include holdings in the steel and cement industries. In fact, one of his companies, Pressed Steel, made 90 percent of the car bodies for the leading British automotive manufacturer, and another, Alpha Cement, was one of Britain's largest cement companies.

Not surprisingly, his business dealings traversed North America and Europe and he built up a vast international network of friends and business contacts, which included bankers, financiers, industrialists, and politicians. His business dealings also provided him insight into German steel production, which later proved vitally important in assessing Hitler's war production capability. This sensitive business knowledge, as well as his extensive travels, brought him in contact with the Industrial Intelligence Centre in London, which was focused on gathering information on strategic commodities. This new contact, supported by his business associations and friendships, became an important access point into the influential British inner circle of security and governmental mandarins.

Nonetheless, it was his ability to open doors in the United States that remained closed to the British that made him an extremely valuable asset to Prime Minister Churchill, who trusted Stephenson unconditionally. And, much like the SOE recruitment overall, Stephenson was in the inner circle — part of an influential clique. As Stephenson himself conceded, "We were all friends, you see. Churchill and the rest." He explained, "We were a group of friends who saw the war coming."[4]

Rather than being a pedantic bureaucrat that would slavishly follow process, the Canadian's uncanny ability to identify the heart of any specific problem, combined with his proclivity to go straight to the top of the hierarchy of an organization to solve it, made him that much more attractive to an action-oriented leader such as Churchill. As such, the British prime minister decided that Stephenson would be his man in the Americas.

However, Stephenson's first trip to the United States in the spring of 1940 was actually as a representative of SIS, at the direction of Stewart Menzies, Britain's chief of intelligence.[5] Menzies directed Stephenson to re-establish a high level liaison with the J. Edgar Hoover, the director of the Federal Bureau of Investigation (FBI). Although Hoover was amenable to working with the SIS, he stated he was under strict orders from the State Department not to collaborate with Great Britain in any way that could be seen as contravening the US Neutrality Acts.[6] As such, Hoover stipulated that the liaison would be a personal one between him and Stephenson and that no other US government department would be involved.[7]

As a result of his successful first foray to New York, Menzies returned Stephenson to the US in June 1940 as the British Passport Control Officer (PCO), the time honoured cover appointment for the senior SIS representative in New York. Although Menzies was the individual that dispatched Stephenson to New York as the SIS representative, the prime minister was fully involved with the decision. In fact, by all accounts, Stephenson was Churchill's choice. Stephenson himself makes reference to Churchill's final direction to him prior to his departure. Stephenson recalled it was clear and simple:

> You [Stephenson] know what you must do at once. We have discussed it most fully, and there is a complete fusion of minds between us. You are to be my personal representative in the United States. I will ensure that you have the full support of all the resources at my command. I know that you will have success, and the good Lord will guide your efforts as He will ours. This may be our last farewell. Au revoir and good luck![8]

Although Stephenson's original assignment to New York was singularly to act solely as the SIS representative, in December 1940, the director of the SOE, Sir Frank Nelson, asked Stephenson to also act as the SOE representative in the Western Hemisphere. The SOE task, which was soon to be just one of many, became a major undertaking for the Canadian. Stephenson's task certainly was not as straightforward as the direction he purportedly received from Churchill, simply "to do all that was not being done, and could not be done by overt means, to assure sufficient aid for Britain, and eventually bring America into the war."[9]

Stephenson's first hurdle was manpower. The staff he inherited as PCO was meagre at best and did not come close to providing the necessary horsepower to fulfill all the activities envisaged. As such, to begin to meet his mandate, he deepened the Canadian connection even more. He looked to fill his staff requirements with Canadians. He turned to his Canadian business associates, as well as his First World War squadron mate and friend Tommy Drew-Brook, a Toronto stockbroker, to help recruit Canadians from all realms of life — business executives, technicians, newspaper and communication experts, university professors, and police authorities, as well as office staff.[10] Overall, approximately eight hundred Canadians were recruited, mostly through newspaper ads, to work for Stephenson.[11]

With the expanding manpower pool and portfolio of tasks, Stephenson's cover as PCO was beginning to fray. His organization ballooned and could no longer be housed under the cover of PCO. In essence, Stephenson was building a new secret organization from scratch. It now had three main components: the secret intelligence division, the special operations division, and the security division. In discussing the issue with Hoover, the director of the FBI suggested he name his new organization British Security Coordination (BSC).[12]

In fact, Hoover had become an invaluable ally. His patronage in the early stages proved to be significant. He directed his officers to assist the BSC in any way possible, and he provided a wireless channel for telegraphic communications between BSC and SIS headquarters, which was the only means of transmission during the early start-up period. In essence, Hoover and the FBI were engaged in a full-up alliance with British intelligence.[13]

The next major problem for Stephenson was one of accommodations. The original suite of PCO offices was inadequate. In fact, he used his own wealth to move the PCO from a cramped set of offices in the Cunard Building off Wall Street to the thirty-fifth and thirty-sixth floors of the Rockefeller Center on Fifth Avenue. His new organization, still known to the casual interloper as British Passport Control, as it was the actual location to sort out passport and/or visa problems, was, in fact, behind the chimera, Britain's "intelligence window" into America. The BSC responded to the Security Executive, officially designated the Home Defence (Security) Executive. It was created by Churchill in May 1940, as one of his first acts as prime minister, during the panic of the German invasion of the Low Countries and France. The impetus was, first, his dissatisfaction with the existing security and intelligence agencies, and second, the belief that the German success in Europe was partially due to fifth column activity. As such, Churchill wanted to ensure a coordinating body existed that would make certain no fifth column activity was possible in England, particularly should the Germans invade. The Security Executive cast a wide net over any and all activities that had a national security nexus, such as communications, censorship, travel, ports, shipping and internment of foreign nationals. It also provided guidance and direction to the BSC.[14]

Stephenson and his BSC had to tread carefully and work within the confines of the US Neutrality Acts, or at least not get caught violating the statutes. The embryonic BSC represented a number of British departments and organisations. Specifically:

    a.   SIS;
    b.   Security Executive;
    c.   SOE;
    d.   MI5 (Security Service); and
    e.   Passport Control.[15]

BSC was also responsible for Station M, which was in the business of fabricating "forged" letters and documents that were used by agents behind enemy lines. Station M had a laboratory in Canada that was established with the help of the Royal Canadian Mounted Police (RCMP), under the cover of the Canadian Broadcasting Corporation (CBC).[16]

Late in 1941, BSC added yet another division to its organization — Communications. It was created to meet three basic needs. First, to create a means of secure, rapid communication between BSC and its Washington, DC, office. Second, to purchase special wireless equipment that was available only in the US for the British war effort. And, finally, to create a secret communication network in Latin America in case underground activities were required should the Axis alliance take power or inspire *coups d'états*. Once established, the BSC Communications Division also fulfilled the function of transmitting the exchange of intercepted enemy messages between American and British intelligence agencies.[17]

With all of these activities on the go, in January 1941, the British government changed Stephenson's appointment from Passport Control Officer to Director of Security Coordination in the US. From a British perspective, the BSC was a critical conduit to the Americans. A British government report elaborated on its official role:

> BSC is represented on the Western Hemisphere Security Committee, which meets regularly in Washington, New York and Ottawa in rotation. BSC maintains close liaison with the US Services in Washington and New York and as a member of the Joint Intelligence Committee in Washington is in touch with the Joint Chiefs-of-Staff and Joint Staff Mission. Contact also maintained with OSS (New York and Washington), the Coast Guard Service, FCC, and the Departments of State and Justice in Washington. Through Washington office liaison is established with the Embassy and British Missions.[18]

Churchill initially gave Stephenson rather broad direction, to get the White House to approve a list of essential supplies Britain needed immediately; investigate enemy activities in the US; institute adequate security measures against the threat of sabotage to British property and organize American public opinion in favour of aid to Britain.[19] On February 15,

1941, an official directive laid out more specific tasks for the BSC, namely to establish an SOE network throughout Latin America, recruit likely SOE agents in the United States and other American countries, help influence public opinion in the US in a pro-Allied direction, and to make contact with various European refugee and exile movements in the New World, as well as to help create secret communications channels for SOE networks.[20]

Stephenson took to heart Churchill's driving desire to get the Americans involved in the war. As such, he felt that a key element of his appointment in New York was to generate American public support for the British war effort and cultivate a pro-British American sentiment.

Although Stephenson had a good working relationship with Hoover, he astutely realized that Colonel William J. "Wild Bill" Donovan, a First World War veteran, winner of the Congressional Medal of Honour, renown lawyer and politician, as well as one of the president's trusted advisers, was his single most important contact in the US.[21] As such, he sponsored a trip to London, England, for Donovan in July 1940, so that Donovan could assess the British war effort and ability to defeat the Nazis. Stephenson then accompanied Donovan on his second trip to London in the early spring of 1941.[22] One British historian went so far as to assess that the Stephenson/Donovan relationship "was eventually to form the basis of a full-scale Anglo-American intelligence alliance."[23]

Stephenson also cultivated a close working relationship with Robert Sherwood, one of the president's key speech writers. Sherwood, a devout Anglophile and anti-Fascist, made a habit, with the president's full knowledge, of allowing Stephenson to read the draft of speeches written for the president and provide comment to capture the British point of view to ensure the speeches supported the British war effort.

Franklin D. Roosevelt, the American president, also assigned his close friend, millionaire businessman Vincent Astor, as his personal liaison to Stephenson so that he could be regularly informed of specific British concerns or requirements that could not be passed through normal diplomatic channels. This conduit also allowed him to get briefed on BSC investigations into enemy activities in the US.[24]

The impact Stephenson had in the United States proved to be dramatic. SOE historian M.R.D. Foot observed, Stephenson played "a leading part in persuading the owners of the United States news media that it was a more constitutional line to take to be anti-Nazi than to be isolationist." He insists, "This transition, which the bulk of the American newspapers and broadcasting stations made between the summer of 1940 and the summer of 1941, encouraged American opinion to follow suit, with world-shaking results."[25]

Stephenson was also instrumental in obtaining American assistance in the form of a hundred Flying Fortress bombers for the Royal Air Force (RAF) Coastal Command, over a million rifles for the newly formed Home Guard, as well as kayaks, landing craft, sub-chasers, wireless equipment, radio valves, parachutes, and war materials for the Middle East. Lord Mountbatten, Commander Combined Operations Command, confided, "I believe too that he [Stephenson] was the man who persuaded President Roosevelt to declare that the Persian Gulf and the Red Sea were no longer combat areas within the meaning of the American neutrality Act, so that it was possible for the Americans to send war material to the British in the Middle East Theatre, and the ships the whole way escorted by American ships."[26]

Stephenson himself commented on the importance of BSC and its ability to advance the British war effort at a very critical juncture point when Britain was at its weakest point and the Americans were still officially neutral. He wrote:

> During the period under review, an organization in the Western Hemisphere restricted in its authority to collecting intelligence by established means would have been altogether inadequate and that the success of secret activities was primarily dependent upon the coordination of a number of functions falling within the jurisdiction of separate government departments in London. It was only as a result of such coordination that the British Security Coordination had the necessary elasticity to meet the urgent demands of the situation and to adapt itself readily to swiftly changing needs.[27]

Stephenson and his BSC performed immaculately. By the end of the war, "not a single British vessel was lost or seriously held up by sabotage in a United States port throughout the war." Yet, the damage inflicted by Stephenson's organization "to German property and nationals certainly exceeded the total damage caused by the Axis powers on the whole of the American continent."[28] Major-General Colin Gubbins, who became the last director of the SOE, described Stephenson's exploits as, "a series of brilliant individual coups against Axis powers." He went so far as to acknowledge that Intrepid's "slightest wish is to me more than a command."[29]

In the end, Stephenson and the BSC, staffed with a multitude of "quiet Canadians" fulfilled a number of key functions:

1. The establishment of a secret organization to investigate enemy activities and to institute adequate security measures in the Western Hemisphere;
2. The procurement of certain essential supplies for Britain;
3. The fostering of American intervention; and
4. The assurance of American participation in secret activities throughout the world in the closest possible collaboration with the British.[30]

In achieving these key tasks they furthered the British war effort in significant ways. The manner in which Stephenson and the BSC achieved the largely SIS- and SOE-type operations is the subject of the next chapter.

4

OUT OF EUROPE:
BSC AND SOE OPERATIONS IN THE AMERICAS

Undeniably, William Stephenson and the BSC fulfilled a vital function for the Allied war effort. First, Britain was in critical need of war supplies and the United States as well as Latin America represented an important storehouse. Stephenson and the BSC ensured access to these supplies. Second, the BSC denied the same to the Axis powers. Most importantly, Stephenson and the BSC were influential in promoting pro-British sentiment that was essential in drawing in American support and, in accordance with Churchill's grand design, participation in the war.

Prior to the Japanese attack on Pearl Harbor on December 7, 1941, which was followed shortly afterwards by a declaration of war by Germany against the US, BSC undertook the following tasks in the Americas:

1. The collection of intelligence concerning United States and Latin American affairs — both foreign and domestic — affecting British interests;

2. The collection of external intelligence — intelligence that is to say, derived from sources within the Western Hemisphere but relating to areas outside the Western Hemisphere;

3. The penetration of unfriendly, as well as enemy, diplomatic and consular missions;

4. The establishment in Latin America of an SOE organization, with the primary purpose of preparing for underground activities in the various republics against the possibility (which at the time seemed far from remote) of Axis invasion or Axis-inspired revolution;

5. The organization of free movements among foreign exiles and minorities in the Western Hemisphere for the purpose of encouraging and strengthening resistance in the occupied countries;

6. The direction of subversive propaganda from American sources both to Europe and the Far East;

7. The institution of measures to prevent the enemy from smuggling supplies both to and from the Western Hemisphere;

8. The institution of security measures in Latin American ports where British ships called;

9. The recruitment of agents in the Western Hemisphere to undertake either SI or SO work in enemy-occupied countries;

10. The training of agents for the establishment in Canada of a special training camp which was opened coincidentally with Pearl Harbor; and

11. The procurement in the Western Hemisphere of special supplies for the underground in occupied countries.[1]

The tasks Churchill entrusted to Stephenson and the BSC were significant. The British assessed the threats in America as a clear and imminent danger — though the US government disagreed as to the severity. In the United States, there were six million German-speaking Americans and four million Italian-speaking Americans. Many of these American citizens with ties to the Axis powers were employed in factories that produced British war materials. Others worked in the freight yards, railways, and on the docks through which Allied war material travelled.

The risk was substantial, as Britain placed orders for four billion dollars' worth of war materials.[2] As the BSC history noted, "It was a dangerous situation; for a wide-scale sabotage campaign in the private factories producing arms for British account or against the large proportion of Britain's 20,000,000 tons of shipping which used American ports could have proved disastrous."[3]

Although the British Purchasing Commission was technically responsible for prevention of sabotage in the US, aside from minimizing risk in the factories that produced war materials for Britain, it had little means of securing the myriad of ports from which the material was sent. Moreover, the American authorities showed little concern for protecting British property. Not surprisingly, BSC absorbed the British Purchasing Commission and immediately expanded its scope of activities. Security officers, designated as Consular Security Officers (CSOs), were posted to all American and South American ports where British ships called to load war supplies. The CSO's primary task was to protect British ships from saboteurs. As an example of the scope of activity, in a single three-month period, CSOs and their staffs in North America carried out over 5,000 inspections on nearly 800 ships, while in South America, they conducted over 2,500 inspections on 859 vessels.[4] In the end, throughout the war not a single British ship was lost or seriously held up from sailing due to accident or sabotage in an American port.

To assist with security and cut down on smuggling, the BSC also instituted the Ships Observers' Scheme. Under this program, the BSC recruited an "agent" (or observer) from amongst the crew of all ships flying a neutral flag that departed from an American or Latin American port. The BSC carefully debriefed their observers in all of the major ports the respective ships visited. Of interest to the BSC was any information on smuggling, Nazi subversion, communist agitation, the sighting of enemy ships, suspicion radio traffic, and potential Axis agents. The program met with some significant intelligence coups, but overall fell short of expectations. As the program entailed agents working in the US, once the Americans passed legislation restricting the activities of foreign agents operating on American soil, the BSC shifted control of the program to the US Office of Naval Intelligence.[5]

Security aside, Stephenson focused much attention on the important task of swaying American opinion toward joining the war. He sought out sympathetic journalists and media moguls — papers such as the *New York Post, New York Herald Tribune, New York Times,* and *Baltimore Sun* became important allies. Conversely, hostile papers that could not be co-opted were targeted for actions to put them out of business.

The same approach extended to radio stations. In fact, a New York–based radio station, WRUL, which possessed a powerful short-wave transmitter, was subsidized by BSC and became an important propaganda tool. Stephenson recruited foreign news editors, translators, and announcers, and he went so far as to provide news bulletins and commentaries.[6]

BSC also took aim at American isolationists and German-American clubs. By the late spring of 1941, BSC tallied approximately seven hundred chapters and a million members of American isolationist groups. In fact, Britain's ambassador to the US reported nine out of ten Americans favoured staying out of the war.[7] Stephenson and the Canadian-heavy BSC certainly had their work cut out for themselves.

Undaunted, the BSC infiltrated the isolationist groups in an effort to turn up information that they could use to discredit the organizations and prove they were a front for the Nazis. In fact, BSC was eventually able to demonstrate that there was active Nazi activity in New York, Washington, Chicago, San Francisco, Cleveland, and Boston. In fact, in a number of instances they actually traced the German money transfers to the groups.[8] This information was readily provided to J. Edgar Hoover and Bill Donovan.

The BSC agents were not above harassment. For example, when Senator Gerald Nye spoke in Boston in September 1941, agents distributed thousands of handbills labelling him an appeaser and "Nazi lover." In addition, agents tried to disrupt an America First Rally at Madison Square Garden by printing phoney tickets.[9]

Following the apparent SOE philosophy that the ends justify the means, the BSC also recruited agents to penetrate enemy or enemy-controlled businesses, propaganda groups, and diplomatic and consular missions. BSC agents and representatives were posted to key points in Washington DC, Los Angeles, San Francisco, and Seattle. One such agent, code-named

Cynthia, was directed to renew her relationship with Italian naval attaché Alberto Lais, who was posted to the Italian embassy in Washington. Cynthia is given credit with warning the Americans of the plans to scuttle ships harboured in the US and for assisting in obtaining Italian ciphers. Later, posing as a journalist, she infiltrated the Vichy French embassy and obtained copies of secret correspondence and the French naval ciphers.[10]

No potential avenue for disrupting enemy activity in the US was overlooked. The BSC established contact with several minority groups with the aim of creating pro-Allied movements and recruiting agents. For example, Austrian-Americans were approached and an organization known as "Austria Action" was formed in an attempt to unite all anti-Nazi Austrians. In spite of differences between the various groups, this project rendered pioneering service insofar as it was the first minority organization to receive benevolent recognition from the US Department of Justice, which was then keeping a watchful eye upon all foreign minorities in the USA.[11]

In addition, the BSC, working with American Yugoslavs, established the *Slav Bulletin,* and created a centre for anti-Nazi activities among the Serbs, Croats, and Slovenes in the US. Lectures were arranged by democratic Slav leaders and groups were established to watch Nazi agents among the Croats and Slovaks. In the same vein, close contact was established with the main Ukrainian democratic group, known as the "Defence of the Ukraine."

The BSC also established contact with members of the Hungarian Communist Party, as well as running a Hungarian-language newspaper to counteract pro-German feelings. The BSC also developed ties with anti-Nazi elements among the Carpatho-Russian clergy, developed a close co-operation with the Mazzini Society, and extended contacts to the various labour organizations with young Italian Socialists in an attempt to persuade them into a more active anti-Nazi policy.[12]

Attention was also focused on winning over Arabs. As the BSC official history captured, "at the time when a British crusade to liberate Syria was considered imminent the principal American Arab newspaper *Al Hoda* was persuaded to become entirely pro-British." In addition, a Near East Information Bureau was established in New York, and broadcasts over WRUL were subsidized in all the principal Near Eastern languages.[13]

Subversive propaganda was also directed against enemy agents. For example, Dr. Kurt Rieth, a German diplomat who arrived in the US in 1934, had been given the double mission of buying up American-owned oil properties in Eastern Europe and contacting all US political groups favouring isolationism in an attempt to hinder application of the Lend-Lease Bill. In May 1941, SIS handed a document of Rieth's activities to SOE for appropriate action. The SOE conducted a press campaign, breaking the story of Rieth's mission as an exclusive to the *New York Herald Tribune,* and then feeding out other angles to other newspapers and agencies. As a result, Rieth was harassed by media for ten days, after which he was arrested by the FBI and subsequently expelled from the country.[14]

The SOE also conducted a pressure campaign against IG Farben, a German chemical company that the British perceived as a powerful and dangerous concern doing much harm, especially through its connections with the various companies of Standard Oil. Its vice president was a German named Von Rath, a naturalized American who had also been a German agent during the First World War, who acted in the capacity of a commercial counsellor at the German Embassy in Washington, DC. As an American citizen, a wealthy man, and a member of all the best clubs in New York, the SOE believed he was possibly the guiding brain behind the activities of Farben in the US. After two weeks of pressure, in which his name and activities were publicized, he resigned. Additional pressure was kept on the company for several more weeks with similar successful results. IG Farben's interests in the US were eventually taken over by nominees of the US government.[15]

In short, the BSC/SOE stopped at nothing to achieve their aims. They even conducted break-ins of those they assessed as threats to the Allied war effort in an attempt to access information, codes, and correspondence. Those stopped once the Americans joined the Allied war effort following the Japanese attack on Pearl Harbor and the subsequent German declaration of war on the United States on December 11, 1941. Stephenson and the BSC no longer had to focus on swaying American opinion or conducting investigations into enemy activity.[16] The Americans actively took this mission on themselves.

The US shift in public opinion toward supporting the war came none too soon, as the days of BSC activity in the US were coming to an end. First, the US State Department had finally taken notice of the BSC activities inside the country. By the spring of 1941, they ordered Stephenson's and the BSC's operations to be curtailed. Their concern was that a "... full size secret police and intelligence service is rapidly evolving."[17]

In early 1942, Senator Kenneth McKellar introduced a bill that required all agents of foreign governments working in the US to register with the US Justice Department and detail the activities they were undertaking. The bill passed on January 28, 1942, and it did not differentiate between friendly or unfriendly powers. As a result, the BSC/SOE were required to curtail some of their activities and pass them to the Americans to conduct. Stephenson and his organization could now focus on Latin America. But this was not without its own problems.

From the perspective of the BSC/SOE, Latin America represented a powder keg — there were significant economic and political interests at play. Latin America was a source of war supplies, as well as being a sanctuary for naval vessels far from home. However, Latin American countries were sensitive to their sovereignty and resented foreign power interference or intrigues.

Complicating the matter was the reality of Clausewitzian *realpolitik*. Both American and British economic concerns piqued national interests at odds with their status as allies, and the US State Department worked hard at blocking British actions in Latin America and the British Foreign Office, perceptive to the Latin American and US political sensitivities, also worked hard at blocking SOE action in the region, while simultaneously trying hard to protect British economic and political interests.

However, many in the British government, and particularly the BSC and SOE, saw the threat at the time as a clear and present danger. As a result, it became a focus for Stephenson. "It [South America] is at the same time the source of supply of many commodities essential to the war effort of the United Nations and the area of investment of £1093 millions of British capital."[18] For example, oil wells in Venezuela and the Dutch West Indies supplied 80 percent of the fuel used by the Royal Navy and a significant portion of the Royal Air Force aviation fuel. Furthermore, bauxite mines in the British and Dutch Guianas represented 70 percent of the Allied aluminum supply.[19]

There was also the issue of enemy activity. Lord Louis Mountbatten confided to General George Marshall that "it was clear that the Axis agents were having a free run in these [South American] States and it was most important that the position should be reversed as soon as possible." Sir Charles Hambro, the second director of the SOE, agreed "that the situation there was serious and required drastic action."[20] Another senior British government official acknowledged, "... the situation in South America worried us greatly.... Our problem in South America would be the obverse of our policy in Europe. We had to prevent sabotage, and SOE's contribution to that could be to attack, by underground methods, the people in South America who were about to organise sabotage."[21]

The SOE's assessment of the situation echoed those of the senior British leadership. It spelled out the dire situation they perceived. As a backdrop, the SOE had fortuitously obtained key German documentation. BSC agents had followed a German courier, who met with an "accident." His satchel was taken and among a myriad of documents was found a map drawn up in Berlin showing the proposed partitioning of South America by the Axis powers.[22] A formal SOE threat assessment explained:

> Latin America is now the only considerable neutral area in the world and, since the loss of the East Indies and Malaya, it has become an indispensable source of many products vital to the Allied war effort. It is therefore essential that these supplies should not be sabotaged and that there should be no breach of the peace in South America, which would inevitably cause their interruptions.... Unfortunately, the Governments in all the South American countries are unstable and their armies weak and often divided in loyalty, while physical, political, economical and ethno-graphical conditions are ideal for subversive operations.... Moreover, the continent is permeated by hostile minorities of which the German and Japanese are highly organised, armed

and prepared for subversive action, ranging from the supply of raiders and submarines and sabotage of exports, to military and political action on the largest scale.... The [US] State Department considers that their 'good neighbour policy,' combined with economic pressure, can secure all that the Allies require. For this reason, United States action is confined to the activities of the FBI, which is a branch of the State Department concerned with secret intelligence. Colonel Donovan's organisation, which includes the American counterpart of SOE, with whom we work in close and most friendly cooperation in other parts of the world, is not at present allowed to operate in South America, although this decision may be reconsidered in the near future.[23]

The British perception, which now became Stephenson's issue to deal with, was simply that the "Axis agents were having a free run in these States and it was most important that the position should be reversed as soon as possible."[24] The SOE was not alone in its assessment of the importance of Latin America. Another official document reinforced, "South America is one of the few sources of war supplies still available to the United Nations and it is a matter of vital importance to see that the enemy takes no successful action to impede their production and free flow to the USA and to the UK."[25] Even arguably SOE's biggest critic, the Foreign Office, recognized the danger. One of its own documents revealed:

Nowhere in the world are the physical, political, economic and ethnographic conditions so suitable for subversive operations by either side as in Latin America. In all States there are large colonies of Germans, Italians or Japanese, and these, particularly the Germans and Japanese, have for years past been organised, prepared, and in some cases strategically placed in order to assist the Axis war effort when required.... There is ample evidence of these dangers based on reports by H.M.

representatives in Latin American States and by SIS and the following factors may be taken as axiomatic:

1. Axis minorities are preparing subversive action ranging from the supply of raiders and submarines and sabotage of exports to military and political action on the largest scale.

2. The existing governments in most Latin American States are unstable and the armies and police forces are weak and of doubtful loyalty. While more than one pro-Axis putsch might succeed, any internal disturbance, even if small and unsuccessful, would seriously interfere with essential supplies to the Allies.

3. The South Chilean coastline and Magellan region, the largely unexplored North East coast of Brazil, the Caribbean cost of Venezuela and Colombia, and the Caribbean islands, afford excellent hiding places and supply bases for enemy surface raiders and submarines. The Admiralty have already expressed concern about the preparations which it is believed are being made and the activities of fishing and coastal vessels in these areas. This danger is emphasised by the recent alarming submarine activities in the Caribbean Sea.[26]

The British ambassador to the United States, Lord Halifax, reported, "It is common knowledge that there are extremely well organised Nazi groups in every one of the Latin American countries which, in the event of an attack, would probably be capable of taking over the country." He warned, "If United States diplomacy and action is not able to convince Latin American nations that these Nazi agents and fifth columnists must be dealt with, these countries, without the slightest doubt, will be lost the moment any of the Axis Powers is in a position to launch an attack."[27]

Although no direct evidence was found, there remained strong suspicion that the Axis forces were using local bases, notably in the mouth of the Amazon, to supply submarines and surface vessels. Suspicions focused primarily on Brazil, southern Chile, Venezuela, Ecuador, and Mexico.[28] As far as the British were concerned the German colonies in Brazil, Argentina, and Chile, as well as the Japanese communities in Brazil and Peru "constitute serious problems."[29]

Specifically, the British perception of threat in Latin America was far from reassuring. An SOE assessment concluded:

> In each of these countries [Peru and Bolivia] there is an unstable Government which is nominally pro-Ally but enemy interests are intriguing to replace them by pro-Axis Governments. Our information indicates that these plans are well advanced, particularly in Bolivia.... Those countries are supremely important as any stoppage of their supplies, especially the rarer metals, would bring many United States war industries to a standstill. The strong German colonies in both countries and the Japanese colony of about 80,000 in Peru therefore form a latent menace, and reports have already been received of their having established refuelling bases on the Peruvian coast.[30]

Brazil was similarly fraught with risk. One British official wrote, "Neither we nor the Americans have any proof that Axis forces are using local bases for supplying submarines. Consul at Para suspects that German submarines are using bases in the mouth of the Amazon." He went on to assess that "No Axis coup on a big scale is expected unless Germans gain victory in (Atlantic) when an attack in the Natal region might be staged with the help of fifth column elements and *integralistas.*" He warned, "I think that enemy sabotage may take place in country on large scale and that preparations to combat it are more likely to be effective if concerted action is taken on large scale also."[31]

More worrisome was the assessment of Japanese infiltration. The SOE assessment noted that "Japanese colonisation, especially in the important State of Sao Paulo, appears to have been carried out on a tactical plan and, as a result, they have a well equipped secret army of over 100,000 men." The SOE report explained:

> A Japanese military force of somewhere near 100,000 men with modern automatic light weapons, including anti-tank guns, hand grenades, machine guns, a completely organised army-staff and all men properly regimentated, at present living apparently peacefully in the State of Sao Paulo. This is located in positions which threaten the principal forts protecting the port of Santos. Strategic stretches of coastline (Japanese fishing colonies), are in Japanese hands and similar colonies occupy lands surrounding important points such as bridges, a dynamite factory, etc. In addition, they have other similar organisations which are in a position to control the ports of Pars and Parintins on the Amazon.[32]

In Chile, the German minorities were perceived as being "fully organised, especially south of the Concepcion-Los Angeles area, where the population is almost entirely German." The SOE believed that in this area the Germans had "not only prepared refuelling bases but definite 'frontier' defences to prevent any interference from the North." In the North, the assessment put smaller German colonies that threatened the important copper and nitrate supplies in the area, as well as the two railways to Africa and the "Antofagasta," which provided the only outlet for the vital supplies of Bolivian tin.[33]

The SOE appraisal listed the Colombian government as "weakly pro-Ally," but rated the defence of the Panama Canal and particularly the maintenance of oil supplies from Venezuela as being "vulnerable to submarine attack."[34] Cuba was considered "the last sanctuary for Axis refugees from the United States." The Cuban Government was considered corrupt and the SOE assessed "every possibility of a successful pro-Axis coup d'état." Moreover, the SOE suspected the enemy was using Cuba "as a clearing house for Axis agents in South America and as a supply base for Axis vessels in the Caribbean."[35]

Mexico was no better. The British representative in the country sent a dismal evaluation of the situation:

> There are increasing reports to the effect that enemy submarines have been seen off Mexican coasts, that parties have been landed, and that local organisations exist for the purpose of refuelling.... It is known that German and Japanese carried out business of coastal studies a few years ago particularly on west coast.... I do not believe in the possibility of a spontaneous internal coup although present government are none too firm in saddle. Units of army could probably be bought for a small outlay by an invading force once it had established an actual foothold in the country. Germans number 5,000. They are lying low at present but are said to be well organised especially in southern frontier state of Chiapas where coffee industry is largely in their hands, and where there may be numerous air fields constructed by Germans for the purpose of flying their coffee to United States. I regard this as the real danger spot and have suggested to United States Ambassador the advisability of setting up with the consent of Mexican Government an agency in Chiapas with the object of purchasing the whole coffee crop and only paying out enough to German growers to keep the industry going. High profits they are now making and passing to Nazi funds could be held by the agency till the end of the war. Japanese number 4,000 and the Chinese Minister (whose agents have access to Japanese Counsels) tells me that all Japanese ex-service men in Mexico are organising in the districts under leaders

who have orders to act on their own initiative until their efforts can be co-ordinated, presumably by an invading commander. Should a landing ever be effected, invaders would undoubtedly be aided by Spanish falangistas, by such German and Japanese as are within easy reach and probably by armed Mexicans who still detest the United States. Much might be done now to reduce the danger here by persuading Mexican Government and United States Government to begin freezing out enemy firms.[36]

The British saw Paraguay as another tinderbox, but one less in danger of Nazi domination. "Danger of revolution is always present here," noted an official report, "but unless allies lose control of the Atlantic Nazis could hardly induce an independent people like the Paraguayans to submit to what would amount to Foreign domination."[37] Peru was seen in a similar light. The local British representative assessed, "considerable [threat] probably in the form of submarine raid on oil field putting a commando ashore." However, once again, "the extreme touchiness of these people in matters affecting their sovereignty and 'face'" made the prospect of a Nazi coup unlikely.[38] Finally, in Venezuela, the SOE concluded that the enemy "are known to have prepared landing grounds."[39]

And so, the BSC/SOE, armed with what they considered a compelling threat picture, set forth to tackle the problem. The SOE lines of operation for South America were fairly straightforward:

1. Countering Axis organisations by secretly contacting and supporting the parties and minorities sympathetic to the Allies. This will involve organising them and supplying them with money and arms;

2. Exposing the activities of pro-Axis parties so that the Governments concerned can be pressed to take action against them;

3. Protecting sources of supplies for the Allies from sabotage by Axis agents;

4. Neutralising Axis strongholds and bases already formed;

5. Causing the confiscation or destruction of supplies and dumps destined for Axis use.[40]

And, they were relatively successful. In Bolivia, the SOE was able to warn the anti-Axis government of a planned Nazi-inspired revolt, which not only strengthened the British position but led to the adoption of numerous security measures and encouraged a wave of anti-Nazi feeling. In Brazil, the SOE secured correspondence that was then shown to the president with the subsequent consequence that the Italian *LATI* airline concession in Brazil was revoked. In addition, providing information to Brazilian police authorities in January 1942, including complete dossiers on all Germans in the strategic Natal area, led to the arrest and incarceration of many Germans and the break-up of the Stoltz espionage group. The SOE also revealed that the governor's newspaper was receiving subsidies from the Nazi propaganda minister Joseph Goebbels. The governor was subsequently removed.[41]

The SOE had similar success in Colombia, where their disclosure of information led to the arrest and deportation of many Germans, as well as the destruction of a rising Fascist party. Additionally, German agents Erich Guter and Wilhelm Dittmar were arrested for possessing an illegal wireless transmitter, photostatic equipment, and compromising documents. Furthermore, a consignment of two thousand anti-British books imported from Argentina were destroyed. Significantly, the SOE were also able to convince the government to implement new restrictions on Japanese colonies within the country and the SOE broke up Accion Nacional, a totalitarian party, by disclosing the party's activities and ties. Finally, the SOE was able to influence the government into passing a law to expropriate property of Axis nationals.[42]

Elsewhere, SOE agents used personal influence to persuade Chilean Cabinet ministers to push the government into rupturing relations with the Axis powers and implementing a law to liquidate all German businesses. In addition, files on German agents were supplied to the police. In Ecuador, the government was provided with evidence on individuals involved in pro-German activity, including the president's own brother-in-law. Individuals were either deported or incarcerated. In Venezuela, the same techniques of disclosing information resulted in the expulsion or blacklisting of several important Germans and German firms. Also, four thousand anti-British pamphlets were destroyed, and the Spanish ciphers were stolen from the Spanish ambassador. In Uruguay, the "Radio Continental" in Montevideo, a powerful Axis propaganda station, was completely destroyed.[43]

In Central America, SOE agents conducted a partial survey of the region and prepared a long list of targets. They were also able to influence the Costa Rican government to pass a law expropriating all property belonging to individuals from Axis powers and the elimination of all German commerce.[44]

Concurrently, throughout the region, the BSC/SOE agents were also laying the foundation for an underground organization to carry on resistance should the Axis invade Latin America, or in the event that any, or all, of those countries declare themselves allies with the Axis. As such, careful knowledge of all strategic targets that would hamper the enemy were catalogued (strategic communications such as bridges, railway lines, airfields, wireless, telephone, and telegraph stations; war industry related electric plants, waterworks, mines, and factories).

Stephenson and his BSC/SOE, however, were fighting an uphill battle. The British Foreign Office, trying to balance maintaining British friendly relations with Latin American countries and the United States, as well as protecting British economic and political interests, saw SOE operations as endangering their efforts. The fear of discovery of SOE meddling, much less SOE operations, or even simply the potential discovery of SOE intent to conduct activities, not to mention subsequent consequences, rattled British diplomats. As such, the British Foreign Office worked hard at discrediting SOE assessments of the threat and the requirement for active operations in the region. One Foreign Office diplomat asserted, "the likelihood of some Axis-inspired coup is generally dismissed, except either (a) with outside assistance, or (b) in the event of the war taking a much more serious turn."[45] Another agreed. He explained:

Our paper shows that the Axis threat to our supplies from South America is not as great as SOE would have us believe.... For many months past SOE have been very keen on operating in South America. As we both know, life in South American countries can be quite jolly and there is no Gestapo there. Consequently, it is a more agreeable and facile theatre for SOE operations than enemy-occupied countries in Europe. If SOE were to be given carte blanche in South America the result would be that we should have endless quarrels with the State Department who are very touchy about the Western Hemisphere, Pan-America etc and also with the local governments, as a result of which our supplies might be endangered to a far greater extent than by sabotage on the part of German or Japanese residents.[46]

As far as the Foreign Office was concerned no BSC/SOE action was worth undertaking. They argued the threat was minimal and the pursuit of operations, which entailed great risk of detection, would only jeopardize relations with the Latin American states, as well as the US.

They argued that "possibly our greatest asset in Latin America today, in view of the unfavourable course of the war, is our reputation for respectability. This asset would be lost if we were to be detected in exactly that form of ill-doing of which we have so successfully accused our enemies, and relations between the UK and these countries, including economic relations, might suffer considerably, both during the war and the postwar periods."[47] The situation festered and the rivalry between the Foreign Office and SOE continued.

Adding to the debate on actions required and the necessity of an SOE presence in Latin America was the US hostility to any British presence, which the British perceived was largely based on economic interest. In the end, the British view perceived the Americans as "a bit too complacent about the situation in Latin America."[48] And, although they questioned the US motives, they acquiesced to the American pressure. There was a concern not to antagonize their rich, resource laden, and powerful new ally. One government official sent to Latin America to try and coordinate Foreign Office and BSC/SOE activities summarized the situation. He counselled:

> We should embark on no SOE activities at all — not even the importation of toys [special equipment for sabotage and surveillance] in Latin America without the concurrence of the [US] State Department ... if importation is undertaken without their consent and then discovered, we certainly cannot afford to risk the displeasure of the State Department, who would of course get to know of it ... this SOE problem, which is essentially a military and naval one, should be placed fairly and squarely before the Americans and that if the American authorities, who will of course include the State Department, agree that something of an SOE nature should be undertaken in Latin America, then it can be undertaken jointly with the United States, and if the authorities object, then SOE would have to desist.... The risks of detection are very great and, given the enormous area to be dealt with, the vast Axis organi- sations and our very slender resources, what we could do under the most favourable circumstances would be a mere pinprick, and certainly not worth endan- gering our good position with the Latin American Governments, and above all the State Department.

The report also commented on Intrepid, namely William Stephenson. The government representative believed that Stephenson was "probably irretrievably compromised with the State Department" and recommended that with all Intrepid's other tasks and responsibilities, he should "devote his activities to close collaboration with Colonel Donovan in North America and Africa — and possibly the Far East." The recommendation also called for a new appointment, to be deployed to Washington, DC, to be responsible for the whole of Latin America. This new appointment would "work closely with the State Department and superintend both SOE and SIS organisations. These two organisations, in so far as the State Department agreed, would work in close cooperation in the various countries concerned, thus putting an end to the existing rivalry between them and the constant troubles which are at present continually cropping up."[49]

More than any other factor, concern for American displeasure drove the end result. A British "in country" representative memorandum seemed to put the final nail in the coffin for BSC/SOE operations in Latin America. It clearly spelled out the primacy of US decision making in Latin America:

> Today more than ever the USA looks upon South America as being within her sphere of influence and resents the undoubted advantages which Great Britain enjoys by reason of the longer association, greater commercial ties and larger financial interests which exist between her and nearly all the countries of this continent.... In the present struggle, the fundamental basis of our policy should be the most complete collaboration with the USA and it is submitted that the American contention as regards South America should be accepted with all the responsibilities which it involves, and that our organisations throughout South America should be placed at the disposal of the USA in order to help carry out whatever action is decide as being best suited to prevent interference by the Axis Powers. The problem is essentially a naval and military one, but in the absence of the necessary ships and armed forces, the Joint Chiefs of Staff may well consider that there is a role in which an organisation such as OSE can play a useful part.... It is submitted, however, that this part must be known and approved by the US authorities, that a directif [sic] to this effect should be issued from a responsible quarter and that the provision of the necessary tools should be made from the USA.

Perhaps before the Joint Chiefs of Staff have issued their directif, steps could be taken to get in touch with the competent American authorities and discuss this general question. Unfortunately, the affairs of South America are not in the hands of Colonel Donovan, with whom SOE is on the friendliest terms, but in those of the FBI under the US State Department, with whom relations have recently become somewhat strained.

It is possible that the idea of covert activities in South America may be distasteful to the US State Department as being contrary to our good neighbour policy.... In the event the Joint Chiefs of Staff giving their approval to the activities of this body and soliciting our assistance, then an increase of the existing British SOE Organisation will be necessary.... American cooperation in South America is a fundamental and without it nothing worth doing can be achieved.[50]

The controversy finally came to an end in December 1942, when the head of the SOE reported that the SOE organization in Latin America would be reduced and their operations suspended. Only a minimum of SOE representatives, enough to enable activities to be resumed in the event of unexpected future developments, would be left behind.[51] BSC/SOE closed down their operations in entirety in Latin America on October 1, 1944. Nonetheless, the impact on the war effort of BSC/SOE efforts in this region of the world was considerable. The head of the SOE wrote:

We have been instrumental, through our local represen-tatives and facilities in Canada, in conceiving and setting up the Security Scheme (now administered by Security Executive) for the protection of British strategic raw materials, their sources and supply lines. Our decision to suspend SOE activities for the time being will in no way affect the progress of this scheme which it is hoped

will shortly cover all British Railways, Oilfields, Power
Companies and essential industrial undertakings.[52]

Clearly, Stephenson's BSC/SOE operations in the United States and
Latin American furthered the British war effort, particularly during the
dark days before American involvement in the war. The Canadian nexus
was instrumental to this success. But the Canadian connection did not
end there. Even as Stephenson and his largely Canadian staff at BSC were
managing the Latin American portfolios, he was also busy working on
cementing his relationship with the Americans, particularly Donovan
and the FBI. He once again reached back to Canada. Specifically,
Stephenson developed a plan to create a special training school, close to
the Canadia-US border that could train both Canadian SOE agents as
well as Americans. This school would become a key component in training Canadian agents, as well as to the establishment of the American
special operations capability.

5

KILLING TWO BIRDS WITH ONE STONE: THE CREATION OF CAMP X

Undisputedly, Sir William Stephenson and the BSC were well invested in advancing the Allied war effort. As Churchill's man in the Americas, Stephenson worked without respite to ensure the security and protection of vital war supplies sourced from the US and Latin America, as well as to strengthen pro-British sentiment. But Stephenson was not the only Canadian who the British solicited to assist with the SOE. As more and more Canadians were pulled into the SOE net, Stephenson realized there was a need to ensure that Canadian recruits were operationally prepared. He also saw the training as another opportunity to tie in even closer with the Americans. After all, the SOE experience and expertise developed so far would go a long way in helping the Americans, particularly his close colleague Colonel "Wild Bill" Donovan, create their own equivalent to the British SOE. Canada became a focal point in accomplishing the dual mission of selecting and training volunteers, as well as drawing closer to the Americans.

Even as Churchill and the SIS were recruiting Stephenson, the SOE realized it was lacking the necessary personnel with the specific skills they required. By the end of 1941 there was a dire need for expert linguists, who were always at a premium in England. However, the requirement was more than just language proficiency. The SOE needed "men and women who were not only thoroughly acquainted with the countries to which they were to be sent, but possessed courage and physical stamina of a degree sufficient to enable them to live the lives of hunted outcasts with the threat of torture and death constantly in the offing."[1]

As early as March 12, 1940 — four months prior to the SOE being created and during its embryonic, although limited, foray into irregular warfare in the dark days of the Phoney War period — the British War Office had approached the Canadian Military Headquarters (CMHQ) in London to inquire if the Canadians could recommend personnel for "irregular leaders or guerilla warfare jobs." The War Office elaborated that the individuals would receive "social and political" training with regards to particular German-occupied countries. The intent was to employ the trained agents for political missions, "especially at the end of the war when conditions may be somewhat chaotic."[2]

Initially, Major-General Andrew McNaughton, the Canadian overseas commander, refused. Philosophically, he was not a supporter of special operations forces or special warfare.[3] However, the following year, in 1941, with no imminent employment of the Canadian troops in the offing, he relented and allowed soldiers from the Canadian expeditionary force to volunteer for special service.

The fact that the British had approached McNaughton is not surprising. Canada, with its diverse make-up, dual founding nationalities, and heavy immigrant population, provided a rich recruiting ground. Specifically, the British were looking for French Canadians for service in France, Canadians of Eastern European descent for the Balkans, and Chinese Canadians for Far East operations. The British also tapped into their offices in North America, specifically BSC. With the consent of the Canadian government, a number of volunteers among Canadian Yugoslavs were recruited. These Canadians actually became the first to be selected for SOE operations in the war. They were later followed by other Canadians with ethnic roots in Italy, Hungary, Romania, and Bulgaria.[4]

By late 1942 the shortage of French-speaking wireless operators was acute. One SOE staff officer advised, "I know the difficulties encountered in the recruiting of personnel for the field. May I suggest that all efforts should be made to approach the Canadian Forces and all other possible sources of supply to obtain men with the necessary qualifications."[5]

With McNaughton's approval, the War Office directly approached the chief signals officer of the Canadian Army to identify likely candidates. As it worked out, the vast majority of Canadian SOE agents were wireless operators who were nominated by the chief signals officer. The other Canadian agents who volunteered were vetted by the senior intelligence officer at Canadian military headquarters (CMHQ) in London.

The Canadians provided the British with a ready solution to their manpower dilemma. In many ways, they were ready-made operatives, since they possessed linguistic and cultural attributes that the SOE were looking for. As such, the SOE needed only to train them in the art of sabotage and subversion. At first, Canadian volunteers were released from the Canadian military and taken on by the British SOE. Incredibly, the terms of service were simply verbal and the subsequent administration was shoddy. Although the need for haste and secrecy was evident, the lack of attention to detail very quickly proved to be unsatisfactory for the Canadians. As a result, some of the first enrolees found themselves utterly abandoned if they were hurt, deemed unfit for service, or if they decided to voluntarily withdraw. By the end of 1942, the Canadian government stepped in and developed a system by which volunteers were "loaned" to the British War Office for terms of six months and they maintained their administrative file with the CMHQ.[6]

Like the other volunteers who joined the SOE during the war, the Canadian enrolees "were quickly made to forget all thoughts about Queensbury rules and so-called 'gentlemanly' warfare ... [and they] were taught a vast range of sabotage techniques and bizarre methods of killing."[7] Their training focus centred on advising, arming, and assisting members of the various resistance movements in the enemy-occupied countries, as well as evading the German police and counter-intelligence services.

Training, not surprisingly, was a critical component of SOE success. As such, they developed an elaborate framework. Preliminary schools were created to provide elementary training, as well as to act as a filter to weed out candidates before they learned too much of their mission or the SOE. Next, paramilitary schools provided training in demolitions, weapons, tactics, and communications. For those going to occupied Europe, a trip to the commando school at Arisaig in the harsh, remote western reaches of Scotland was also in the cards. Upon completion, candidates proceeded to Manchester for their parachute qualification. Finishing schools gave training in the art and science of leading a clandestine existence. Final briefings were conducted in country-section flats. Raiding parties did only the paramilitary course and were then sent to a holding school. The commando school at Arisaig, which belonged to MI(R), became the first of the paramilitary schools. The first courses for SOE were conducted in December 1940 at Brickendonbury and Arisaig.

Most of the SOE special training schools (STS) were located in the United Kingdom. However, a few were opened in other overseas locations. STS 101 was opened in Singapore in July 1941, but its staff and students were forced into the jungles to carry out guerrilla warfare once the city fell to the Japanese in February 1942. In December 1942, the SOE also opened STS 102 in Ramat David near Haifa in the Middle East to train agents for operations in the Balkans and the Middle East. Its third overseas school was based in North America. Once again, the Canadian nexus was all important. Arguably, it would become the most important of the external schools.[8]

The idea for opening a secret agent training school in Canada was raised in a substantive way on September 6, 1941, when Stephenson hosted a dinner at his residence at the exclusive St. Regis Hotel in Manhattan. One of his guests was Tommy Davies, from SOE headquarters in London, who had come to discuss a number of issues, one of them being a training school in North America. Another key guest was Alfred James Taylor, a wealthy Vancouver businessman who is credited with turning Camp X from an idea into reality.[9] Taylor, already known to Stephenson through his business dealings, was working with the British Supply Council in Washington, DC, at the time, which brought them even closer together. Taylor had used his business contacts to help recruit administrative assistants for the BSC and he had arranged for cover positions for some of the executives who were appointed to some of the most sensitive positions in the BSC.

The morning following the dinner, Davies and Taylor met with two BSC executives (as Stephenson was unavailable), and decided on the location of the camp on the shores of Lake Ontario, near Whitby, Ontario.

The location was deemed ideal because there was ample isolated land for training, yet it was easily accessible from Toronto, which offered thrice-daily air service to New York allowing for communications with BSC headquarters and American organizations. Davies briefed Taylor on the exact nature of the training to be undertaken and the requirements of the camp itself. Taylor went immediately to work, upon Davies's agreement in principle, pending London's approval, that Taylor be given a free hand to find a site and build the camp and have it ready, fully furnished, by November 1941.

Taylor's first act was to make a series of phone calls. The first was to his brother who owned a construction company in Toronto, the second was to a senior partner of the Toronto architect firm Allward and Gouinlock.[10] The proverbial train had left the station. Five days after the original dinner that set the idea in motion, SOE HQ in London approved the project. The following day, SOE HQ authorized twenty-five thousand pounds for preparation of the site and construction of the necessary buildings. Less than a week later, Taylor, through a nebulous entity known as the "Rural Realty Company Ltd.," simultaneously purchased two lots comprising 260 acres in the Broken Front (lakefront) concession near Whitby. Taylor paid for the property himself and he agreed to provide it free of charge to the British government for the duration of the war.[11]

The issue of official Canadian approval was never seriously considered. It was almost an afterthought — other than Stephenson and Taylor, there were no other Canadians or government officials at the dinner or subsequent deliberations. Nonetheless, once apprised of the situation, the Canadian authorities quickly agreed. An official SOE document from October 1941 noted, "We have ascertained that SOE have come to an arrangement with the Canadian Government for the setting up in Canada of a Special Training School to be known as 207 Military Mission."[12]

In fact, they had. In October 1941, Colonel W.H.S. Macklin, director of staff duties in Ottawa, on behalf of the Chief of the General Staff (CGS), informed Major-General Charles Constantine, the commanding general of Military District No. 2 (M.D. No. 2) that the British government was setting up a Special Training School at Whitby, Ontario. Macklin informed

Constantine that the accommodations were already under construction and that the commandant would be accompanied by instructional staff and sixteen students. Macklin also explained that "the Minister has approved all this and has also approved a proposition that we do not set this unit up as a distinct unit of the Canadian Army." He added, "The Minister's intention is that we give the British every assistance in running this school, which is regarded as an important one."[13]

The Canadian Army cover name for Camp X became Military Research Centre No. 2.[14] The manning of the school was a combination of British and Canadian personnel. An SOE document laid out, "the other ranks staff of which will be partly Canadian and partly British. As regards the Canadian other ranks, these will be provided by the Canadian Military Authorities, and we understand all the arrangements are agreed."[15]

Colonel Macklin soon addressed the manpower bill. He wrote Major-General Constantine, "we have been asked to find certain assistance in the way of administrative staff and transport." Quite simply, the personnel were to be sourced from M.D. No. 2. Macklin explained, "you should select them carefully with a view to picking reliable men who can keep quiet about their duties."[16] The staff was required for duty no later than November 15, 1941.

Macklin's final point set the tone for the entire endeavour. He reinforced, "CGS asked me to impress the need for every precaution as regards secrecy."[17]

For administrative purposes the school was controlled by the BSC in New York. Decisions on training policy and practice, however, were in the hands of SOE's director of training in Britain. He also appointed the commanding officer (CO) and instructors.[18] The school's non-teaching staff were provided by the Canadian Army. To the SOE, Camp X was an extremely important post. As such, they sent their top instructors from Beaulieu, their premier finishing school in England, to the new facility. These appointments were an indication of how important they considered the school and its American connection.[19]

Unlike most SOE schools, STS 103 was purpose-built, rather than taking over established buildings and manors. Instructors and students occasionally called the facility "Camp X," but most commonly they referred to it as "the Camp" or "the Farm," as much of the property had been farm-land. Locals, based on the high level of security and frequent explosions, believed it to be a demolitions training area.[20]

The purpose of Camp X, however, was more complex than that. Its "clientele" was one indication of its important role. The "students" at Camp X included:

a. South American Security Scheme personnel;
b. European expatriate Canadian volunteers;
c. Canadian military volunteers;
d. SO and SI Operations personnel (Canadian and American);
e. Office of War Information (OWI) personnel; and
f. members of the FBI.[21]

In fact, an official SOE report captured the wide training audience:

> In December, 1941, a school was opened in Canada for training personnel in SOE methods of warfare. Officers from the New York Head Office, Chief Agents in Latin America and members of OSS and FBI were trained at this school. Canadians, Yugoslavs, Italians, Hungarians, Romanians, Bulgarians, etc., recruited in Canada, were trained at the school and it was then arranged for the majority of them to be infiltrated into Europe.[22]

The training at STS 103 was diverse and exacting. Canadian volunteers recruited in Canada were first sent to Camp X for assessment and elementary training. They normally spent four to five weeks training before being sent to the UK for advanced instruction. Overall training, depending on specific assignments, could take up to six months. All agents had a thorough grounding in unarmed combat and the use of small arms, as well as on the use of explosives and modern industrial sabotage. All had to be parachute qualified, and they all received extensive instruction on their target country.

Although the training was essential, equally important to the establishment and existence of Camp X was solidifying and advancing the American connection. In November 1941, the US was not yet directly involved in the war, and the country's Neutrality Acts made direct co-operation challenging. Moreover, the American special operations and intelligence regime was woefully immature, if not non-existent.

The British were clearly ahead of the Americans in this regard. In fact, the US president consistently lamented his inability to know what his potential enemies were doing. He railed at the deplorable state of US intelligence. President Roosevelt revealed that he had no idea of German plans, German potential, the threat to Pearl Harbor, or the intentions and plans of neutral countries.[23] Roosevelt blamed the inadequate intelligence collecting agencies (the State department, Military Intelligence Division (MID), Office of Naval Intelligence (ONI)). As one official noted, "We knew nothing about what the enemy was doing, while for instance every traveller leaving Japan had definite orders as to what to report and what to look into while travelling."[24]

Due to the perceived failure of his intelligence apparatus, in 1939 President Roosevelt urged the MID, FBI, and ONI to coordinate their intelligence activities. He demanded intelligence that would provide him more situational awareness of the increasingly dangerous and hostile world that was emerging. At first, the Roosevelt administration had no clear idea of what information it thought the intelligence services should be gathering, but as the Axis countries achieved a cascade of military successes without the administration having adequate warning, the US realized the enormous problem it faced. At the heart of the failure of the intelligence system was the rivalry and internecine conflict between the various players. Not surprisingly, each agency jealously protected their domains. In addition, all were focusing on subversion, sabotage, and espionage.[25] As a result, President Roosevelt was basically blind to the capabilities and intent of other nations.[26]

Despite constant reassurance from the various intelligence agencies that coordination had been achieved, the president continued to be surprised by enemy activities. On April 4, 1940, President Roosevelt officially directed the heads of the MID, FBI, and ONI to examine the creation of an intelligence coordination capability similar to the British model in the event that the US would enter the war. Concurrently, Colonel "Wild Bill" Donovan began to advocate — despite the vociferous objections of the three existing agencies — for a centralized intelligence collection and analysis organization.[27]

These actions were occurring at the same time the British intelligence services were requesting better intelligence coordination between the two countries. As noted earlier, this request led to the dispatch of William Stephenson to meet with the director of the FBI and develop a mutually beneficial relationship.[28] By June 1940, the three intelligence agencies (MID, FBI, ONI) had worked out the division of intelligence work abroad. The FBI was responsible for the Western Hemisphere, while the MID and ONI divided up the remainder of the world.[29]

Nonetheless, through the winter of 1940–41, President Roosevelt remained unhappy with the level of intelligence he was receiving. He was, once again, surprised by the German invasion of the Soviet Union in June 1941, particularly its amazing initial success. He found himself lacking the information to anticipate events and make the necessary decisions.

As a result, on July 11, 1941, the President ordered the creation of the office of the Coordinator of Information (COI).[30] The chief branches included research and analysis, geography, economics, psychology, foreign nationalities, oral intelligence, and foreign information service.[31] The Presidential Directive read:

> There is hereby established the position of Coordinator of Information, with authority to collect and analyse all information and data, which may bear upon national security; to correlate such information and data, and to make such information and data available to the President and to such departments and officials of the Government as the President may determine; and to carry out, when requested by the President, such supplementary activities as may facilitate the securing of information important for national security not now available to the Government.[32]

The British War Office.

Electra House, 84 Moorgate, London, England.

Hugh Dalton, minister of economic warfare, responsible for the creation of the SOE.

64 Baker Street, headquarters of the SOE.

Hugh Dalton (right) and Colin Gubbins (centre) speak with Czech officers.

Above: *PROHIBITED AREA* sign at the entrance to Camp X, near Whitby, Ontario.

Left: *An aerial view of Camp X.*

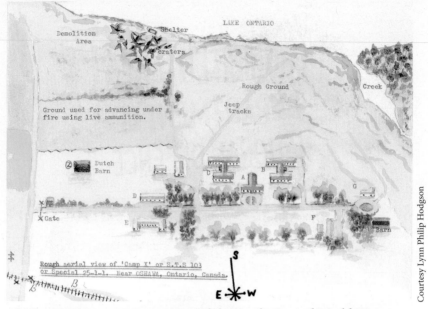

The layout of Camp X, as it appeared during the Second World War.

Sinclair House, a training facility at Camp X.

The main gate at Camp X.

Camp X buildings.

*Camp X
commanding
officer's quarters.*

Some Camp X instructors.

Camp X trainees practising placing explosives.

Right: *Demolitions training at Camp X.*

Facing top: *"Spot check" — preparing for operating behind enemy lines.*

Facing centre: *The hay wagon as a mode of covert transportation.*

Facing bottom: *Yugoslav Canadians at Camp X training for missions in their former homeland.*

American trainees at Camp X.

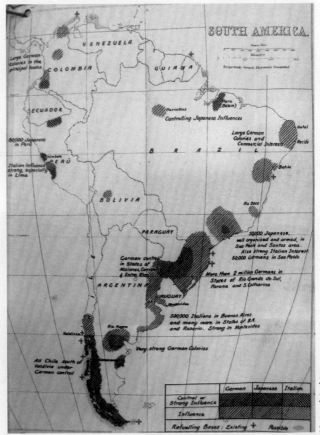

*SOE map of
South America
showing areas
of enemy
infiltration and
influence.*

Colonel Donovan accepted the appointment of director. However, he requested three guarantees before he would undertake the new task. First, as director of the COI he would report directly to the president; second, that the president's secret fund be made available for some of the work of COI; and third, that all departments of the government be instructed to give him such material as he might need. The president agreed to all of the conditions.[33]

For Donovan the pressure was immense. Many, including the president and the Chiefs of Staff, expected Donovan and his COI to produce immediate results, despite the fact that he had not had the time or authority to make the necessary preparations. In the end, Donovan's survival was based on the support and assistance of Stephenson and the BSC, at least in the early stages, and arguably at least until June 1942. Specifically, BSC provided Donovan and the COI the bulk of COI's secret intelligence before Pearl Harbor, as well as for several months following the attack. In addition, BSC controlled, through intermediaries, two short-wave radio services — one for broadcasts to Europe and Africa and the other for broadcasts to the Far East. These networks were made available to COI immediately after Pearl Harbor and they were the foundation of all American short-wave radio propaganda.

As well, the BSC trained the COI officers, both of the SI and SO Division, as well as COI agents at Camp X. The BSC also supplied the COI with all the equipment which it needed for special operations for a lengthy period after Pearl Harbor when such equipment was not yet in production in the US. Stephenson and the BSC also assisted Donovan and the COI with the establishment of its SO division and the creation of its worldwide system of clandestine communications.[34]

And so, the close personal connection between Stephenson and Donovan and the BSC/SOE and the COI ensured that the neophyte American secret intelligence organization got off the ground.[35] Despite the success of the COI, approximately a year later, on June 13, 1942, President Roosevelt directed a change. He created the Office of War Information (OWI) responsible for all overseas propaganda other than "Black" (covert) propaganda, and COI was transformed into the Office of Strategic Services (OSS) and it became an arm of the US Services. Donovan remained the head and his responsibilities were "to collect and analyse all information and data which may bear upon national security, to correlate such information and data, and make the same available to the President and to such departments and officials off the government as the President may determine, and to carry out when requested by the President such supplementary activities as may facilitate the securing of information important for national security not now available to the government."[36] However, he now reported to the Joint Chiefs of Staff.[37] This change gave the JCS the most detailed and relevant information available to them prior to the planning of operations.

As such, the OSS mission was primarily to collect information that would be of operational value.[38] But, with no experience of its own, or with its sister agencies, the OSS looked to the SOE. In fact, as one historian observed, "the conception of coordinated operations in the field of secret activities, which BSC originally exemplified, was the basis upon which the Americans built, with astonishing speed, their own highly successful wartime intelligence service."[39]

Central to building this capability was Camp X. As it had with the COI, Camp X became both a schoolhouse and template for the OSS. In fact, an SOE document revealed, "In order to assist in the establishment of Colonel Donovan's organisation [OSS] special courses were drawn up and carried out at the SO Training School in Canada [Camp X]."[40] A British report on the co-operation between the SOE and OSS noted, "In February 1942, OSS had no training-schools, and the need for them was urgent ... two special courses for OSS personnel were arranged by the commandant of the SOE school in Canada, STS/103." The report assessed, rather condescendingly, that it was "a parent-child relationship."[41] In sum, the report summarized the substantive assistance the SOE provided to the OSS, largely through Camp X and its staff:

a. SOE trained the first OSS instructors;
b. SOE trained the first OSS field agents;
c. SOE officers spent many weeks, during the crucial period of the growth of the organization, in lecturing, demonstrating, and advising at OSS schools;

    d. The revisions by which, in 1942–43, the OSS training scheme was set on its feet were planned by SOE officers;

    e. The lecture-books used by SOE were handed to, and adopted by, OSS schools; and

    f. SOE provided the equipment with which the OSS schools got started.[42]

And so, the SOE, primarily through Camp X and the Canadian connection, provided to the Americans training for their personnel, made available their entire suite of lectures and publications, and furnished the special devices developed for special operations. Throughout, the SOE reinforced its operating philosophy, which was also captured in the school syllabus, "Employ all methods of irregular warfare. END JUSTIFIES THE MEANS [capitalization in the original]."[43]

6

SHROUDED IN SECRECY: TRAINING AND THE INTRODUCTION OF HYDRA AT CAMP X

"We learned how to kill a person smartly — in a short time."[1]
— Les Davis

For William Stephenson the establishment of Camp X was a critical accomplishment. It provided a vehicle for selecting and training Canadians designated for SOE operations in occupied Europe, preparing them for a hazardous environment where the "game" of cat and mouse had deadly consequences. Of equal, if not greater, importance to Stephenson was the ability of Camp X to provide an intimate link and support to Donovan and his embryonic special operations organization. It would become another Canadian contribution to furthering the co-operation and assistance of the United States to the Allied war effort.

The first course at Camp X was scheduled to start December 1, 1941, but the school actually opened on December 9.[2] The training syllabus at Camp X was broader than any of the other SOE establishments. American students were given the Group B (Finishing School) training, as well as advanced instruction on propaganda. Canadian volunteers recruited for SOE employment in enemy-occupied territory were given only the Group A (paramilitary) training. The rest of their instruction was completed in Britain. An official SOE report noted that "Courses at the school [Camp X] consisted of training in Intelligence, creation of an SOE organisation, unarmed combat, small arms, demolitions and incendiaries, and wireless telegraphy."[3] The official BSC history explained:

> The new recruit [at Camp X] was taught the importance of accurate observation; and his own powers of observation were frequently put to practical test by moving or removing objects in his room. He was taught how to shadow a man and how to escape surveillance himself, how to creep up behind an armed sentry and kill him instantly without noise; and how to evade capture by blinding an assailant with a box of matches. In the unarmed combat course he learned many holds whose use would enable him to break an adversary's arm or leg, or knock him unconscious or kill him outright. He learned to handle a tommy-gun and to use several different types of revol-vers and automatic pistols, as well as the use of a knife. Much of his time was spent in mastering the arts of sabotage. He was taught the simplest way of putting a motor car out of commission without leaving trace of his interference. He learned how to attach explosives to a railway track or an oil tank in the way to cause the greatest damage; how to make simple types of grenades and explosive and incendiary devices using material that could easily be purchased. He was also taught how to make and write with secret inks, use different kinds of codes and cyphers for communication with agents and how to interrogate a prisoner to best effect. He was trained in parachute jumping. Practical tests were conducted too, in the city of Toronto with the help of the Toronto City Police.[4]

Joseph Gelleny, a Hungarian-born Canadian, attended Camp X. He described the camp as an unimpressive collection of wooden huts and out-buildings out in the brush. He remembered it had very tight security, despite the fact that there didn't appear to be anything of any particular interest or value there. "When I arrived at the camp," recalled Gelleny, "I was made a part of a group who were largely Canadians with Hungarian backgrounds. I also met some Yugoslavs while I was there, but we pretty much stayed with our own because that's the way it had been arranged." The SOE trained its agents in Camp X in cultural groups because of the language and knowledge of the culture. But first came basic training that lasted a few months. Gelleny described:

> The first objective was to be in absolutely top shape. We had a tremendous amount of physical exercise: running, jumping out of towers, climbing, scaling walls — anything and everything. Then we were given training on a whole range of weapons, including German guns of all kinds. We had to know them inside and out, how to load and fire them, and how to dismantle and reassemble them blind: Sten guns, automatics, whatever, which we did over and over and over again. Then came explosives. It was important to our repertoire of skills that we know how to attack such targets as trains, roads, bridges, and transmission lines. And, we learned how to kill a person a dozen ways, including how to do it without your victim being able to make a sound…. We had to learn to recognize German uniforms, planes, vehicles, whatever. We were shown how to disguise ourselves and how to stop someone from following us. In short, we were taught anything you could possible need if you were working behind enemy lines. As a final exercise, we were dropped off blind in the bush, twenty miles from camp, with nothing to work with, then told to find our way back. There'd be a time limit.[5]

Gelleny summarized, "We were trained to live by our wits, in any circumstance…. On one occasion I was dropped off in Toronto, dressed in the uniform of a German soldier. My assignment was to take photographs of war materiel production factories. If picked up by the Toronto police, I was expected to be able to talk my way out."[6]

Andy Durovecz, another Camp X alumnus, agreed. He asserted, "The training physically and mentally was of the highest order." Durovecz confirmed that each national group was trained separately, isolated from other, similar groups, usually small in number (about a dozen at a time). He emphasized the training "was intense and very rough." Durovecz explained, "In this service a trained agent was somewhat of a one-man unit, his own 'army', handling everything from the decision-making of a general down to the dirtiest routines. He had to know how to do his own killing, demolition, plan his attack and retreat, and above all — stay alive to carry out the next assignment."[7]

The instructional staff paid close attention to the peculiarities of the countries they targeted for operations. It was a simple dictum — the more current knowledge you possessed of your target country, the more advantageous it was for you as an agent. For example, in the dormitory, two individuals shared a simple room, whose furnishings were austere to the extreme. It was simply not a place of luxury or comfort. Durovecz quipped, "Everything suggested that we would have to adjust ourselves to Spartan ways."[8] There was a larger mess area with an attached kitchen that served for whatever leisure activities time off permitted. Durovecz recalled:

> We had suspected all along that our enterprise would be connected with Hungary, still, we were surprised when we entered the mess hall. There was a feeling of "home" about it. A large map of Hungary confronted us on the wall. There was a long table with a Hungarian folk-embroidered cloth. And, what was even more surprising, the table was laden with Hungarian drinks — different kinds of wines and bottles of fruit brandy. Hungarian folk-art objects, a woven rug on the floor, pottery, objects and smaller tablecloths all gave the place a homely Hungarian look.... We really felt transported back to the place most of us had left ten or fifteen years ago.[9]

The training had some perks, although everything had an aim and a purpose. For example, a social evening including drinking was more than just a social affair. First, it allowed the instructors to see how each potential agent took to alcohol. For instance, did anyone have a weakness for it? Second, the agents in training were required to get used to Hungarian and European drinks once again. And, finally, and according to Durovecz most important, the agents had to get used to drinking, period. "Being able to hold one's liquor," asserted Durovecz, "is one of the principal defensive and offensive weapons of a secret agent. One must be able to out drink one's opponent and remain fit for action."[10]

Drinking aside, a key element of the training was physical fitness. Durovecz remembered, "Physical training got tougher as we progressed. The idea was to survive not only punches but also the blows of a club or the butt of a rifle. There were exercises to maintain mobility in the most impossible situations." He also recounted, "There was every kind of hide-and-seek, climbing through pipes and fences, through the narrowest of gaps, over standing or moving objects, hanging on by the skin of one's teeth, then jumping down and disappearing — things a normal human being would not even attempt, thinking them impossible. But the impossible became possible after proper practice."[11]

Weapons familiarization was another key element of the training program. "We were taught at Camp X," recounted one agent, "that any object of everyday use could be a weapon: a box of matches, a lighter, a nail file, fountain pen, pencil — or anything else within reach. Even a newspaper, a hat, a glass of water, or a handful of sand could be a deadly weapon. One could blind an enemy for a moment, or divert his weapon wielding hand when it mattered. The key was to catch on quickly and act with determination and speed."[12]

Foreign and Allied weapons were also an integral component of the training plan. One agent described, "We had to learn to handle our weapons blindfolded, by touch alone. We took them apart and reassembled them blindfolded.... We learned how to conceal weapons, even when subjected to close observation and body-searches, as when entering a building."[13] The agents were also instructed in close-quarter combat in shooting ranges that resembled rooms. One agent depicted:

We shot at standing or moving man-sized dummies attached to a wire stretched between two walls. When the doors were closed and the lights switched off, and it was pitch dark, we had to shoot at standing figures that we had a chance to take a good look at in the light. Later they were moved in the dark, which meant we had to guess at their location, listening to every sound, smelling the air and trusting instinct. This took perfect mind-body coordination.[14]

In the end, the training was simply about killing. Major William Ewart Fairbairn, the unarmed combat specialist, consistently reminded the aspiring agents, "You're interested only in disabling or killing your enemy.... There's no fair play; no rules except one: kill or be killed."[15]

One operator noted, "All of us who were taught by Major Fairbairn soon realised that he had an honest dislike of anything that smacked of decency in fighting."[16] Another agent in training echoed Fairbairn's sentiments. He explained, "We had lots of classes on what to do if you were behind the lines. We learned all the things that could give you away. There was the use of weapons, close-up and hand-to-hand.... It was all stuff that was dirty, not the kind of thing you learned in infantry school. You played dirty here. We learned how to dislocate someone's arm while you had a knife under their rib."[17]

The training itself was conducted largely within the confines of the camp, but also external to it. One agent clarified, "beyond the guarded fences of Camp X, our training fields stretched out in all directions of the compass to faraway areas, covering hundreds of square miles from our central location." He stated, "The area from Oshawa to Toronto and the whole countryside tens of miles to the north provided all kinds of targets for the practicing of demolition, destruction, diversion, dissipation. We built imaginary situations that resembled similar targets and situations in the country to which we would be sent."[18] In fact, Toronto, particularly its railway station, was a popular venue. The agents studied the roundhouse, as well as the turntable platform that placed engines on their tracks. The agents were also taught how to start, get up steam, and stop a locomotive.[19]

Another favourite target was the Oshawa General Motors plant. The plant was a substantial contributor to the war effort, manufacturing tanks, armoured personnel carriers, armoured vehicles, and motorized artillery equipment. It was also a great practice target. Durovecz explained:

> We first went on a survey of the works with a view to formulating plans of action. Places of entry and retreat had to be found. Finally, the plan of action, including calculated risks was worked out. Similar surveys were carried out at the Toronto Telephone Exchange, power stations, oil and gas depots and similar sites. Everything was, of course, merely simulated, but the experience gained was nevertheless invaluable.[20]

Similarly, Frank Devlin recalled another training mission outside of Camp X. He reminisced:

> One of our missions they told us that we had to blow part of the Canadian-Pacific railroad. There were a set of rails right before a bridge. They said that this area was completely guarded and we haven't told the guards that you are coming and they have loaded weapons. We had to rehearse it, work it out in the woods so when we did it we didn't get shot. It worked like clockwork. We planted all the charges under the rails and didn't blow it up of course but we could have done it.[21]

As interesting as the physical training was, there was a dark side to the work of the agents that also had to be covered. As part of the psychological preparation, the SOE instructional staff had to speak to the reality of working as a spy behind enemy lines — namely, the likelihood of capture and subsequent torture. "As part of our psychological preparation," clarified Durovecz, "we were shown a terrible film obtained from France by the SOE. It was made by the Germans in a torture chamber and it showed what they did to the likes of us if caught." The film clearly spelled out the unbelievably sadistic torture methods to which Allied agents were subjected. "When the lights were turned on," elucidated Durovecz, "we all looked pale and were covered in sweat. We were asked if we still wished to carry on with the job.... None of us threw in the towel, but the film taught us to hate the enemy even more."[22]

The psychological preparation ensured all the agents were clearly aware of the potential consequences of their intended actions. It did not, however, detract from the mission focus. One SOE staff visit to Camp X revealed, "The spirit of STS 103 is good and the discipline is high. The Camp is well kept and it compares favourably with training establishments of a similar character in England, particularly in view of the difficulties with which the Commandant is faced in having Canadians under his command who are not trained in the same way as English troops."[23]

Aside from the apparent issues working with Canadian troops, which were not explained in the report, there were some administrative matters that created concerns to the inspection party. Although satisfied with the level of training, the inspection party had some issues with the command and control of Camp X and the training regime. The report noted that the "higher control" of the school was confused. It elaborated:

For financial purposes it [Camp X] is under the control of New York [Stephenson/BSC] and it is also under the direction of New York as regards certain administrative functions. On the other hand, as regards training and policy it is responsible directly to DCD(O) in England. The officers at STS 103 have a tendency to regard themselves as a separate Training Mission sent out from England, responsible only to DCD(O) and that they may train whomsoever they please. They regard co-operation with New York rather as a matter of courtesy than as an obligation. Up to the present no difficulties have arisen, but the principle of having a school in Canada operating under a loose arrangement which makes it partly responsible to London and partly to New York is unsatisfactory. The solution would appear to be to make it responsible to New York for all purposes and New York would then be responsible to London.[24]

Despite the apparent concern, nothing was ever done to change the reporting relationships.

Other concerns also surfaced, specifically about the press and potential discovery. The commanding officer, Lieutenant-Colonel Arthur Terence Roper-Caldbeck, devised a cover story should the local press begin to ask questions. He explained to the district officer commanding, Major-General C.F. Constantine, "I now feel that it might be easier to keep the Press quiet if your Press Liaison Officer could take them into his confidence and tell them a slightly fuller story about our activities, saying he knows they will keep the information to themselves. If they are not told a story of some kind, I am rather afraid that they will start guessing and their speculations might appear in the Press in a form likely to attract considerable attention."[25]

Secrecy was such that even the district commanding officer was not even completely in the know. Major-General Constantine wrote, "Incidentally, I have not told him (Press Liaison Officer) of your special activities, but informed him that they were of such a nature that even I did not know exactly what you were doing and it was imperative that the press not 'speculate in print.'"[26] The camp's true purpose was never revealed during the war.

Camp X was also the main pipeline for intelligence traffic between London, Washington, and Ottawa. The communications centre within Camp X was code-named Hydra, and it was manned entirely by Canadians.[27] By late 1941, the BSC found itself faced with a series of serious communications problems. Up to that point the BSC had an agreement with the FBI that SIS and SOE telegrams between New York and London were passed via Washington DC over an FBI wireless channel, which linked FBI headquarters and a British communications centre in England. A landline from New York to Washington was used to relay the telegrams, where a staff of six worked in a code room to encode the messages. BSC traffic to locations other than London were sent over Western Union cables.[28]

In October 1941, two issues strained the existing arrangement. First was the severe shortage of special wireless communications equipment in England. Moreover, Colonel Richard Gambier-Parry, who was the head of Section 8 (communications) of MI6 (SIS), believed he could not rely on the telex link between New York, Washington, and London because the coded Typex messages being sent were passing over American lines and it was just a matter of time before these were cut or intercepted.

The second issue was London's concern that the Nazis would seize parts of South America and, as such, wanted to install a secret communications network in the event that an underground resistance movement would need to be established in South America. As a result, Stephenson agreed that Camp X would be an ideal site to co-locate a secret radio station capable of sending coded messages. After all, the camp was isolated and had several acres of level ground ideal for erecting antennae as well as room to build transmitting and receiving buildings. He appointed another Canadian to solve the immediate BSC communications problems by purchasing secret wireless equipment from the US and providing expertise into the establishment of the secret communications network for South America.[29]

A month later, in December 1941, when the initial training staff for Camp X arrived in Whitby, Ontario, their number included three members of the Royal Corps of Signals. A large two-and-a-half-kilowatt transmitter was acquired in Toronto from an amateur radio enthusiast, and months later a ten-kilowatt unit was obtained in Philadelphia. By May 1942 the link was in full operation.

Initially, the station used the somewhat cumbersome Typex machine. However, the communicators quickly adopted a new machine developed by Canadian professor Benjamin (Pat) deForest Bayly, who was the head of the BSC communications system. The new cypher machine was called the Telekrypton. It was a tape-driven system, rather than a keyboard-operated system like the Typex machine. Edward Travis, the head of Bletchley Park, visited Stephenson in New York and obtained the details of the machine so that it could be produced in Britain.[30]

In the end, Hydra outlived its host, STS 103, which closed its doors in April 1944.[31] Hydra remained in existence and became part of Canada's contribution to the North Atlantic Treaty Organization (NATO), specifically for monitoring Soviet communications.[32] However, the camp was renamed the Oshawa Wireless Station after the war and it was turned over to the Royal Canadian Corps of Signals as a wireless intercept station.[33]

Camp X trained five hundred students and conducted fifty-two courses before it closed in April 1944.[34] Furthermore, it was a shining example of civilian-military co-operation. One official report noted, "The relations between STS 103 and the local military authorities and the RCMP [Royal Canadian Mounted Police] appear to be excellent. The camp appears to be able to obtain within limits anything it requires in the way of men, material and facilities from these sources."[35]

Camp X trained not only Canadians recruited for SOE work, but also Americans from OSS, ONI, OWI, US Military Intelligence, and the FBI, as well as Canadians from the RCMP, Military Intelligence, Department of External Affairs, and Wartime Information Board.[36] In fact, Camp X provided the instruction, as well as the template for the OSS and OWI, as well as other American organizations to train their personnel and set up their own schools.[37] Not surprisingly, Stephenson described Camp X as the "clenched fist" of all Allied secret operations in the Second World War.[38]

7

DOWN TO BUSINESS: OPERATIONS IN EUROPE

Stephenson's motives for establishing Camp X may have been varied; however, central to his focus was preparing Canadians and others to conduct special operations overseas. After all, talented agents were the key to successful missions in Europe, and Camp X was an important vehicle for both screening and preparing many of these. As indicated earlier, most agents were recruited based on linguistic or cultural expertise early on in Camp X's existence. Since the art and science of special operations was in its infancy, it is not surprising that SOE selection was inefficient. Initially it consisted of as little as an informal interview, or, at most, attendance to a three- to four-week selection/training course that SOE leadership eventually deemed too leisurely and ineffective.

Many of those who took the course were failed at the end of the process, which proved a waste of time and resources. Therefore, by July 1943 a four-day selection course (student assessment board (SAB)) was developed that applied a variety of psychological and practical tests to candidates over a four-day period. In this manner they screened questionable volunteers out early. The SAB took less time and provided better results. John Debenham-Taylor, an instructor at the SOE finishing school at Beaulieu, explained what they were looking for in a potential agent:

The sort of thing that we looked for were indications of how people reacted to surprise situations: whether they managed to treat the whole thing quite calmly and not give any indication of being rattled by them. Secondly, was simply the general intelligence and quickness of people to grasp what you were trying to tell them and to carry it out when they did exercises to show that they'd absorbed the lesson. Thirdly, the question of temperament and readiness to accept instructions and orders. Some people did exactly as they were told and others queried it or tended to be excessively laid back about it, as though it was unimportant. It seemed to me this was an important factor in judging to what extent you know the agent was likely to be obedient to the instructions he got. It was a bit of a hit and miss business assessing an agent, but I feel that if you applied those three maxims, you were getting near an accurate picture.[1]

For those who volunteered to be agents, wireless operators, and organizers working behind enemy lines, the rewards were paltry. Recruiters and instructors noted there were many demands placed on those risking their lives behind enemy lines, yet little but a patriotic sense to drive them. After all, the life of an agent required anonymity, as well as the absence of reward. It also meant that individuals had to shed their moral compass and adopt the SOE philosophy of the "end justifies any means." Instructors continually emphasized to candidates that the "rules of this game are different." In addition, agents had to develop habits of exactness, punctuality, attention to detail, as well as personality traits of imagination, ingenuity, cleverness, leadership, loyalty, and patriotism. Finally, for agents a great sense of personal courage was also necessary.[2]

Not surprisingly, the SOE found that successful work was only accomplished through the efforts of high-calibre men and women. The requirement for excellent personnel was to be expected as the enemy also used highly capable individuals and the competition in, as well as consequences of, the deadly cat-and-mouse game of espionage and counter-espionage was severe. The SOE and OSS instructors drilled into their students that "survival and success go to the quickest, cleverest, most ruthless and most patiently persistent" individual.[3]

The hunt for high-calibre agents was not easy. The SOE found that "with a few notable exceptions the members of foreign minority groups in the Western Hemisphere had insufficient interest in the land of their origin to be prepared to return to it, at the sacrifice of their existing comforts, on an arduous and dangerous mission." Moreover, many had forgotten their original language or could speak it only with an accent. Interestingly, anti-fascist intellectuals who had sought sanctuary in the Western Hemisphere were, in general, "not of tough enough fibre to be suitable either for SOE or SIS work, while the majority of the roughnecks did not seem to care greatly who won the war."[4]

The difficulty in finding the necessary agent "raw material" was somewhat mitigated for the British by their colonial offspring. The official BSC history identified that "Canada was by far the most fruitful field of recruitment, and Yugoslav Canadians the most successful recruits."[5]

For the few Canadians deemed potentially capable of becoming agents, they were initially screened, selected, and trained at Camp X. Upon completion of training there, the next step was dispatch overseas. "We were shipped overseas to the UK for the final stages of our training," remembered Joe Gelleny. He continued:

> Our first base was a large commando-training centre in Arisaig, near the Isle of Skye. We spent some twenty-some days there and never once did we see sunshine; it rained every day at least once.... The training at Arisaig was more rigorous than at Camp X. We were taken through paramilitary exercises, such as trying to run in full kit across a boggy swamp with live rounds and explosions going off around you. But after going through such training, you began to build enormous confidence in your ability to handle any physical challenge.... From Arisaig, we were sent to parachute training near Manchester, England. But unfortunately

that course was only a week or so. Then the SOE started to separate us according to skills.[6]

After finishing specialty training, everyone was sent to SOE "finishing school" at a series of manor houses southwest of London. There, trainees were grouped according to their specialty.[7] Training became a continuation of what they had learned at Camp X and Arisaig. Agents were taught to use their head and each limb as a weapon of attack and never to stop just because an opponent was crippled. One Canadian recruit commented, "It [the philosophy] turned our values upside down." Agents were sent from the Group A schools (aggressive techniques of subversive warfare) to the Group B finishing schools for three to four weeks. There, they learned the defensive skills of how to survive in a hostile environment (counter surveillance, police methods and techniques, inconspicuous behaviour).[8]

Even after all that, there was more. As Gelleny recalled, everyone also underwent parachute training at the Parachute Training School at Manchester at Ringway airport. The SOE agents were called "specials." They arrived in groups of thirty and undertook an abbreviated course that lasted only four days, rather than the normal three weeks. They were concealed in safe houses, and after preliminary instruction on parachuting conducted two drops from a balloon from seven hundred feet, two daylight drops from a Whitley bomber, and a night drop.

Throughout their training the agents were kept under close scrutiny. "We were put under intense observation, testing and review," Gelleny reminisced. "Psychiatrists and psychologists were always checking us over, asking questions, and challenging us."[9] The agents were given briefings on what to expect once operating behind enemy lines, as well as practical instruction on disguising one's appearance — remaining the "gray man" — and avoiding scrutiny or suspicion. They were also shown techniques on surviving interrogation and torture without giving up key information. Finally, they continued to refine their self-defence and killing skills. Gelleny asserted that in a three-week training period alone, "they taught us such skills as arson, blackmail, B&E [break and enter], more extensive shooting from the hip techniques, forgery, invisible ink, sabotage, assassination, and even more ways of silent killing."[10]

Unquestionably, expert preparation of the agents that would be dropped behind enemy lines was a critical component of success for SOE operations in Europe. However, so too was the command and control of the various missions. Ironically, despite the assistance the SOE and particularly Stephenson and the BSC gave to the Americans, a complicating matter became the emergence of the OSS.

Although slow to start, once the Americans realized the need, mobilized the capacity, and created their organization, it quickly took root. From the start, the British chief of the Imperial General Staff, Field Marshal Sir Alan Brooke, "stressed the importance of the closest liaison between anything which was set up by Colonel Donovan and the corresponding British Services." He cautioned, "There would be great danger in too many organisations dealing with the same subject." In the same vein, early on Colonel Donovan reassured the British "that he intended that his organisation should work in the very closest touch with the British. He did not intend that there should be any 'crossing the wires.'"[11]

As such, talks between American and British authorities took place in London in June 1942 to delineate SOE and OSS operations. As part of the agreement, American missions were set up in British zones in order to contribute "such services and equipment as are best available from America and will be used by the Head of the British Mission in whatever way he thinks most advantageous."[12] Expressly agreed upon was the caveat that "The Head of the American Mission was forbidden to take action without the approval of the Head of the British Mission, to whom the former was bound to look for all directions and instructions." Although the agreement was initialled by Colonel Donovan, before long the British began to doubt whether it was actually ratified by the American Chiefs of Staff. To the British it appeared that "the Americans never made any serious attempt to implement it."[13]

By March 1943, the then director of the SOE, Sir Charles Hambro, was required to address the wayward agreement. As such, he sent a letter to his subordinates, stating, "We can dot the i's and cross the t's indefinitely, but that we should not try to tie OSS down too rigidly." Hambro asserted that the OSS "must keep their own identity as a separate organisation and that our chief aim must be that they should do nothing without consulting us." He insisted that the emphasis be on "'consulting' and 'working with,' rather than obtaining our 'approval' and 'consent.'"[14] For some of his subordinates the writing was on the wall. One opined, "Personally, I think they [the Americans] are simply paying lip service to the idea of agreement to keep us quiet and that as soon as they have got their personnel, schools, equipment for War Stations, W/T [wireless] sets and aircraft etc. they will throw off this paper control and do just what they like."[15]

Nonetheless, despite the growing pains, the SOE and OSS initially worked closely together. For example during Operation Torch, the invasion of North Africa in November 1942, a combined SOE/OSS organization supported the operation. The special operations orders specifically stated, "The joint OSS/SOE organization will assist by subversive action the landing and subsequent operations of the three Task Forces and the subsequent advance of the 1st Army into Tunisia."[16] By spring 1943, OSS had access to the SOE War Station in England, which allowed them to communicate in their own cyphers with any of their own agents in Western Europe.[17]

Issues continued to arise with control and coordination of operations in Europe, however. SOE seniors had a myriad of complaints, including the observations that: ranks in the OSS were generally one above the corresponding SOE rank; the OSS had limited experience, while the SOE had the advantage of a three years' start in Europe; and SOE had the bases, the schools, the communications, the air liaison, and the experienced staff to do the operation. As a result, as one SOE senior articulated, "I do not think there is any reason why cooperation or efficiency should suffer by authorizing the SOE commander to act as the coordinator for operations. On the contrary I think it may be of assistance to OSS in developing and exercising a very complex and delicate type of organization."[18]

Philosophical approach was another point of friction between the two organizations. One SOE executive complained to Churchill, "the American temperament demands quick and spectacular results, while the British policy is generally speaking long-term and plodding." He warned that "OSS's hankering after playing cowboys and red Indians could only lead to trouble for the alliance."[19]

The continuing tensions finally came to a head and led to the eventual drafting of a new agreement. For the Americans, the "hard and fast delineations of spheres as in the present 1942 agreement [were] undesirable."[20] This is not hard to understand, since the original 1942 agreement was heavily skewed to British control since they had the advantage of having an organization already in place at the time. For instance, the original 1942 agreement stipulated:

> Where the Americans have little interest in an area it would be assigned exclusively to the British organisation and the Americans would either stay out or be represented at most by a liaison officer and a small staff. Where the Americans have a major interest there would be a separate American mission but it would work under the direction and control of the British mission.[21]

Once the OSS was operational, the US predominance began to take effect and a new agreement was put in place. The American position, approved by the American Chiefs of Staff, was basically, "To avoid the confusion resulting from two completely independent organizations working in the same field initial assignment of US and British areas of operation would be made, but the US could assign its own missions, with headquarters, stations and agents to British territory to operate under direction and control of the British 'Controller' and vice versa."[22]

Furthermore, to assist with the command, control, and coordination of special operations in Europe, a Special Force Headquarters was also created. An official letter from Supreme Headquarters Allied Expeditionary Force (SHAEF) explained:

> Special Force Headquarters is a combined United States/ British Headquarters formed from an amalgamation of those divisions of the United States SO Branch of OSS and of the British SOE, concerned with those countries

(less Germany) in the Supreme Commander's sphere. Under the operational control of Supreme Headquarters, Special Force Headquarters is under the joint command of British and United States directors. The main concern of Special Force Headquarters is the organisation and issuance of orders to Resistance behind the enemy lines. This is carried out from the Headquarters in London, assisted in the case of Holland by Special Force Staff Detachments at Headquarters of 21st Army Group and First Canadian and Second British Army.[23]

Turf battles aside, the main purpose of both the SOE/OSS remained to disrupt the German war machine and to shape the Continent for the eventual return of Allied forces.[24] And the Allies believed that subversion, sabotage, and the raising of secret armies would go a long way to achieving the aim. An SOE brief explained:

The Axis Powers, by the enormous extension of territory which they at present control and by their brutal behaviour to the occupants, have laid themselves open to all forms of subversive warfare. Without outside support however it is quite impossible to continue such warfare for long, owing to the lack of direction and control, of materials, of communications etc.

S.O.2 [SOE] is the organisation which is now endeavouring to exploit that situation. Sabotage and explosive materials and devices have been despatched to most countries in Europe in large quantities; money has been provide to subsidise opposition parties; wireless sets and courier services have been established to facilitate communications. In the case of emigre Governments, S.O.2 has direct contacts with them all so as to assist and to direct their own efforts.... S.O.2 is, in fact, acting not only as the counter to German Fifth Column activities, but also as its counterpart. The Axis is waging total war and must be answered in the same way; its Fifth Column must be 'out-columned,' and all oppressed peoples must be encouraged to resist, and assist in the Axis defeat. This can only be done by inciting them, and organising them, and providing the means and training for effective action. This S.O.2 is endeavouring to do, and the time will come when the combined efforts of these peoples, suitably timed and staged, will play a valuable part in the eventual defeat of the Axis.[25]

It was to this end that the SOE (later in conjunction with the OSS) set their sights. The British intended that the occupied populations assist in their liberation, but the SOE realized this could only be done with the proper direction and support.[26] The total war nature of the conflict also meant that the SOE and its agents would make "use of any method which may suit the circumstances."[27] In essence, SOE undertook "direct action," which embraced all operations requiring some degree of force, as well as "indirect action," which covered all means from subversion, such as moral disintegration, to sabotage, as well as the raising of secret armies.[28]

The aim of subversion was simple — encouraging occupied populations to rise against their oppressors and undertake direct and indirect actions to assist the Allied cause. Subversion was intended to foment silent/passive resistance. It included the insertion of British news items in the local press; the dissemination of leaflets in enemy territory; the spreading of subversive whispers; the encouragement of foreign General Staffs to take special measures against possible German invasion; the subsidization of political opposition parties in neutral or semi-neutral countries; labour disruptions, attacks on the morale of the enemy forces, encouragement to join resistance movements and undertake sabotage.[29]

The SOE viewed sabotage as an especially effective tool to disrupt the German war effort. Hugh Dalton, the SOE's first political chief, believed firmly that supporting guerrilla forces behind enemy lines was an integral element of any sabotage organization. He affirmed as early as July 1940 that "we must organise movements in every occupied territory."[30] Sabotage was of particular value to the SOE as it varies from highly technical *coup de main* acts that require detailed planning and the use of specially trained operatives, to innumerable simple acts that the ordinary individual citizen-saboteur can perform. As the SOE/OSS sabotage manuals explained:

> Where destruction is involved, the weapons of the citizen-saboteur are salt, nails, candles, pebbles, thread or any other materials he might normally be expected to possess as a householder or as a worker in his particular occupation. His arsenal is the kitchen shelf, the trash pile, his own usual kit of tools and supplies. The targets of his sabotage are usually objects to which he has normal and inconspicuous access in everyday life.... A second type of simple sabotage requires no destructive tools whatsoever and produces physical damage, if any, by highly indirect means. It is based on universal opportunities to make faulty decisions, to adopt a non-cooperative attitude, and to induce others to follow suit.... This type of activity, sometimes referred to as the 'human element,' is frequently responsible for accidents, delays and general obstruction even under normal conditions.[31]

It was the simple acts of sabotage carried out by thousands of citizen-saboteurs that the SOE hoped to generate. In essence, the slashing of tires, draining fuel tanks, acts of arson, abrading machine, malingering, were all seen as effective ways of wasting materials, manpower, and time, thus degrading the German war effort. "Occurring on a wide scale," the SOE/OSS planners believed that, "simple sabotage will be a constant and tangible drag on the war effort of the enemy."[32]

The SOE looked to a Canadian to assist with the task of imbuing knowledge of sabotage on their agent candidates. The Canadian instructor was Bert "Yank" Levy, an expert on guerrilla warfare who served in the British Home Guard, possessed experience with the British Army in Palestine and Trans-Jordan, and undertook nefarious activities in Mexico and Nicaragua prior to joining the military. He explained the intricacies of sabotage and guerrilla warfare:

> As a guerilla you must be a dim but sinister shadow, a mosquito in a darkened tent that stings first here then there, his victims unable to trap him. Silent, lurking in tiny bands in riverbeds, ditches, ravines, hillsides, empty railway cars, flitting from cover to cover, and like a gadfly pricking the bulky body of the enemy force, striving to goad it into wastage of effort and material. It is our job to buzz around the enemy, stabbing him here then there, with sudden unexpected jabs, destroying or appropriating his stores, munitions and supplies, cutting his communications, trapping his messengers, ambushing his convoys or trucks. In general, creating a considerable amount of hell, and wearing him down.[33]

An SOE training document underscored the importance of guerrilla warfare as part of its irregular warfare activities that included sabotage and subversion. It asserted, "Guerrilla warfare is one of the great war-winning weapons; virtual impossibility for enemy to combat subversive movements on a large scale simultaneously in all his conquered territories."[34]

The importance of guerrilla warfare and sabotage as part of irregular warfare was also underscored by the support it received from the research and development community. BSC's Station M, working with the Canadian National Research Council and OSS, provided six million dollars' worth of special devices, as well as forged identity papers for agents. It also sourced authentic clothing from enemy countries, as well as articles such as knives, fountain pens, and suitcases.[35]

Special weapons and devices were also developed for SOE at Station IX, known as "The Frythe," a small private hotel in Welwyn Garden City in Engalnd. This was the same location in which from August 1940, SOE wireless research was based. Station IX was also known as the Welwyn Experimental Laboratory, which also lent its name to some of its exotic creations such as the Welrod silent pistol and the Welbike (portable motorcycle), as well as the Welfag, a .22 calibre firing device concealed in a cigarette. Special weapons and devices were also manufactured at Station XII (Experimental Station 6 (War Department) ES6 (WD)) at Aston House near Stevenage.[36]

The research community also developed contaminants to sabotage lubricants and fuel. When it was determined that sand and sugar were not effective (in the case of sugar, it was hard to come by in wartime Europe), they developed special compounds such as "turtle eggs," which was bad lubricant contained in a small palm-sized rubber packet that could be slipped into the oil aperture of an engine. When heated, the rubber melted and the bad lubricant mixed with the engine oil. "Special grease" was also manufactured that had a disastrous effect on engine bearings and the axles of rolling stock. Additionally, plastic explosive was developed by the Royal Arsenal at Woolwich. It consisted of an explosive called RDX (Research Department Explosive), which was mixed with oil in an approximate 85 to 15 percent ratio. This mixture gave the explosive a consistency of plasticine. It was superior to dynamite or any other commercial explosives since it was extremely stable and required a well-embedded detonator to trigger an explosion.

Researchers also developed such devices, or "toys" as they were called, as explosive coal, explosive cow/mule/camel dung, as well as explosive "stone" lanterns or Balinese carvings. Not to be outdone by their SOE colleagues, the OSS also developed an explosive flour, nicknamed "Aunt Jemima," that was a mixture of 75 percent RDX and 25 percent wheat flour. It could be baked to look like a loaf of bread. In extremis, it could also be eaten.[37]

The governing principle of the sabotage operations was to cause maximum damage and confusion to the enemy in the shortest possible time. However, agents and their saboteurs were carefully instructed that this objective did not give them "unlimited authority to blow everything at sight." The concern was that numerous obvious small acts of sabotage that would irritate the enemy and prompt them to take increased security precautions. As such, the SOE reminded its agents that "in every case the importance of the objective must be weighed against the possible consequences of the act."[38]

Another methodology that was successfully implemented, but that did not require agents or their networks to actually risk action themselves, was the implementation of the "Blackmail Policy." Quite simply, organizers targeted industrialists. Agents proposed to the owner, manager, or some junior competent authority in a vital factory, that they should immobilize a particular machine tool or vital producing plant so as to deny production to the enemy. If the proposition was refused, the alternative, the agent would explain, was that the Royal Air Force (RAF) would bomb the factory in totality, thereby, greatly increasing the suffering to personnel and the cost of lost property owing to the infinitely lesser precision afforded by aerial bombardment compared with ground sabotage.[39]

Yet another means of sowing chaos was the anonymous letter. SOE/OSS instruction explained, "An anonymous letter is a weapon which is readily available to any literate person. No special materials are required except those which are accessible to all persons....The anonymous letter writer and the amount of damage which can be accomplished amongst enemy personnel is only limited by the ingenuity of the writer applied to the environment in which he is living."[40]

As useful as these methodologies were to the SOE, they were far from the only methods used. It was the raising of secret armies that the SOE saw the greatest potential for investment producing great dividends. If properly prepared, they could tie down large numbers of enemy troops and assist with the liberation of occupied territories. Prime Minister Churchill spoke to the importance of secret armies in an address to the Canadian Parliament. He extolled:

> The second phase which will then open may be called the phase of liberation. During this phase we must look to the recovery of the territories which have been lost or which may yet be lost, and also we must look to the revolt of the conquered peoples from the moment that the rescuing and liberating armies and air forces appear in strength within their borders. For this purpose it is imperative that no State or region that has been over-run

should relax its moral and physical effort in preparation for the day of deliverance.[41]

But the SOE knew that "Insurrections, of popular uprising type, feebly armed and without modern weapons, are foredoomed to unsuccess [sic] as the quick arms of enemy forces may frustrate the insurrection, execute reprisals and exterminate the population as well as destroy the region of insurrection."[42] However, the SOE also realized that support of insurrectionist movement through modern weapons and a communications system could dramatically assist liberating forces. As such, the SOE listed the main tasks of a secret army as:

a.   seizure of aerodromes and landing grounds;
b.   piecemeal destruction of small and isolated German garrisons;
c.   providing a cordon to prevent German troops from being sent to reinforce vital areas; and
d.   supplementing their supplies of arms and equipment from German garrisons and munitions factories.[43]

Having worked out the theory, the SOE next worked on creating the organizations on the ground. Their plans were ambitious. The SOE proposed to build up and equip sabotage organizations that would work as a corollary to the secret armies to the fullest extent that local circumstances would permit by October 1, 1942. They planned to act in the following countries, with the listed number of personnel:

a.   Norway, 525 personnel;
b.   Denmark, 430;
c.   Holland, 1,050;
d.   Belgium, 700;
e.   France, 2,800;
f.   Poland, 1,820; and
g.   Czechoslovakia, 1,225 personnel.

Moreover, the SOE intended to increase or commence the establishment of similar organizations in the Balkans, Switzerland, Tunisia, French West Africa, Algeria, Tangiers, French Morocco, Turkey, and Iran, and further afield in India, the Far East, and South America.[44] In addition, the SOE planned to, by October 1942, raise secret armies in the following locations with the hopes of filling the ranks to the following amounts:

    a. Norway, 19,000 personnel;
    b. Holland, 5,000;
    c. Belgium, 6,000; and
    d. France, 24,000 personnel.[45]

The ambitious plans clearly required a large support base of SOE agents and wireless operators. It also required the SOE agents to recruit and organize resistance cells in the occupied countries in order to grow the sabotage organizations and secret armies. This was always a risky proposition. As such, the SOE provided sage counsel on the selection of host nation agents:

> The type of agent whom you should look for will be the "organiser." First decide, when you have assured yourself of his reliability, for which particular category he will be best adapted, e.g. "Political subversion," and train him to do that work only. A good organiser should have:
>
> a. Personal qualifications:
>   i.   fanatical antipathy to the Germans and every-thing German,
>   ii. courage, resource and determination,
>   iii. leadership and ability to command respect, and
>   iv. a flair for underground work.
>
> b. Technical qualifications:

i. he must be under no suspicion, must have excellent cover and should have no conspicuous features,

ii. an expert knowledge of the territory he is going to work,

iii. he must have the right connections, and

iv. technical knowledge of the branch he intends to organise.[46]

The SOE organizers cautioned, "above all," to guard against recruiting individuals who possessed too strong a personality because "there is always the danger that he will be conspicuous."[47]

Despite an institutional bias, if not animosity, towards the SOE and what it stood for, the British Chiefs of Staff Committee built in substantive roles for SOE agents and their resistance networks in the plans to re-take the continent. They specifically directed that all SOE/SO activities within the sphere of operations of the Supreme Commander Allied Expeditionary Forces fall under his operational control.[48] Their guiding principle, however, was "to inflict the maximum casualties, in men and material, on the withdrawing enemy and thus to undermine his morale by spreading a spirit of defeat among his withdrawing forces." Specific targets included railway demolitions, sabotage of telecommunications, attacks on headquarters, and harassing road transport and small parties of enemy troops.[49]

The British Chiefs of Staff also used the SOE to manage the delicate issue of resistance activities and the desire of the governments of the occupied countries to have more control over events within their borders. An official correspondence explained, "Contacts with Allied Governments and exiled Military Staffs or Commanders on questions relating to subversive activities, resistance groups or secret armies are made through SOE channels. This practice is essential in the day-to-day arrangement of SOE operations, in view of the complex system which has built up in the past few years."[50] Not surprisingly, many of the Allied governments felt aggrieved by the snub; however, it was the SOE that was now maximizing on the investment it had made in agents and resistance networks as the Allies prepared themselves to return to the Continent.

Both the SOE and OSS took on major activities, both at the strategic and tactical levels, as the invasions began. SOE parties were attached to army organizations at the corps or army level to assist with operations. For example, during Operation Husky, the invasion of Sicily, the SOE dispatched a small party called G (Topographical Liaison) Unit to 13th Corps. This group kept military representatives at the corps headquarters and deployed a number of plainclothes parties into the Allied occupied territories to contact anti-fascist elements and to recruit personnel for work further forward on the island or on the Italian mainland. They succeeded in recruiting a small number of local sympathizers with contacts on the mainland, who were prepared to infiltrate into Italy in order to "prepare the ground for Allied troops."[51] Specifically, they were to organize and carry out sabotage and other subversive activities.[52]

At the more tactical level, the Army Force Headquarters (AFHQ) provided direction to the SOE:

(a) Your primary task will be to establish contact with your resistance groups and to bring about, with all the resources at your disposal an immediate hampering of the movement of German troops in or into the Pantaloon area; and

(b) Your subsequent tasks will be:

(i) To gather together and strengthen your contacts with subversive elements within our own lines and to recruit from amongst them personnel to work on attacking vital military objectives, behind the enemy lines, and especially to make attacks on communications;

(ii) to establish contacts with your resistance groups in territory still occupied by the enemy, to supply them with sabotage material, and to direct their activities in such a way that they conform to the military situation; and

(iii) through your political contacts, to keep the army commander continually aware of the possibilities of a 'coup d'etat' within a given town or district.[53]

For the subsequent invasion of Italy, the British Chiefs of Staff directed, "Special Forces, [an official designation given to the SOE by the War Office] will be directly under command of Commanding General, Fifth Army and will at all times keep the Army Commander and his staff fully informed of Special Force activities."[54] The Fifth Army in turn directed the SOE/OSS to conduct two specific types of tasks:

Tasks. There are of two types, and must be kept entirely separate:

(a) Military:
  i. to concentrate on causing the maximum disruption of communications of the German forces in Italy;
  ii. destruction of aircraft;
  iii. undermining the morale of the German forces in the field;
  iv. attacks on fuel.

(b) Political:
  To build up, without the knowledge of the Italians, clandestine networks based on existing groups to prevent, for obvious military reasons, any form of chaotic conditions due to political upheaval in the country.[55]

In the simplest terms, SOE agents were to be deployed prior to the collapse of the Fascist regime and "spread defeatism and confusion among Axis troops, and to disrupt in every possible way German com-munications and transport."[56] Their main tasks were:

a. the contacting of subversive elements (particularly political contacts) which have been working for SOE in Italy during the past eighteen months;
b. the employment of these elements to assist in the weakening of enemy resistance behind the enemy lines by attacking vital military objectives, espe-cially communications; and
c. recruiting of individual agents from among the local populations to assist in (a) and (b) above.[57]

The SOE's main contribution to the defeat of the Axis powers was argu-ably in its assistance to the defeat of the Germans in occupied Europe. The countries that endured the Nazi occupation — such as France, Holland, and Belgium, to name a few — were where the investment in agents and resistance movements provided the greatest dividends. The main tasks SHAEF allotted to resistance groups for D-Day centred chiefly around "the disruption of communications, principally railway communications." The general anticipated tasks were described by the SOE:

1. Attacks on Luftwaffe personnel and aircraft (this is now a priority...);
2. Delay in Road Transport (tyre bursters, ambushes, etc);
3. Attack, or if necessary, very temporary preservation of Aerodromes;
4. Attacks on petrol and ammunition depots;
5. Reception of Airborne or Parachute troops and the provision of local guides who would be able to give a commanding officer up to date information regard-ing local conditions; and
6. Neutralisation or suppression of Civilian author-ities who might prove unfavourable to us.[58]

As D-Day approached, SHAEF provided more specific direction. In April 1944, the SOE was told to begin to shape the theatre. SHAEF directed the SOE to make every effort:

a.   to lower the morale of the German occupying troops;
b.   to ensure the maximum degree of dispersal of the German occupying troops; and
c.   to disrupt and destroy the German Air Force.[59]

SHAEF also set a priority of targets to sabotage to prepare for D-Day:

Between D-14 and D-day — priority targets:

a.   to attack local headquarters of the enemy;
b.   to mark headquarters by ground signs conspicuous from the air;
c.   to mark landing grounds suitable for paratroops;
d.   to cut telephone and other communications;
e.   to erect simple road blocks;
f.   to start fires, particularly in coastal towns;
g.   to prevent demolition of bridges and installations of value to the Allies, but not to prevent the demolition of railways and railway communications; and
h.   to harass the enemy generally in these areas.

On D-Day — priority targets:

a.   The disruption and destruction of the German Air Force;
b.   U-boat supplies and U-boat crews;
c.   petrol and oil dumps; and
d.   enemy military communications.[60]

Prior to D-Day, the SOE briefed the Chiefs of Staff Committee and explained that in excess of a million people in resistance groups in Europe were available for clandestine operations against the Axis forces. The SOE briefers postulated that although the Resistance personnel were only lightly armed and operating in small detachments, they "should be able, if well controlled, to immobilize many enemy divisions." The SOE concluded, "The direction and equipment of resistance groups may therefore prove to be of high value in diverting enemy forces and facilitating Allied military operations."[61] They were proven correct. The great majority of SOE missions prior to D-Day were actually conducted by Allied nationals and very few by British officers.[62]

As the Allied operations struck deeper into Europe after D-Day, pushing the Germans out of the occupied countries, the SOE began to focus on Germany itself. To this point, the SOE's weight of effort was almost exclusively on building up the resistance networks and secret armies in the occupied territories. One assessment explained, "We had in the past concentrated on subversion, loss of confidence in the [Nazi] regime and a split between the [Nazi] Party and the Army.... Apart from these main courses of action there was little else SOE could do to hasten a German downfall."[63]

By August 11, 1944, Germany had become SOE's first priority target. "We must start upon the penetration of the Reich itself," asserted the director of the SOE, "upon means of disrupting it and upon building up inside it a suitable organisation to use during the post-armistice period and perhaps to lead to future clandestine subversive work by whatever agency is charged by H.M.G. [His Majesty's Government] with these functions in peacetime."[64]

The methodology devised was a multi-pronged approach. It included:

a. mass subversion of German Administrative officials in Occupied Territories;

b. Subject to the directives of SHAEF any activity that will cause large movements of people in Germany or create administrative chaos;

c. Attacks on the German Security Services especially the S.D. organisation and all its branches;

d. Organisation of each country's Nationals inside Germany;

e. The recruiting from the local Underground Movement of Agents who, for money or revenge, will be willing at a later date to go into Germany and carry out specific tasks allotted to them;

f. Demoralisation of German troops and mass desertion;

g. Attacks on any German assets and holdings in occupied countries; and

h. Development of channels to handle supplies of "black" propaganda.[65]

With all the Allied movement into Europe, the SOE was given the opportunity to prove its worth and strategic purpose through operations in occupied Europe. The years of preparation, training, cultivating, nurturing, and supporting agents, resistance movements, and secret armies, as well as maintaining a persistent campaign of sabotage and subversion, all came to the fore during the Allied invasions and subsequent operations. However, achieving the end goal was not easy. As with any great endeavour, there were impediments. Not surprisingly, they were exacerbated in war. For the SOE, Clausewitzian "friction" was substantial.

8

"THE SIMPLEST THINGS IN WAR ...": CLAUSEWITZIAN FRICTION

The concept of subversion, sabotage, and raising large resistance networks made eminent sense to many. Luckily for the SOE, many of those individuals carried enough authority and influence to not only protect the SOE, but to also provide it the resources to prosecute its plan. And so, the SOE was given the opportunity to prove its worth and strategic purpose through operations in occupied Europe.

The myriad of challenges in running operations was captured in an SOE memorandum. It explained, "Like all human enterprises, the work of SOE depends greatly on the human factor."[1] This summed-up, without explicitly stating, one of the greatest "frictions" the SOE had to overcome to succeed — namely, human frailty — which expressed itself in many ways, including vice and self-interest. Some individuals and nations preferred others take the risks and do the fighting; some individuals and organizations saw only rivalry and potential competition for power and resources; and some individuals sold out to the enemy to save their own lives. These challenges all severely tested the SOE.

The failure of conquered, occupied nations to assist in their own liberation seems counterintuitive, but it was a very real problem for the SOE. One report noted, "The fact remains, however, that the people in occupied Europe are unsatisfied by our appeal to fight for 'democracy' which as a political creed was never well suited to their temperaments and which now corresponds less than ever to the ideas or needs of the time." The author explained that many of the people of occupied Europe "identify the appeal to fight for democracy with the failures of the older generation before the war."[2]

Nowhere was the reluctance to support a subversive campaign against the Germans greater than in Denmark. An SOE analysis assessed, "It has been rightly said that the Danes are a stolid, unimaginative people, and hardly made of the kind of fuel that will by itself kindle and burst into flames. If the Danes are to be inspired to action now or later, they must be given as much encouragement as possible."[3]

Denmark's lethargy was an irritant to the SOE, who saw subversive action in Denmark as important. They had three principal objectives to achieve. The first was to reduce to an absolute minimum the Danish contribution to the German war effort. The second was to prepare the way for Danish co-operation and assistance for Allied landings or expeditions on Danish territory. Finally, they desired to undermine German authority and the veil of invincibility. An SOE report asserted, "by striking action (for example, the blowing up of the H.C. Orsted Electrical works in Copenhagen) to bring home to the Danes the power of Allied arms and the existence of another dominant factor in the world situation besides the Axis and its awesome theatricalities."[4]

However, their efforts seemed futile. The SOE began operations in Denmark in January 1942, yet they met little success. "Our greatest difficulty," one SOE report noted, "has been to persuade the Danish people that sabotage is a necessary instrument of war, and it was the non-cooperative and at times hostile attitude of the pro-British community that tied the hands of our small band of agents in the Field."[5] The SOE was able to convince and recruit a small band of conspirators and collaborators, but the majority of the population "held the views that, for good or evil, since the King and Government had capitulated to the invader, it was un-Danish for the people to take the law into their own hands and so prejudice the position of their King."[6]

As a result, the SOE took an innovative approach to convince the Danes of the need to co-operate. In January 1943, the RAF conducted a Mosquito bomber raid on the Burmeister & Wain's shipyards in Copenhagen. The Danish attitude literally changed overnight. They realized that the Allies were seriously concerned with Danish industries being exploited by the Germans. The bomber raid sent home the message that if the Danes would not assist in limiting German production by their own efforts, then the RAF would do the job for them. As an SOE report captured, "It was a grim choice of Sabotage or Bombs, and they chose the former because of the lesser risk to human lives."[7] Notably, results were almost immediate. "Our rising record of sabotage," lauded an SOE assessment, "over the last twelve months, which would not have been possible without the help of thousands of local collaborators, dates directly back to that one bombing raid, which has not since been repeated."[8]

Although the SOE was apparently able to overcome the human element in Denmark, the Germans did not take it lying down. One SOE assessment reported:

The situation today is that the Germans have launched a powerful and subtle anti-sabotage campaign, which is, unfortunately gaining considerable ground among important industrialists, as well as police and other officials, amongst whom rank many of our former collaborators. It is a very insidious form of propaganda directed by Danes to Danes and its main theme is that, whilst it is the duty of every good Dane to preserve a very correct attitude to the German invader, sabotage is only of nuisance value to the Allies and constitutes a major threat to Denmark's post-war economy. The latest victims of this form of propaganda are the Danish police, without whom our saboteurs could not have existed in the past, who are now cooperating with the Gestapo to put down sabotage. The Gestapo in their turn are integrating all branches of the Danish police to ensure proper control. This argument against sabotage is a real one and the only one which the materialistic Dane will comprehend, but it would fall to the ground if the Danes were made to realise that their post-war economy will be affected anyway; if not by sabotage, then at any rate by bombing. If the situation in Denmark is allowed to deteriorate still further, then all our efforts to prevent the Danes from collaborating with the Germans will have been wasted and sabotage will eventually come to a standstill through lack of popular support.

The Danes must once again face the choice between being sabotaged or being bombed, and one good raid against a well-chosen target would at once alter the whole situation. This is required particularly now, when Denmark is being subjected by the Hun to a greater degree of humiliation than ever before in her history, If such a raid could then be repeated at regular intervals it would be possible for us to drive home the lesson with a campaign of black-mail sabotage, and German production could be brought almost to a standstill. On the other hand, if the Danes are not given some demonstration of the RAF's striking power their present attitude will deteriorate into one of apathy and German war production in that country will eventually be able to proceed unmolested.[9]

Additional pressure was placed on the Danes, particularly through Danish resistance groups, to understand the ramifications of their failure to take action with regard to the postwar world. "It should be pointed out to the Danes," counselled one Foreign Office [FO] working group, "that, so far, they [the Danes] have done nothing to justify anything other than a very back seat if indeed a seat at all, at the Peace Conference table, and only by action during the remainder of the war, indicating clearly their unity with the Allied Nations, would they deserve, or achieve, such a seat."[10] In a letter to a Danish resistance group, the SOE was equally abundantly clear that some form of action was required, and soon. "It would be most dangerous for Denmark," the letter warned, "if people started to say that the Danes were not prepared to do anything to help the United Nations cause until after the war was won, or until it was practically won."[11]

The Danes were not the only group with which the SOE had difficulties. Personal interest, particularly with regards to safety, livelihood, and economic gain, continually created friction, and the French proved to be a very wily and difficult group with which to work. After the initial shock of defeat in the spring/summer of 1940, some French officers, prior to demobilization, had time to plan underground resistance in general terms before being separated from each other and their men. The planning was, not surprisingly, rather vague, being more theoretical than practical considering the time available. However, it planted the seed. By the autumn, resistance began to sprout. It was at this time that the French ("F") Section of the SOE was first established. The policy of the section was not clearly articulated, but operated under the general operating imperative "to foster subversive activity by all means against the enemy."[12]

By February 1941, a list of possible organizers in country was developed from individuals who were known and whose loyalty could be vouched for. In addition, another list was established based on reports from escaped prisoners, both British and foreign, who provided the names of those who had helped and facilitated escape from occupied Europe.[13] F Section also undertook the compilation of a list of important targets throughout France.[14] However, there were three main challenges:

a. how to confirm that worthwhile resistance movements existed;
b. if they did exist, how to establish contact; and
c. how to provide the sinews of war to those in occupied territories prepared to fight.

F Section deduced the first and third challenges postulated the establishment of physical means of communication; the second, the ability to transmit and receive at an acceptable speed messages, information, and orders.[15]

However, the challenges proved to be more complex. General Charles de Gaulle became the de facto leader of Free French forces and he was anything but co-operative with the SOE. As one SOE report captured:

Owing to the policy of the Government that French arrivals in UK should be placed at the disposal of General de Gaulle, we [SOE F Section] were prohibited from attracting men of French nationality who would have been suitable for radio work, and we, therefore, had to look for that extremely rare phenomenon, an Englishman — or at any rate a national other than French — speaking French as fluently as his own language, with a suitable temperament for radio work and a desire to volunteer for this particularly dangerous and difficult task.[16]

Not surprisingly, French Canadians were seen as a perfect replacement to act as SOE organizers for resistance movements in France.

Aside from the difficulty of working with exile governments and leaders, SOE officers soon found that internal divisions within the French Resistance itself also created no end of frustration. Quite frankly, the SOE were never quite sure with whom they were dealing. Self-appointed resistance leaders, hidden agendas, and political manoeuvres, compounded by petty personal jealousies, made the task of the SOE agents extremely difficult.[17] An SOE assessment bluntly opined, "Now, at this particular time, I would defy anyone to say who has betrayed anybody, or rather who has not betrayed everybody."[18]

The Albanians were also a challenge. One report stated, "They [the Albanians] are extremely venal and are liable to take pay from, and deliver the goods to, both sides."[19] The SOE also had difficulties with the Norwegians who also had their limits of what they were prepared to do and suffer to support the Allied cause. Again, a SOE assessment determined:

We believe that if interference with the business [Herring Oil Industry] were organised so as to interfere with the livelihood of the Norwegian fisherman, we should do our cause harm — not only in Norway itself but possibly among the many thousands of Norwegian seamen upon whom we depend for the movement of a

great deal of ocean going tonnage for our own war supplies. We consider that any attack upon the Herring Oil
industry should be designed in such a way as to interfere
with the delivery of the oil to Germany after it has left
the hands of the fishermen, and then only if they have
been paid for it.[20]

The SOE also had to contend with internal frictions. Chapter 2
articulated the rivalry and difficulties the SOE faced in its creation from
internal competition. The rivalry, particularly with the Foreign Office
and the Secret Intelligence Service, never let up. In fact, the tensions and
lack of co-operation between FO/SIS and SOE even created delays in
operations in Greece.[21]

Similarly, the disdain from the RAF also never diminished. Senior
individuals, such as Air Chief Marshal Portal, resented the SOE, not
only because of the threat they posed to the diversion of aircraft from
the strategic bombing of German cities, but also because of philosophical differences. Portal remarked of SOE operations that "the dropping
of men dressed in civilian clothes for the purpose of attempting to kill
members of the opposing forces is not an operation with which the Royal
Air Force should be associated ... there is a vast difference, in ethics,
between the time honoured operation of the dropping of a spy from the
air and this entirely new scheme for dropping what one can only call
assassins."[22] Indeed, what aircraft the RAF provided was normally done
reluctantly and only after firm direction from higher authority.[23]

The SOE also felt pressure from the British Chiefs of Staff Committee.
They assessed that the SOE organization suffered from:

   a. Lack of Experience. An embryo organisation was
       started shortly before the war as an offshoot of SIS.
       This new Section was transferred from the Foreign
       Office and the present SOE organization was set up
       in mid-1940. Since this date its expansion in per-
       sonnel and activities has been very rapid whilst
       the resources from which suitably qualified and

experienced personnel can be recruited have been strictly limited.

b. Conflict of Interest with SIS. Clashes of interests between SOE and SIS occur owing to the nature of their different activities and owing to overlap and competition in such limited facilities as recruitment of personnel, transport and inter-communications. These clashes, even with the closest liaison, cannot always be resolved as the two organisations are not in a position to assess the relative importance of their respective activities in each case;

c. Control being Exercised by a Ministry not in the full Strategical or Political Picture. In this respect SIS is at an advantage as it is under the Foreign Office and the Foreign Secretary is intimately concerned with the high direction of the war in all its aspects. On the other hand, SOE is outside the central war machine and its representatives are not always fully conversant with the strategical and political background. The issue of Chiefs of Staff directives which lay down priorities and indicate the work which the Chiefs of Staff would like to see carried out, cannot ensure that the day-to-day activities are closely related to the immediate operational requirements. Whilst closer liaison between the Service Departments, SOE and SIS in London might be achieved, we do not believe that this can provide a solution in itself.

d. Control of Resistance Groups and National Armies actively engaged in Operations against the enemy. Experience has shown in the Balkans, and especially in Yugoslavia, that whereas SOE are able to initiate the formation and preparation of resistance groups, a time will come when either these resistance groups will develop in size or their activities will increase in scope to such an extent that SOE will no longer be able to exercise operational or administrative control satisfactorily. In such circumstances those groups must be transferred to the operational control of the Commander-in-Chief and fostered by the normal Service administrative machine. It is advisable that this transfer of responsibility should take place at an early rather than a late stage if full advantage is to be taken of their potentialities.

e. Availability of Transport Facilities. The activities of SOE at present curtailed by a lack of suitable aircraft and sea transport. The Chiefs of Staff from time to time allocate craft to SOE indicating by the means of percentage the purpose for which SOE are to use them. A further difficulty, however, occurs because planned operations cannot always be carried out either owing to unsuitable weather conditions or hazards of the selected route. This uncertainty which is inevitable reacts unfavourably on our Allies.[24]

The greatest "friction" to SOE operations, however, was the Germans themselves, particularly their counter-intelligence activities. The Allies harboured no illusions regarding German capabilities. A 1943 training manual clearly noted:

Experience shows that the German C.E. [counter espionage] authorities are highly organized and methodical; impossibility therefore of leaving anything to chance. Conversely, the very rigidity of the system gives Agent certain loop-holes, provided he conforms to regulations and controls and has an idea of methods used by the police and a cast iron story.[25]

Agents were instructed that "security cannot be taught by rule of thumb. It is a frame of mind attainable through self-discipline, self-training that will make the taking of precautions a habit."[26] Importantly, they were constantly reminded to be "inconspicuous. Avoid all limelight by being an 'average' citizen in appearance and conduct."[27]

However, this was not always enough. The German counter-espionage organization was both skilled and ruthless. The CE used various methods to catch and trap agents. Surveillance of individual premises, railway stations, and public places for both locating suspects, as well as any suspicious individuals, was a staple of the CE methodology. They also controlled hotels, lodging houses, and taxis. In addition, they followed suspects, as well as keeping a watch on their relatives and friends. House and individual body searches were a common occurrence.

Beyond surveillance, the Germans also focused on interception. They routinely vetted the postal system, including everything from censorship, random check of letters, and targeted interception of suspect addresses, names on blacklists, as well as letters to neutral countries. They would use burglary to access courier and official mail. The CE authorities would also intercept telephone and telegraph traffic. Significantly for the SOE agents, the Germans became highly skilled at Direction Finding (D/F) of wireless radio transmissions to the point that they could detect and locate a set within a radius of thirty-two kilometres and be able to narrow down the search to a point where the operator could hear the key strike at approximately one hundred metres.[28]

The German CE agents would use provocation to unearth enemy agents. They would routinely provide bogus offers of service and pass on false information. For example, they would offer to supply boats to facilitate escapes, provide rendezvous points for escapees, or try to organize acts of sabotage and resistance to identify anti-German elements. They would also penetrate cells by utilizing agents who would offer their services or use double agents, notably Allied agents who had been captured and turned. On some occasions, the Germans would arrest an individual and then have them rescued by strangers who purported to belong to the Resistance. This method worked several times. The detainees gave away a great deal of information through sheer relief and excitement after their staged rescue. Similarly, the Germans also used fake arrests and releases to buy credibility for their agents.[29]

The darker side of the German CE efforts included interrogation. The interrogations focused on anyone they thought might be of assistance to the CE campaign. This group included prisoners of war, captured SOE agents, persons whose names had been mentioned in other interrogations, or friends and families of those who had been detained and implicated.

In fact, the SOE soon realized one of its gravest miscalculations in recruiting agents in the occupied territories. An SOE manual explained:

> The basic principle that recruitment should be confined to personal friends, whilst admirable in theory, received a severe and unexpected jolt in practice. The German C.E. authorities made a habit of asking an arrested agent who his personal friends and acquaintances were and then arresting these persons without further pretext. Though the arrests were haphazard and fortuitous, they led incidentally to many casualties in the ranks of the underground.[30]

The German CE authorities were also not above kidnapping suspects in neutral countries.[31]

Interrogation became a major issue for SOE agents as the methods used by the CE authorities, mostly the Gestapo, were brutal. Questioning was normally carried out by four or five interrogators. They frequently made their detainees an offer of immediate release in return for vital information. If two agents were arrested simultaneously, one was invariably told at the beginning of his interrogation that the other had confessed. The alleged confession of a colleague was habitually produced to bluff the detainee into giving further information.

The fact that interrogations were brutal is undisputable. The example of the torture of the Norwegian guerrilla leader called Skogen is informative. An SOE report revealed:

> Skogen was interrogated in sessions lasting, on an average, 20 hours each by three and sometimes four

members of the Gestapo. At the outset the Gestapo were friendly. Later kindness alternated with bullying; and finally bullying predominated. At this stage bright lights were shone in his face; he was continually presented with incriminating confessions signed by his friends and by false statements that they were alleged to have made. When these methods proved ineffective, he was beaten up and a screwing apparatus gradually tightened round the bones of both legs until an attendant doctor stated that he could take no more torture without dying. During all this, Skogen gave away not one word of the important information which he had in his possession. Another victim was placed in a room where the temperature had been raised until it was barely tolerable, and interrogated by relays of Gestapo questioners. On refusing to divulge information, his head and entire body were submerged in a bath of ice-cold water where he was held until on the point of suffocation. His head would then be released and he would be asked the question which he had refused to answer. If he refused again, his head would again be submerged. This man talked.[32]

In another case, a captured agent recounted his interrogation. He described:

With my hands still cuffed behind me I went up two flights in the apartment house, kicked at every step. Then they gave me the works: rawhide whips, clubs, and fists rained on me. They spread my radio equipment out in front of me and tried to force me to acknowledge it, and to admit my relations with the others who had been arrested. I denied everything, or remained silent, not having time to say anything but "No." Then they took me by the hair and beat my head against a radiator. I could not ward off these blows because my hands were still cuffed behind me. Then they took me upstairs to the top of the apartment where they had another nice trick. I was hung by a strong rope tied around the middle of my body and run through a pulley in the roof just over the stair shaft. Then I was whipped hanging in space with nothing to hold on to. My feet, my face, my head, my back were beaten until I was unconscious. They broke several clubs on my back. From time to time they let me down to the bottom and between whippings interrogated me.[33]

Few interrogations were conducted without physical violence. The use of two-foot-long wooden sticks and rubber truncheons to beat a detainee was more common than specific torture. Many would argue that violence was often successful in the extraction of vital information, and that each success encouraged further brutality. For example, the use of wooden sticks to beat an agent led to the "blowing" of the entire Oslo Clandestine Press Organisation in December 1943. The success of this particular incident encouraged interrogators to beat victims even more severely than before.[34]

In the end, the German CE efforts were successful to a degree. For instance, the German *Funkspiel*, where they used captured wireless sets and either their operators or a German imposter to continue to communicate with London, turned up a number of agents working for the Allied cause. The Germans called it "the England Game."

Starting in mid-1942, the Nazi intelligence service, the *Abwehr*, began controlling the SOE's network in the Netherlands, capturing most of the agents parachuted into the country and forcing them to transmit false intelligence back to London. The scale of the disaster was only discovered when two captured Dutch agents escaped from a Nazi prison and made it to Switzerland, where they informed the British that their network in Holland had been infiltrated. In all, forty-six consecutive agents dropped into Holland were immediately captured.[35] In Belgium, the situation was little better. All eight working circuits were run by the Germans. In France, seventeen agents from SOE F Section dropped straight into the arms of the Gestapo. By 1942, half of all SOE agents deployed to France had been eliminated.[36]

The capture of Canadian agent Frank Pickersgill, code-named "Bertrand," and his wireless set, provides but one example. Pickersgill was captured with his wireless operator, John Macalister. Fortuitously for the Germans, they also seized Macalister's codes, as well as his security checks.[37] The Germans then played a *Funkspiel*, pretending to be Bertrand, and proceeded to arrange for the drop of a large amount of material, which was subsequently taken by the Germans. They also captured a number of SOE agents and resistance members.[38]

The Germans maintained another tactic to thwart SOE efforts — reprisals. Ironically, a German lessons-learned document captured the necessity of winning "hearts and minds" in current parlance. The report noted, "The fight against partisans would be simplified if the German forces succeeded in gaining the confidence of the inhabitants through correct and prudent treatment."[39] Nonetheless, theory was quickly cast aside and reprisals became a reality.

The SOE was very conscious of the impact of sabotage on the population. For this reason, its general policy recognized that "Reprisals are almost certainly bound to ensue, and in each case the importance of the target must be weighed up against the effect of such reprisals on the population."[40] To mitigate the impact of reprisals, the SOE enacted specific policies. For instance, the underlying premise was that "All acts of sabotage are subject to such immense reprisals that sabotage work must of necessity be limited to comparatively few attacks on objectives. It is, therefore, highly important that each of these objectives be scientifically selected and the direction come from the highest authority."[41]

The SOE's concern for reprisals was as much humanitarian as it was pragmatic. The SOE leadership fully realized that their operations would meet with resistance from governments in exile, as well as their resistance cells in the respective occupied countries, should reprisals take too great a toll. Experience had already taught them this lesson. One report to the Chiefs of Staff Committee revealed, "German reprisals against acts of sabotage and subversive activity have, however, been of such a brutal character, and the spread of German influence in the

Balkans has been so marked, that Polish and Czech subversive activities supported by us have been seriously handicapped of late."[42] As a result, a careful consideration of all actions was always undertaken.

And so, despite the enthusiasm and commitment to the cause of "setting Europe on fire," the SOE faced innumerable hurdles and "frictions" that impeded their abilities to prosecute operations. From internal rivalries, to hesitant allies, to a cunning and brutal foe, the SOE navigated the challenges and worked diligently to set the stage in occupied Europe for the day the Allies would return to the Continent. Their ultimate success depended on the intrepid agents they infiltrated behind enemy lines. It was a question of turning theory into reality.

9

TURNING THEORY TO REALITY: CANADIANS ON SOE OPERATIONS

Theory is relatively simple; it is the execution of the plan that is consistently difficult. Although the SOE did everything in its power to control as many variables as it could, and to mitigate the impact of those it could not, its ability to control actions on the ground, surprisingly, was not necessarily a question of how well agents were prepared or supported. Rather, success on the ground consistently depended on the ability of their agents to adapt to, and operate in, a very complex, dynamic, and lethal environment. As one agent observed, "We learned the rules and made the rules as we went along. Some had no time to learn them; their first mistake was their last." He conceded, "At the start, it must be confessed we thought of the whole business as a game. A serious deadly one, but a game nevertheless."[1]

The first real challenge for SOE agents was penetrating occupied Europe. They infiltrated by being dropped off by parachute or boat, as well as by foot through neighbouring countries. The SOE often used bombing runs to cover the infiltration of agents. The challenge, however, was convincing the RAF to divert bombers from other targets, or even to allow for their bombing routes to be adapted so that they could provide cover for SOE infiltration. For example, in one case the SOE approached the RAF for assistance stating, "It is hoped that the bombing attack on Skoda works will provide the cover for two special operations to be carried out on the same night." The SOE planners argued, "It would greatly increase the chances of success of these operations if a number of the aircraft carrying out the bombing attack could follow the courses suggested on the attached plan after bombing the Skoda plant in order to provide cover for the two aircraft carrying out the special operations."[2] The use of the RAF for cover went one step further. SOE agents were given airmen identity discs in order to give them a chance of being treated as prisoners of war if they were captured by the Germans.[3]

Once on the ground, the difficulties for the SOE agents magnified. Not surprisingly, the casualty rate for SOE operatives, based on operations in France, was 25 percent.[4] All agents learned two lessons very quickly. The first was that without radio communications, an organizer was powerless and almost totally ineffective. This reality was in itself problematic. The wireless radio sets weighed approximately fourteen kilograms and were not easily disguised. Regular German searches, spot checks, and an efficient direction finding capability, merely added to the difficulty. Consequently, the average "life expectancy" of a wireless operator was only three months.[5]

Another rule that agents learned very quickly was that it was essential to prevent leakage of information, plans, and identities between sabotage or resistance cells (or circuits as the SOE called them) — each had to be completely "watertight." Most agents never spent more than three to four nights in the same house.[6] But even constant movement was not always enough. The problem was who to trust. By the end of March 1941, F Section had a preliminary list of only ten reliable Frenchmen selected for training. These men, for the most part, had acted as liaison officers with British units in the early years of the war, and as such possessed background of both French and British military practice.

The first of the SOE individuals to be dropped into France was George Noble, whose actual name was Commandant Georges Bégué. He made contact with SOE headquarters immediately upon landing and was followed by a number of others. Together, they were responsible for reporting on the preparedness of French Resistance organizations and their requirements.[7]

Despite having some SOE-trained French agents on the ground, F Section suffered considerably from a lack of a clear directive on the prosecution of operations, due no doubt to uncertainty on the part of the authorities as to how far indigenous French Resistance could be trusted. Nonetheless, the director of F Section decided to proceed with the dispatch of British officers, "on whom we could rely, in order that they might try out the temper of the local resistants."[8]

Even with their own people on the ground, however, the SOE found developing the resistance circuits and networks exceedingly difficult. The SOE agents were required to select others who could act as leaders, organizers, recruiters, agents, and saboteurs. The question of trust was always a key issue. As such, SOE agents had to first assure themselves of a prospect's reliability. Next, they had to decide the particular category of work the prospect was best able to carry out (political subversion, sabotage), and then train the individual for that particular type of work only.

To assist their personnel in the field, SOE headquarters specifically detailed the attributes and characteristics of a "good" prospective agent/organizer. These were:

    a. Personal qualifications:
       i. fanatical antipathy to the Germans and everything German,
       ii. courage, resource and determination,
       iii. leadership and ability to command respect,
       iv. a flair for underground work. (Above all, guard against using a man with too strong a personality, as there is always the danger that he will be conspicuous); and

    b. Technical qualifications:
       i. he must be under no suspicion, must have excellent cover and should have no conspicuous features,
       ii. an expert knowledge of the territory he is going to work,
       iii. he must have the right connections, and
       iv. a technical knowledge of the branch he intends to organise.[9]

Initially, the SOE leadership maintained a very tight control of sabotage activity in France. As one F Section report explained, "It was our belief that premature explosion of French resistance was our worst danger, as there could at that time be no prospect of an early landing of Allied troops to sustain such a movement."[10] Rather, the early period was designed to build and equip the resistance network so that it could be of the maximum value when actually called upon on.[11]

Then, on January 22, 1943, the British Chiefs of Staff Committee gave the SOE a new directive that contained a key objective, namely "to undertake the sabotage of the German war effort by every means available." The ban on violent sabotage was removed, and pressure was now placed on the recruiting of *coup-de-main* parties. Thereafter, sabotage incidents occurred almost daily in the greater Paris area, including very important attacks on electricity transformers, railways, and oil storage facilities.[12]

As the sabotage campaign kicked off, the SOE agents that undertook the clandestine field work to lead, establish, maintain, and support the various resistance circuits and networks included Canadians. In fact, numerous French Canadians led resistance forces in France. Although not a comprehensive list of all Canadian SOE operatives, this brief snapshot of some of the intrepid Canadian SOE agents provides a small window on the Canadian contribution and the challenges they faced.[13]

The first Canadian officer to serve with SOE in the field was Captain Gustave Daniel Alfred Bieler, a Canadian of Swiss origin and French birth. He had been the director of translation for Sun Life Assurance Company in Montreal when the war began. Although in his late thirties, he volunteered for duty overseas and joined the Régiment de Maisonneuve. In April 1942, while undertaking official business at the War Office fate played its hand. Bieler ran into Major Maurice Buckmaster, the SOE director of F Section. Bieler, due to his French background, maturity, and apparent dedication, made a favourable impression. Despite his age, he was soon offered a position. By the time he completed his training in November 1943, he was forty years old, the oldest candidate on his course.[14]

Later that month, on November 25, the newly promoted Major Bieler dropped into France, near Montargis. His mission met misfortune immediately. His parachute descent was incredibly bad. Bieler hit the rocky ground extremely hard and seriously injured his back. The debilitating injury was so acute that Bieler lay on the ground unable to move for hours until his companions, who had jumped from the same Whitley bomber, found him and transported him to Paris. Linking up with his brother, who was in the French Resistance, Bieler was signed into a Paris hospital under the false identity of Guy Morin. After six weeks of hospitalization he spent a further three months in a safe house recuperating. Throughout, he refused offers from headquarters for air evacuation.[15]

Once able to move with more ease, Beiler relocated to St. Quentin, which was his area of operation (AO). He still experienced persistent pain and was unable to stand on his feet for more than five to six hours a day. Nonetheless, Beiler's focus was singularly on developing his sabotage circuit, known as "Musician." Frustratingly, he had to wait over six months for the arrival of a qualified wireless operator.[16]

Beiler's dedication to duty soon began to pay dividends. He cleverly maintained constant contact with the French railway officials. This connection allowed him to stay up to date with the rail schedule and furnished him with the ability to pick the best, most lucrative targets to hit on the vital rail network that passed through his AO. At the height of their operations, Beiler's circuit was sabotaging the main line between St. Quentin and Lille at least once every two weeks. They also worked with the railway workers to apply abrasive grease to locomotives, resulting in at least ten locomotives being immobilized in the fall of 1943 alone.[17]

Equally important, Beiler and Musician circuit were able to attach underwater limpet mines to a principal canal gate in St. Quentin and take out a target that the RAF had been unable to destroy. Later, they used limpet mines again to demolish forty loaded barges in the canal system. Working with officials in the canal's administration, they were able to time the explosions to do the optimum damage, blocking the canal for several weeks.[18]

Beiler's success was immense. With great achievement, however, came increased attention. By late 1943, German counter-intelligence began to close in. On January 14, 1944, the Gestapo struck, capturing Major Bieler, his wireless operator, and forty-seven other members of the circuit while at their headquarters in the Moulin Brule café just outside of St. Quentin.[19]

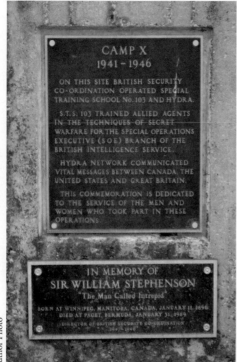

Left: *Camp X memorial plaque erected on the original site of the Second World War secret installation.*

Below: *The Lysander aircraft was a robust workhorse that delivered many SOE agents into Europe.*

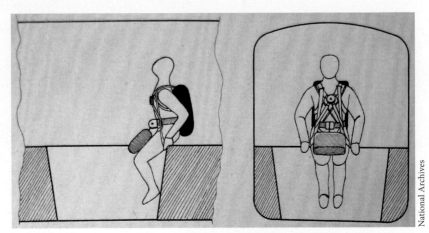

A graphic from an SOE document showing the proper jump position to use when leaving a Whitley bomber.

Dropping of SOE agents into France.

SOE officer meeting with partisans in Albania, August 1943.

A group of maquis, known as the "poachers," Savournon, Haute Savoie. SOE officers can be identified third and fourth from the right.

A Canadian paratrooper links up with a French Resistance fighter on D-Day.

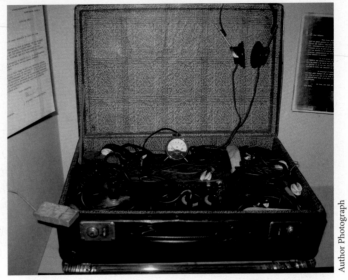

Wireless set hidden in a suitcase.

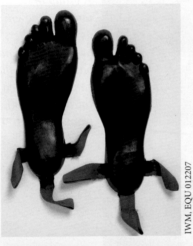

Above left: *Decoy overshoes, commonly called "sneakers," were worn over conventional footwear. They were made specially as a deception device for SOE agents.*

Above right: *A Type IV Limpet Mine camouflaged in a red petrol can.*

Left: *A delay-action fuse in a tin, complete with twelve acid ampules of varying time delays.*

A successful sabotage mission derailing a locomotive in France.

Another successful sabotage mission in France.

Canadian SOE agent Joe Gelleny prior to capture in 1941.

Lieutenant Joe Gelleny in 1943 after capture and torture.

Captain Lionel Guy d'Artois with his wife, Sonya Butt. They met while undertaking SOE training together.

Six SOE members returning from duty in Burma and Southeast Asia.

Seven Canadian SOE officers.

Whitby Archives

Members of the Canadian Women's Army Corps (CWACs) working inside the Camp X teletype room, c. 1944–46.

Courtesy Lynn Philip Hodgson

The rebuilt postwar Hydra building.

His fate was now ordained. He underwent three months of interrogation during which his back injury was exacerbated and one of his kneecaps was broken. His courage under torture was not lost on his superiors. His posthumous Distinguished Service Order commendation notes:

> Despite the most barbarous forms of torture by the enemy over a period extending over at least eight days, he refused absolutely to divulge the names of any one of his associates, or the location of any arms dumps. Despite the intense pain that he was suffering from the injury to his back, he faced the gestapo with the utmost determination and courage.[20]

Bieler and fourteen other British SOE agents were eventually sent to Flossenbürg concentration camp. In September 1944, when headquarters in Berlin ordered his execution, so impressed were his captors at Flossenbürg with his courage and character that they mounted a guard of honour for him as he walked to his execution, which was by firing squad rather than the normal practice of hanging agents. The director of F Section later acknowledged, "This is the only instance known to us of an officer being executed in such circumstances by a firing squad with a Guard of Honour."[21]

The aforementioned Frank Pickersgill and John Macalister were two other Canadians that were inserted into France.[22] Although arguably the most well-known of the Canadian SOE agents of the Second World War, they actually achieved little, since they were captured almost immediately upon arrival. Pickersgill was in Europe at the outbreak of the war. He made his way to France, was interned by the Germans, and then escaped. In November 1942, in London, England, he was commissioned into the Canadian Intelligence Corps and CMHQ subsequently loaned him to the SOE the following month. Macalister was also a student in France at the start of the war. His poor eyesight disallowed his enrolment in the French Army so he returned to England, where he too joined the intelligence corps and subsequently the SOE.

Upon completion of training, the two were deployed into occupied Europe. On the night of June 15, 1943, the two Canadians jumped from a Halifax bomber near Romorantin, south of Loire, France. They were met by a French Resistance member from the Prosper circuit. The SOE tasked Pickersgill and Macalister to develop a sub-circuit of Prosper north of Sedan. Unknown to Pickersgill and Macalister, or to the SOE for that matter, Prosper had been badly compromised due to its large size and inept agents. As the Canadians were led off to a safe house, their safety was already in jeopardy. On June 21, while in transit to the train station for the trip to Paris, the car they were travelling in with members of the Prosper circuit was stopped by a German checkpoint at the entrance of the village of D'Huison. Their cover was quickly blown. Although the two French Resistance members had initially been able to pass scrutiny, upon discovery of the Canadians, the Germans tried to recall the other two, who then decided to make a run for it in the vehicle. German gunfire caused the car to crash and severely injured the two resistance members.[23]

The catastrophe got even worse. Pickersgill and Macalister had with them two of the latest, more lightweight compact wireless sets, radio crystals, the team's codes and security checks, as well as messages in clear to various agents. With the latest information, now reinforcing what they had already accumulated, the Germans decided to pounce immediately on Prosper, arresting virtually the entire circuit. After days of torture at the hands of the Gestapo, one of the French Prosper agents broke down and divulged even more names and addresses. The Germans eventually arrested hundreds of suspects and seized 470 tons of arms and explosives.

Pickersgill and Macalister were severely tortured, but never gave away any information. Another captured agent later affirmed, "Pic and Mac were given the usual beating up, rubber truncheons, electric shocks, kicks in the genitals and what have you. They were in possession of names, addresses and codes the Germans badly wanted, but neither of them squealed."[24] Postwar interrogations of German security personnel who were present confirmed the courage of the two Canadians. The Germans testified, "to the outstanding fortitude and courage displayed by both these officers [Pickersgill and Macalister] under interrogation and have categorically stated that neither revealed a scrap of information that was of the slightest use to the Germans."[25] Pickersgill and Macalister were eventually sent to a concentration camp at Rawicz, Poland.

As previously mentioned, the Germans used the radio equipment and codes to play a *Funkspiel*. An SS officer, Josef Placke, posed as Pickersgill. Placke was a pre-war salesman, rumoured to have once lived in Canada. He spoke excellent English and French, and since no one in the French Resistance had ever met Pickersgill, Placke was able to pass himself off as the Canadian SOE agent. It was not until mid-May 1944 that F Section finally began to suspect that Pickersgill's circuit, as well as several others, were bad. All further drops were suspended.

Pickersgill and Macalister were eventually brought back to Paris in the hope that they would co-operate with the *Funkspiel* and allow the Germans to reactivate their link with the SOE in London. However, when their attempt to get Pickersgill to co-operate failed and he attempted to escape by jumping from a second-storey window (killing a guard and wounding another during the course of the flight), he was shot four times. Surprisingly, the Germans rushed him to a hospital where he eventually recovered from his wounds. On August 8, 1944, as the Allied armies were approaching Paris, Pickersgill, Macalister, and thirty-two other agents were transported to Buchenwald concentration camp. There, on September 11, 1944, they were executed. A report on their deaths revealed:

> The prisoners were brought into a basement of the crematorium on the night of September 11th. There they were beaten atrociously by a half dozen SS. They were then hanged on butcher hooks that had been cemented into the walls, until death came to them. Their bodies were immediately cremated in the furnaces.[26]

Yet another example of a Canadian SOE agent operating in France was Captain Joseph Henri Adélard Benoit, who parachuted into the Saône valley on the night of May 23, 1944. At thirty-eight years of age, Benoit was one of the older Canadians working for the SOE. Prior to enlisting, he was a switchboard inspector and power plant technician with the Montreal Tramways company. As such, he had specific expertise and could easily select vulnerable points on any electric power system.

Benoit organized a circuit at Reims and Epernay. They focused on destroying ammunition and gasoline dumps, as well as disrupting reinforcements and supplies reaching the Normandy front line. Importantly, he twice cut the Reims-Berlin telephone cable, thus disrupting German communications. He also helped destroy a cache of V1 rockets. Having gleaned sensitive information on their location from a senior German officer, Benoit then conducted a careful reconnaissance. As a result, he was able to pinpoint twelve kilometres of tunnels near Rilly-la-Montagne that were full of V1 rockets and their components. A subsequent RAF bomber raid destroyed the entire cache.[27]

Misfortune eventually caught up with Benoit, however. His driver, a member of the *maquis*, was brash, vocal, and enjoyed drinking in bars. This volatile mix ended in the driver's arrest by the Gestapo. As a result, Benoit was forced to escape south to Chaumont. There he organized and led a *maquis* of 250 fighters.[28] Armed with enemy weapons, they assisted the Allied troops in "mopping-up" German forces during the Normandy campaign.

Another remarkable Canadian operating in France was Captain Guy d'Artois. He began the war as an officer in the Royal 22nd Regiment. He returned to Canada in the summer of 1942 to undergo parachute training after volunteering for the 1st Canadian Parachute Battalion. He was subsequently transferred to the newly created First Special Service Force. While on leave in Montreal in September 1943, he was recruited for the SOE. He completed some training at Camp X and then proceeded to Scotland to complete his matriculation.[29] He was undoubtedly one of, if not the, best-trained Canadian SOE operative.

Captain d'Artois was eventually parachuted into France near Lyon on May 1, 1944. He was assigned to the Ditcher circuit. His initial tasks were unenviable. First, he had to encourage the co-operation of the "right" and "left" political elements of the local resistance movement to try to create a more unified, disciplined, and effective fighting element against the Germans. His other responsibility was to create a small security unit responsible for identifying and capturing German agents and the despised French *Milice* in his AO.[30] His group arrested 115 collaborators.[31]

Known as Michel *le Canadien* by the French Resistance members, d'Artois displayed remarkable initiative. He seized a rich French collaborator and held him for ransom, then used the money to finance his entire unit. D'Artois also arranged for large arms drops prior to and immediately after D-Day, which allowed him to equip two battalions worth of fighters. One unit, numbering seven hundred, was commanded by d'Artois himself. He continually cut rail lines, and the night prior to the D-Day landings, d'Artois and his unit blocked sixteen troop trains, disrupted and destroyed railways and telephone cables, blew up canal locks and continually attacked resupply and reinforcement convoys.[32]

By the end of September 1944, d'Artois's work was complete and he reported to advanced SOE headquarters in Paris. He was awarded the Croix de Guerre avec Palme, France's highest award, by General Charles de Gaulle himself at a special ceremony in Canada in 1946. The SOE also awarded him the Distinguished Service Order.[33]

There were numerous other Canadians who operated in France with amazing results. For example, Lieutenant John Dehler dropped into occupied France on August 7, 1944. He organized arms drops for the FFI, enabling them to conduct operations leading to the death or capture of over two thousand enemy troops.

In total, approximately eighteen hundred SOE agents were deployed to occupied France between 1941 and September 1944. Of these, twenty-five were Canadians, seven of whom were captured and executed.[34]

Canadians joined the SOE to serve in theatres of operation other than France. In fact, of a total forty-eight Canadian Yugoslavs volunteered for service.[35] They were deployed singly and were generally attached to British SOE teams as interpreters. Similarly, six Italian Canadians were also recruited in Canada during the war. The intent was to employ them in the same manner as the Yugoslav SOE agents who were trained as interpreters and agents to organize resistance in occupied enemy territory. However, all but one withdrew their service once faced with the actual prospect of dropping behind enemy lines.

Canadians were also dropped into Hungary. The case of Lieutenant Joe Gelleny, who used the cover name Lieutenant Joe Gordon, is instructive, as it provides yet another glimpse into the hazardous existence of a Canadian SOE operative working behind enemy lines.

Gelleny enlisted in the Army at the Canadian National Exhibition in Toronto in 1942. He wanted to be a paratrooper; however, due to his experience with ham radios, he was assigned to the signal corps. Discontented, he transferred to the artillery and was sent to Camp Petawawa where the chain of command discovered he could speak Hungarian. The SOE then interviewed Gelleny, who was a Canadian citizen but Hungarian born, whose parents emigrated from Hungary. The SOE representative persuaded Gelleny to volunteer for a special assignment. The recruiter convinced him that that it would be easy for him to obtain his commission, jump out of an airplane, and do interesting work. He was also told that he would need to temporarily transfer to the British Army, specifically to the SOE, and that he would be able to keep his rank at the end of the war. Enticingly, the recruiter explained that once he completed his basic training he would be promoted to sergeant and once he completed his basic parachutist course he would be promoted to second-lieutenant. As Gelleny recalled, "it all sounded too good to be true, so I was happy to sign up."[36]

At the time Gelleny was recruited, there was little prospect for sabotage or subversion in Hungary. One report candidly assessed, "It must be understood that no appreciable sabotage can be promoted or carried out in Hungary for a long time to come and at least until the general military situation alters drastically in our favour."[37] The report noted that "Any work into Hungary must therefore be along 'long-term' lines, and must aim at influencing the course of events immediately before, and during, the final break-up of the Axis armies in Europe." The report finished by alluding to "certain forces" that if handled correctly at the decisive time would exercise "a powerful influence" for the Allied cause when the Third Reich began to break.[38]

In February 1943, events began to develop. That month, Nobel Prize–winning professor Albert Szent-Györgyi arrived in Istanbul, Turkey, and contacted British representatives. He was acting on behalf of the Hungarian Popular Front and he stated that he was in direct contact with leaders of the Social Democratic Party, the National Peasant Party, the Small Holders Party, the National Democratic Party, and the Peace (Communist) Party. Szent-Györgyi also acknowledged that he had contacted the then minister of defence and notified the Hungarian prime minister of his journey. He then revealed that, with the exception of the Hungarian "fascists[,] all parties and other organizations in Hungary would support a democratic alternative government if the country defected from the Germans."[39]

Apparently, the "peace" initiative by the unofficial Hungarian representative changed the attitude in the SOE, and by June 1943 they began to train agents with Hungarian backgrounds. An SOE detailed assessment of the situation later summarized that "Contact is being maintained with a 'Surrender Group,' representing a part of the Government."[40] The summary and analysis explained that Allied victories in Russia and Sicily encouraged certain elements of the Hungarian "government to offer 'unconditional surrender' to the Anglo-American Allies in the hope of extricating themselves as cheaply as possible from the war."[41] The assessment revealed that the SOE now "hoped that the [Surrender] group can be induced to accept a SOE party." The intent of the team, codenamed "Sandy," was to advise the Hungarian government on means of increasing resistance to Germany, "but not on a sufficiently large scale to provide a German occupation," as this prospect was undesirable to the British government.[42]

Although willing to entertain the peace initiative, the British were understandably leery. As one senior military commander opined, "At this stage of the war, when the satellites will make every effort to climb on the band-wagon, we should exclude any flirtation with their political renegades, who will swarm after us, and confine our activities to direct action."[43] He went on to predict, "I foresee another Bela Kun Red Terror in Hungary when the Axis breaks up. We cannot help that and must use it for our own ends if it will hasten the end of the war."[44]

The flirtations with the "Surrender Group," however, progressed slowly. By early November 1943, British patience was wearing thin, and on November 15, the SOE recommended to the Chiefs of Staff Committee and the Foreign Office a severe bombing of Budapest without delay in order to send a message. The SOE missive stated bluntly, "The time has come to stop these temporising manoeuvres and to tell the 'Surrender Group' in a most categorical manner that Hungary is regarded as an enemy country and will be treated as such unless she proves by action her right to different treatment."[45]

On March 19, 1944, the Germans, aware of political intrigue, occupied Hungary. Regardless, the SOE was now intent on Hungarian operations and the focus became getting "trained SOE personnel with wireless (W/T) sets into Hungary before the withdrawal or collapse of the German Army in order to hinder the withdrawal by all possible means."[46]

Infiltrating Hungary, however, was problematic. SOE agents faced a number of challenges, including vigorous German and Hungarian counter-espionage services; efficient and ruthless police forces; the lack of any established resistance movement and of reliable contacts; and difficulty obtaining forged Hungarian documents outside of Hungary.[47] In addition, the SOE agents faced the apathy, if not the hostility, of the Hungarian population. One report noted, "The country population, were on the whole, hostile and to contact them 'blind' would be extremely dangerous." More ominously, it recounted stories of "American fliers who had bailed out, or force landed [and] had frequently been ill-treated and, in some cases killed."[48] Not surprisingly, the SOE assessed, "Therefore infiltration will remain slow and uncertain. The highest degree of security must be ensured."[49]

The SOE determined there were two approaches to attacking Hungary. The first was by direct attack on targets or personnel whose destruction could handicap the enemy's war efforts. The second was "by seducing or suborning influential elements with the eventual object of bringing Hungary out of the war." Both methods were to be used simultaneously.[50] The first agent, a Hungarian W/T operator trained in England, was successfully dropped in southern Hungary on April 9, 1944.[51]

The SOE found that they had limited success. Nevertheless, they kept trying. Several other missions infiltrated into Hungary in the spring of 1944, but some were captured and others were evacuated for health and/or security reasons. On June 4, 1944, Canadian Gustave Bodo, code-named

Lieutenant Gus Bertram, who was the advance element of the "Dibbler" mission, successfully entered Yugoslavia and linked up with one of the few SOE teams still operating.[52] Bodo moved to his operational area and on July 24 sent a message indicating that he had moved north of Pécs and that he was staying with a peasant in the hills. As a result, the Dibbler commander, British Captain John Coates, decided to send Canadian team members Lieutenant Mike Turk (code named Mike Thomas) and Lieutenant Joe Gelleny, who was the wireless operator, to join Bodo.[53]

Turk and Gelleny made four attempts, guided by Yugoslav partisans under the command of the legendary partisan leader Josip Broz Tito, to get across the border by crossing the Drava River, but heavy patrolling by the Hungarian Home Guard forced them to abort each time. On September 9 they finally returned to their base camp.[54] In the interim, contact was lost with Bodo. Unknown to the Dibbler team, he had been arrested by the Hungarian police. Despite the loss of contact, four days later, Coates, Turk, and Gelleny conducted a blind drop out of an SOE Halifax bomber north of Pécs in an attempt to link up with Bodo and carry on with their mission, which was to create passive resistance and, if possible, uprisings amongst the industrial workers, as well as to form sabotage groups and examine specific targets in the area. They were also responsible for preventing demolition of vital installations and communications by the Germans.[55]

The choice of Pécs was controversial. The area had a considerable population of German origin. However, it was the only district in which SOE had a contact and, therefore, planners felt they were "justified in taking the risk."[56]

The Germans were already aware that the British were planning to drop agents, and their radar easily picked up the Halifax bomber. Adding to the agents' troubles was the fact that the drop was conducted at a higher than normal altitude and, as a result, the Dibbler team and their equipment container were widely scattered. Coates and Turk were picked up almost immediately by the Hungarian Home Guard. Unfortunately for Turk, upon landing he had changed into civilian attire. His lack of uniform, as well as the fact that he was Hungarian, caused him problems once he was captured. His Hungarian captors, as well as the Germans, saw him as a traitor and a spy.

Gelleny was dropped far from his colleagues. Like Coates, he had kept his uniform on. Gelleny tried to signal his colleagues using both his flashlight and calling out "Dibbler," but his efforts were to no avail. Therefore, he buried his wireless set and other equipment, including the mission money made up of gold sovereigns, and decided upon first light to move toward the emergency rendezvous point to find his comrades.[57]

Unable to find them, Gelleny holed up outside the village of Abaliget. Here he was run down by tracking dogs and their handlers. And so, by September 14, the entire Dibbler team was in custody. Coates and Turk underwent a tactical interrogation in the village of Orfü. Coates was bound and then the Hungarians attached wires to his big toes and then to a hand generator. Coates remembered they then began to "ring me up." The electrical current created immense pain without leaving a single mark. Coates agreed to talk and played out his cover story.

On approximately September 15, the Dibbler team was moved to a military detention facility in Pécs. This is the first time the team was reunited. Upon arrival the Hungarians marched Gelleny in front of Coates and Turk to show them that they had captured the entire team. All three underwent interrogation by both the Hungarian 2nd Bureau (security service) and the German *Sicherheitsdienst* (SD, or Security Service).[58]

While in prison, the Hungarian soldiers and senior non-commissioned members were relatively friendly to Coates and Gelleny. Unfortunately, this benevolent attitude did not apply to Turk because he had been captured in civilian clothing. This friendliness did not extend to their interrogators. Gelleny was repeatedly questioned, earning himself kicks and punches when the inquisitors failed to appreciate his vague answers. Growing tired of his lack of detail, the interrogators attached electrical wires to his testicles. Still not satisfied with the results, they proceeded to pour water on Gelleny to increase the pain. He had numbness in his extremities and remained uncoordinated for a long period following the sessions.

On October 5, 1944, the captors moved the entire Dibbler team to Hadik military prison in Budapest. The team was initially incarcerated in the same cell, but were separated the next day. The interrogations continued. The SOE operatives found a large difference between their

Hungarian captors and the Germans — they felt that the Hungarians tried to make things as easy as possible for them.

In fact, two high-ranking Hungarians approached Gelleny to convince him to send a message to his headquarters in Bari, Italy. He was to let them know that on October 15, 1944, Admiral Miklós Horthy, the regent of the Kingdom of Hungary, would make an announcement stating that Hungary was withdrawing from the Axis alliance and calling for an official armistice with the Allies. They wanted to warn off the Allied command and arrange co-operation prior to the actual announcement.[59] Gelleny sent off the missive, and the following day Horthy made the announcement. The commandant of the Hadik prison briefed the Dibbler team, informing them that as far as he was concerned they were free men.

However, events became chaotic. The Germans forced Horthy to resign and installed a puppet dictator. Due to turmoil on the streets, the Dibbler team agreed that the safest place was to remain in the Hadik facility. On November 8, the Hungarians smuggled the Dibbler team into Zugliget prisoner of war camp to evade the Germans. The camp security at this location was extremely lax. It was actually a transit camp to hold Russian, British, and American military personnel on their way to proper detention camps.

Despite the efforts at deception, the Germans found the SOE operatives at Zugliget, and on November 14 they renewed their interrogations. Two days later, coincidently the same day the Dibbler team had planned to escape, the Germans kidnapped the entire Dibbler team and moved them into German-controlled detention cells in the Hungarian 2nd Bureau headquarters building. Surprisingly, on December 7, the Germans returned them to Zugliget. This time, Gelleny and his colleagues did not miss their opportunity to escape. Turk was sent to a Budapest hospital due to his deteriorating health, however, Coates and Gelleny escaped on December 12.

They remained together at a safe house until December 17. The next day Coates moved off to another location to hide, while Gelleny remained. He stayed hidden away in the house until the Russians captured Budapest in early February 1945. His ordeal, however, was not over. Gelleny was eventually arrested by the Soviets and moved into a prisoner of war camp with German prisoners. Fortunately, he was able to convince the Russian commander of the camp that he was in fact British. Given a Russian soldier as an escort, Gelleny walked approximately 230 kilometres to Budaörs, where the British and American delegations were stationed. Upon arrival, Gelleny was taken to the British Embassy and eventually flown to Italy and then transported by boat to Southampton, England. His experience, like so many others, was one filled with adventure, terror, and courage.

With the war in Europe winding down, SOE focus shifted to the Far East. The SOE component in the Far East was known as Force 136. It was larger than a brigade group and has been described as a private army.[60] The organization was very informal, and its commander was a civilian. Force 136 tasks, similar to those of the SOE in Europe, were to establish, train, and arm indigenous underground resistance groups, sabotage industrial and military targets, and conduct subversion, as well as deception. One significant difference was the emphasis placed on Force 136 operatives to undertake tactical and strategic intelligence gathering. Its area of operations included Burma, Siam (current day Thailand), Indo-China (current day Vietnam), Malaya (current day Malaysia), and the eastern portion of Dutch Indonesia (Sumatra, Java). A special organization also existed to assist with the escape and evasion of Allied personnel.

Force 136, which was originally called GSI(k) — ostensibly a branch of British General Headquarters (GHQ) India, was created in the spring of 1941 to prepare for possible operations in the East.[61] As part of this initiative, the SOE opened STS 101 at Tanjung Balai, approximately sixteen kilometres from Singapore, in July 1941 with the intent of training local volunteers in the use of weapons, demolitions, and sabotage. By the time the school was closed down after the fall of Singapore on February 15, its alumni included hundreds of guerrillas. In fact, STS 101 graduates made up the nucleus of the Malayan Peoples' Anti-Japanese Army, which numbered seven thousand by the end of the war.[62]

The SOE efforts in the Far East proved impressive. In fact, SOE-led guerrilla groups killed more Japanese forces than the regular army. One guerrilla force alone is credited with killing an estimated 10,964 Japanese soldiers and wounding another 644.[63]

Despite its success, SOE operations in the Far East proved extremely challenging. First, most western SOE operatives in the Far East had a major disadvantage — namely, skin colour. As such, those of European decent were unable to travel freely in the more populated, urban areas without standing out. As a result, much of Force 136 activities transpired in a rural setting.

The requirement to stay hidden, largely in the jungle, created additional difficulties. The alien culture of the locals, as well as the hostile jungle environment, proved problematic for many, if not most, Europeans to fully adapt to. The heat, disease, and insects endemic to the jungle all had a cumulative effect in wearing down the SOE agents. In addition, the population ranged from indifferent to hostile. This range of emotion is not difficult to understand as many were cowed by the brutality of the Japanese occupation and were terrified to bring undue attention on themselves. And finally, the fanaticism and savagery of the Japanese military proved to be an intractable enemy to combat.

Similar to occupied Europe, Canadian SOE operatives played a commendable role in Force 136. The SOE looked to Chinese Canadians that could easily fit into the surroundings in the Far East. The SOE developed a plan to infiltrate a group of Canadian Chinese into mainland China where they would join forces with the communists to start special operations in the vicinity of Hong Kong. Key to the recruitment of this group was Major Francis Woodley Kendall.[64] He was a Canadian mining engineer who, in 1939, lived in Hong Kong and had done a great deal of relief work for the Hong Kong government. With conflict with Japan imminent, the general officer commanding Hong Kong, General Sir A.E. Grasett, requested Kendall to organize a unit given the code-name "Z Force" to prepare for special operations in the event the colony of Hong Kong was ever occupied.

Kendall, with the assistance of others, prepared six food and ammunition dumps to be used by Z Force, whose name changed to the Reconnaissance Unit in October 1941. He also attended a course at STS 101 in July 1941. He proceeded to recruit Chinese saboteurs and was in the process of establishing a training centre for them when the Japanese overran the colony. During the siege Kendall and another civilian twice rowed out in sampans to attack Japanese ships being used as observation posts. He attached limpet mines, sinking one and severely damaging another.[65]

Kendall's courage and commitment went further. With the fall of Hong Kong imminent, on December 18, 1942, he organized the escape of approximately seventy-five key government and military personnel in five motor torpedo boats and safely led them to guerrilla-controlled territory in China. Kendall taught at the SOE's Eastern Warfare School in Poona, India, until July 1943, when he deployed to London to lead Operation Oblivion.

Operation Oblivion was designed to attach Canadian-Chinese SOE agents to Chinese Communist guerrillas in order to assist them in their fight against the Japanese occupying forces. Kendall was responsible for arranging the recruitment of Chinese Canadians.[66] His first hurdle was the Americans. Kendall travelled to Washington, DC, to obtain US approval of the operation since, as part of the Anglo-American partitioning of theatres of operation, China had been allocated to the US. They objected for political reasons. Specifically, that the SOE mission intended to work with Mao Tse-Tung's communist guerrillas, whereas the Americans had clearly sided with Chiang Kai-Shek's Nationalist Chinese forces.

Undeterred, Kendall stopped by to see William Stephenson at the BSC in New York to discuss the recruitment of Chinese Canadians. He next travelled to Ottawa to speak with government and military officials. This interaction with Canadian officials is where he met his second hurdle. The Canadian government was sensitive to the lack of "enthusiasm" in British Columbia for recruitment for military service of Canadians of East Asian descent. In fact, the government, despite issues with a lack of reinforcements for combat units in Europe and an impending conscription crisis, refused to accept offers of service from Chinese or Japanese Canadian volunteers. It was only after months of lobbying that Kendall finally received ministerial approval for his quest for candidates.[67]

Once approved, the Canadian military authorities, as well as the RCMP, which was actually responsible for vetting all prospective volunteers, provided the necessary co-operation and support. Although given approval, the next challenge became finding the requisite recruits, namely, patriotic Canadians who still had some interest in their country of origin. A serious problem was the level of discrimination that second-generation Chinese Canadians still faced in Canada. The resentment of this poor treatment, compounded by a general apathy to the war in the West, made it not surprisingly difficult to find volunteers prepared to take on dangerous duty on behalf of Canada or the British Empire.[68]

Kendall overcame much of his trouble by drawing on Chinese Canadians that were already enrolled in the Canadian Army.[69] In total, army officials interviewed twenty-five young Chinese Canadians, four from Ontario and the rest from British Columbia. From this group Kendall selected twelve for training at the newly established Lake Okanagan training camp, which was located in a small cove called Goose Bay, approximately sixteen kilometres from Penticton.

Upon arrival at the secret training camp, which was officially called Commando Bay because of a misunderstanding by government officials regarding the actual role of Operation Oblivion, the volunteers, all promoted to the rank of sergeant, were broken into two distinct groups.[70] For the next four months, one group of four was given in-depth training on wireless transmissions, while the other group of eight focused on sabotage and weapons training. The W/T operators next deployed to India for several weeks of training in cryptology at the SOE school at Meerut. The other eight volunteers travelled by ship to Queensland, Australia.

By mid-December 1944, the Canadians had completed their training and deployed to Australia. However, the political dynamic of the American support of the Nationalist army in China once again became an impediment. The American commander of the "China War Theatre" and his secondary role as Chief of Staff to Chiang Kai-Shek, refused to allow the British SOE mission. Concern arose over any possibility of an Allied mission contacting or working with Mao's Communist guerrillas, who were opposing both the Japanese and Kai-Shek's Nationalist Chinese forces. In addition, there were American suspicions that the British were simply trying to rekindle their influence, if not empire, in the Far East. On April 25, 1945, the SOE scrubbed the mission.

A second group of Canadians who served in Force 136 consisted largely of veterans of the SOE French section from the Canadian Army overseas. This group was originally intended for service with the Indo-China section. A number of the French Canadian officers who had parachuted into France subsequently returned to England when their tour of duty was completed and found it difficult to return to regular army life. Therefore, they volunteered for a fresh tour of duty that held the allure of excitement and adventure. After a short course in jungle warfare, the small group of officers was preparing to drop into French Indo-China when the mission was terminated. Force 136 headquarters deemed it suicidal after some French officers were parachuted in to the area and immediately rounded-up by the Annamite Nationalists and handed over to the Japanese.[71]

Some of the French Canadian officers were instead passed to the Burmese section of Force 136 to conduct operations ahead of the south-ward advance of the British 14th Army. As a result, a number of Canadians, Majors J.H.A. Benoit and Captains J.P. Archambeault and R.J. Taschereau, and P.C. Mounier, dropped into the Karenni region close to the Burma–Thai border. Their task, working with Karen guerrillas, was to harass enemy lines of communication, which in this sector passed over narrow and tortuous jungle trails since there were no major roads or railways. Their technique consisted of laying grenades attached to detonation cords at suitable intervals, and then igniting the charges as Japanese convoys passed through. Each officer commanded small forces of native levies from the Burmese Nationalist Army (BNA) who provided diversions for the ambush and completed the mopping up.[72]

Another Canadian operated in the area north of Shwebo. Lieutenant C.C. Dolly was a Trinidad-born South Asian whose parents immigrated to Canada. Dolly, who spoke a number of native dialects current in the theatre of operations, was a natural for Force 136. Although an untrained recruit in January 1945, he was dropped into the field as early as the end of February to report on the movements of 4th and 41st Japanese Infantry Divisions. Often dressed as a coolie and sometimes as a native Burman, Dolly would calmly drive bullock carts for the Japanese supply services. He found the BNA levies unsatisfactory and preferred to work alone. The

Japanese became frustrated with his success and subsequently sent two officers into the jungle, dressed as Buddhist priests, to assassinate him. However, unable to adequately disguise the noise of their weapons under their yellow robes, the Japanese assassins were captured.[73]

Another Canadian initiative commenced towards the end of July 1945, when Major J.H.A. Benoit decided to form the first Canadian Jedburgh Team (consisting of an OC, 2IC, W/T operator, and an interpreter) as part of Operation Tideway Green. Their task was to drop into the northern part of Johore State in Malay, where they were to contact Chinese Communist forces who had proven themselves to be the most aggressive of all irregular armies operating against the Japanese. The Jedburgh's specific mission was to provide day-to-day intelligence on the movement of Japanese forces in western Johore, as well as block three highways in their area. Benoit and his team jumped from a Liberator bomber into Johore on August 5, 1945, the day prior to the atomic bomb being dropped on Hiroshima. The subsequent Japanese surrender on September 2, 1945, rendered the planned Allied invasion of Malaya on September 9 redundant. As such, the mission was terminated.[74]

In all, throughout the war 227 Canadians served as SOE operatives behind enemy lines. Although this chapter is not intended to provide a comprehensive account of all of the missions or Canadian operatives, it provides a window on the challenges and accomplishments of some of the Canadian SOE agents. After all, it was not always the planning or training that made the difference. It was the individual creativity, ingenuity, courage, and daring that led to mission completion. It was the ability of the individual agents to adapt and innovate based on circumstances and environment that led to SOE success. As was shown, Canadians were instrumental in assisting SOE prove their detractors wrong.

10

RECKONING:
THE VALUE OF THE SOE IN THE SECOND WORLD WAR

As the war began to wind down, pressure to minimize, if not shut down, the SOE was omnipresent. The original opponents and rivals of the SOE continued to harbour their resentment and opposition to the secretive organization. By February 1945, the Vice Chief of the Imperial General Staff (VCIGS) challenged SOE manning requirements. His staff wrote, "He [VCIGS] considers that SOE must show in detail just what manpower they are using and where and why; and that they must justify up to the hilt their requirements, in view of the obvious reduction in commitments in Europe. Further, he is not satisfied with the very large figure which is apparently required in the Far East; I cannot, myself, understand how we could conceivably justify 3,000 men for SOE in the Far East."[1]

Other conventional commanders shared a critical eye, if not disdain, for the SOE. One assessment proffered, the SOE was "of little tactical military assistance to direct military operations," insisting that the SOE had "little effective coordination below General Staff Army Group level." It went on to note that the "Secret nature of SOE acted to its disadvantage ... regarding liaison with regular forces."[2] Similarly, the vice chief of the Air Staff revealed, "I think the organization and direction of SOE on the whole was amateur and not half as effective as it might have been."[3] Yet another study group appraised, "the strategic effect of SOE operations was negligible."[4]

Their criticism, however, was a bit harsh, if not heavily tainted by partisanship. At the start of the war, the Allies were in a difficult bind. Having withdrawn from the European continent under German pressure without any of their heavy equipment, facing what was perceived to be an imminent invasion, and with the requirement to completely rebuild and retrain its army, there was little the Allies could do to strike back at the German war machine. The War Cabinet itself had affirmed:

> Our programme of air expansion cannot come to fruition until 1942, and, in order to achieve the strength at which we aim, our first-line expansion during 1941 must be limited. If we try to expand too quickly in the next 12 months, we cannot hope, at the same time, to build up our air power to a decisive strength in 1942. The same considerations apply to a lesser extent to the Army, whose programme cannot be expected to be complete until 1942.... The general conclusion, therefore, is that our strategy during 1941 must be one of attrition.[5]

As such, the SOE was one of a few viable tools to disrupt the German war effort. Beginning from scratch, with no real previous experience in irregular warfare, it is not surprising that the SOE was perceived by many to be amateurish, particularly at the start. Excessive secrecy and a reluctance to educate others as to their utility and methodology, as well as a lack of transparency with the senior conventional chain of command, exacerbated any and all perceived SOE weaknesses and shortcomings. In all fairness, the successes achieved by the SOE were convincing. For example, one 1942 Foreign Office report acknowledged:

> It has been shown that sabotage within occupied countries can be immensely successful when directed, and given assistance from Headquarters in England. Individual acts of sabotage such as the simultaneous destruction of six railways leading from Warsaw to the Eastern Front, the destruction of Radio Paris which

was transmitting vital information for the enemy, the destruction of transformers supplying power to the electric grid system of Southern France, including ship-building yards at Bordeaux, are each the immediate result of one flight of one aircraft across occupied country, and its safe return. The damage achieved is often more than accomplished with the loss of 15 or more planes in mass bombing raids.[6]

Quarterly reports and summaries assembled for the prime minister and chiefs of the general staff shed some light on the impact of the SOE effort. Although not a complete record of what was achieved throughout the entire spectrum of theatres of operation during the entire time period, the following snapshots are indicative of the effect that was achieved. The cumulative total of the sabotage efforts, not to mention the more difficult to measure subversion efforts (work slowdowns, disruption to productivity, non-assistance to the occupying power), undeniably shows that SOE operations caused a continual drain on the German war effort and a requirement for the Germans to spend more time, manpower, and resources in combatting the Allied sabotage and subversion campaign.

For example, from March to June 1942, the SOE had 385 agents in the field. In May 1942, three Norwegian SOE agents landed by fishing boat and destroyed the Bardshaug electric converter station that supplied power for the Orkla pyrite mines and the railway serving the mine. In addition, during this timeframe, the SOE destroyed the only magnesium factory in Italy at Mestre and burned a large dump of Army grain and fodder near Gorizia.[7]

From October 12 to December 31, 1942, the SOE attacked and damaged German barges and merchant vessels in France. They also damaged factories and port facilities, as well as destroying locomotives and railway lines.[8] Often, actual impact and effect can be measured by the reaction of the enemy. To this end, by the end of 1942, the Gestapo headquarters in Paris ordered the German counter espionage personnel to dismantle the SOE. It directed, "The French Section [SOE] organisation in Paris must be rooted out as an overriding priority task."[9]

Nonetheless, SOE success in France continued into the spring. Between March 1943 and May 1943, the SOE continued with the destruction of locomotives, trucks, trains, barges, electric motors, transformers, munitions trains, as well as the killing of German officers and soldiers (583 in April alone), and the destruction of fuel (300,000 litres of oil and 200,000 litres of petrol in May alone). The SOE observed that their efforts had created "a general feeling of alarm and despondency among the German troops dealing with the *maquis*."[10]

The SOE also had an impressive record in Greece. Their April 1943 monthly summary revealed that SOE actions achieved:

1. a two-thirds reduction of Chrome output;
2. an attack on German and Italian troops prompting reinforcement by troops outside of Greece;
3. the destruction of the Gorgopotanos Viaduct;
4. the derailment of trains;
5. the destruction of road and railway bridges;
6. the destruction of ships in harbour;
7. the sabotage of 20 aircraft;
8. the organization of strikes;
9. power houses in Salonika and Athens rendered ineffective; and
10. the placement of mines in Corinth Canal.[11]

SOE success in other theatres was also impressive. In Norway, in April 1943 alone, the SOE sank with limpet mines the 2,000 ton *Ortelsburg* and the 1,460 ton SS *Sanen* and holed and grounded the 5,500 ton *Tugela*. During the same period, in Poland, SOE-sponsored activity was reported to have damaged 202 locomotives, 937 trucks, destroyed a petrol train, and inflicted 28 interruptions to rail traffic headed to the eastern front.[12] A letter from a German soldier on the eastern front to his parents revealed, "Now the Partisans have started their activities in Poland and hardly a train reaches its destination, everything is being blown up."[13] In fact, the Polish Home Army is credited with having put over 5,000 locomotives out of service.[14]

By June 1943, the SOE had 650 agents in the field. Moreover, it had created secret armies that amounted to an impressive number including:

a. Poland, 100,000 personnel;
b. France, 30,000;
c. Norway, 20,000;
d. Holland, 10,000; and
e. Belgium, 5,000.

In addition, the SOE supported a large number of guerrillas in the field, specifically 180,000 in Yugoslavia and 20,000 in Greece.[15]

Meanwhile, SOE's F Section continued to deliver results. From July to September 1943, SOE sponsored activities were responsible for:

1. Members of the French Resistance, with SOE support, killed 650 German officers and men, wounded 4,000, destroyed 150 locomotives, 1,200 railway wagons and 170 lorries;
2. 445 attacks on Axis personnel or premises;
3. 171 train derailments and acts of railway sabotage;
4. 289 acts of incendiarism;
5. 219 acts of sabotage in factories or against public works;
6. 141 acts of subversion;
7. destruction of the Lannemexan aluminium factory in July 1943 (as of end October only 50 percent capacity);
8. sinking of a minesweeper in Rouen;
9. the burning of 3,600 tires at Michelin works in Clermont-Ferrand; and
10. the destruction of 1,000,000 litres of aviation fuel and 10,000,000 litres of oil.[16]

Moreover, October was rated as a "record month to date for sabotage including the blowing up of aircraft, transformers, break-down trains, lock-gates, locomotives and powder factories."[17] In addition, five thousand tons of munitions were destroyed at Langres.

The remainder of the year for SOE activity in France was no less successful. SOE actions achieved the substantive destruction of:

1. Lock gates, which immobilised 50 barges;
2. Pimento's power plant;
3. 35 locomotives;
4. 50,000 litres of ether;
5. 14 tankers;
6. 800 aircraft wings;
7. 19 transformers; and
8. a steel works.[18]

In addition, many smaller targets were attacked, including forty-four locomotives, three trains, and numerous vehicles, pylons, and electric motors. Furthermore, the Peugeot factory in Sochaux, France, that made tank turrets was put out of commission by sabotage.

These snapshots of major accomplishments in France and a few other countries begin to paint a larger picture.[19] The persistent strikes had a cumulative effect on the German war effort, as well as morale. The "war of the flea" is both physically and psychologically exhausting. As such, SOE operations were making themselves felt.

Moreover, SOE efforts provided the Allies a major boost during the invasion of occupied Europe (D-Day) and the subsequent Normandy Campaign. For instance, on the coded announcement by the BBC on the night of June 5, 1944, SOE-supported resistance cells conducted hundreds of sabotage attacks in preparation for the invasion. The FFI cut the French railways at 950 points.[20] In total, there were three thousand confirmed rail cuts in France and Belgium between June 6 and 27, 1944.[21]

One immediate impact of the SOE actions was to deny the Germans the ability to rapidly counter-attack. For example, the 2nd SS Panzer Division, *Das Reich*, was short of fuel due to the attacks on petrol dumps. As a result, it turned to the railway, but found the lines between Toulouse, where it was stationed, and the front-line cut. A normal three-day trip took sixteen days. Similarly, the 11th Division took three days to move from the eastern front to the Rhine River. It then took three more weeks to reach Caen on the Normandy coast.[22]

SOE teams also arranged the reception of three-man Jedburgh teams that were designed to assist local resistance networks to coordinate their efforts. The Jedburghs provided a wireless link, supplied arms and ammunition, and provided training on the use of weapons and basic tactics. Fourteen teams dropped into Brittany alone and helped organize twenty thousand resistors. A large part of German effort was simply to fight the Resistance forces.[23] Significantly, eight thousand Frenchman were fighting in Massif Central alone.[24] The Chiefs of Staff Committee acknowledged:

> There can be no doubt that at a time when the Germans were exerting every effort to obtain more manpower, the dispersion of troops in protective and internal security duties had an effect on the land battle. In June 1944, the Germans were forced to employ 5,000 troops to disperse the guerillas in the Correze and approximately 11,000 with artillery, were engaged against resistance in the Vercors in July. On 20th July, the 11th Panzer Division was still operating against resistance groups in Dordogne.[25]

By June 10, 1944, the SOE claimed a degree of success. An internal assessment reported, "Virtually all organisers have carried out successfully their D-day tasks, which have included the derailment of at least two trains in tunnels, the mining of road bridges over which German armour was expected, the blowing up of transformers supplying power to electric railways, and the cutting of telecommunications in widespread areas."[26] Their assessment was understated. The Chiefs of Staff Committee was far more elaborative and generous. It acknowledged that SOE supported resistance assisted Allied operations as follows:

1. It sapped the enemy's confidence in his own security and flexibility of internal movement;

2. by diverting enemy troops to internal security duties and keeping troops thus employed dispersed;
3. by causing delay to the movement of enemy troops: (a) concentrating against the Normandy beach-head; (b) regrouping after the allied break-out from the beachhead;
4. by disrupting enemy telecommunications in France and Belgium;
5. by enabling Allied formations to advance with greater speed through being able to dispense with many normal military precautions, e.g. flank protection and mopping up;
6. by furnishing military intelligence; and
7. by providing organised groups of men in liberated areas able to undertake static guard duties at short notice and without further training.[27]

A SHAEF report issued just after D-Day lauded, "The actions of the Resistance groups in the South resulted in an average delay of 48 hours in the movement of German reinforcements to Normandy, and often much longer. The enemy was facing a battlefield behind his own lines."[28] The Supreme Allied Headquarters later elaborated, "The widespread and continuous sabotage caused outside the capabilities of Allied air efforts … it [sabotage] succeeded in imposing serious delays on all the German divisions moving to Normandy from the Mediterranean, and forced the enemy to extensive and intricate detours … both main railway lines up the Rhone Valley were closed for a good part of the time, the route on the right bank at one time for ten consecutive days."[29]

Of immense importance to the Allied war effort, the SOE-supported resistance action provided a major contribution towards the attrition of the German pool of locomotives, as well as the destruction of irreplaceable machine tools and heavy cranes. In fact, sabotage in France alone between September 1943 and September 1944 accounted for almost as many locomotives being disabled as the total disabled by air action during the same period. Moreover, the increase in repairs made necessary by sabotage overwhelmed the repair facilities. It forced the deployment of railway troops, reserve troops, defence workers, and German railway-men to guard and rebuild the vital lines and thereby overwhelmed the German administrative system for the occupied countries.[30] As well, the SOE through its connections with the Société National de Chemin de Fer, encouraged slow-downs, absenteeism, and strikes. In fact, the German director of French Railways cited this as one of the significant contributory factors that led to the German failure to maintain transport facilities adequately to contain the Allied bridgehead in Normandy.[31]

The SOE achieved similar results during Operation Dragoon, the invasion of Southern France, in August 1944. The American 3rd Infantry Division history noted, "A major factor aiding the speed and success of our movement was the activity of the French resistance groups."[32] The 3rd Infantry Division considered the efforts of the SOE-supported resistance network equivalent to that of four to five divisions. In fact, with regard to Operation Dragoon, British general Sir Henry Maitland Wilson, Supreme Allied Commander in the Mediterranean Theatre acknowledged that the FFI "reduced the fighting efficiency of the *Wehrmacht* in southern France to forty per cent at the moment of the Dragoon landing operations."[33] In addition, the FFI were credited with capturing approximately forty-two thousand German prisoners of war during the operation.[34]

The example of Denmark, which was actually slow to fully commit to SOE activities, is also telling. Major operations included the attack on the Burmeister & Wain power station in Copenhagen, which was engaged in U-boat production in 1943, that put it out of commission for nine months; the destruction of thirty German aircraft, the aero mechanised workshop and special tools at the Aalborg West aerodrome in 1944; the destruction of material and machinery of the Torotor factory in Copenhagen, which was engaged in V1 and V2 rocket manufacturing; the destruction of the Rifle Syndicate armament factory; and the complete destruction of the Always Radio factory during U-boat production. In addition, there was also minor sabotage, particularly against Danish railway traffic. During February 1945, for instance, as the Germans were attempting to withdraw forces from Norway to reinforce their crumbling front lines elsewhere, they were repeatedly attacked and stalled in Denmark. The 223 Panzer

Division and the 166 Infantry Division were successfully attacked over one hundred times. In fact, in a period of one week, more than half of their forty-four trains were immobilized in Denmark.[35]

The SOE also accomplished other significant coups during their tenure. For example, they orchestrated the assassination of SS Obergruppenführer (lieutenant-general) Reinhard Heydrich as part of Operation Anthropoid on May 27, 1942, in Czechoslovakia. Heydrich was head of the Reichssicherheitshauptamt (Reich Security Main Office), which meant that he was responsible for the entire Nazi secret police apparatus. In this capacity, he was second-in-command to Reichsführer Heinrich Himmler, commander of the SS. Heydrich was also a leading proponent of the "Final Solution," namely the extermination of the Jews.

Perhaps the most singular spectacular achievement of the SOE was its destruction of the German atomic weapon program. Not surprisingly, Churchill was aghast at the idea of the Nazis creating an atomic bomb. In fact, he acknowledged the fear of a German atomic weapon "lay heavy on my mind."[36] He was not alone. Allied leaders and scientists were equally concerned. After all, Otto Hahn, a German physicist, had successfully discovered atomic fission as early as December 1938.[37] His work was given an exponential boost once German forces overran Europe in the spring of 1940. German physicists now had access to heavy water (deuterium oxide)[38] from the Norsk-Hydro plant in Vemork (Rjukan), Norway; thousands of tons of uranium ore from the Union Minière in Belgium; the use of the only cyclotron[39] (albeit one that was not completely finished) in existence in Paris; and access to Niels Bohr, a recognized intellectual giant among nuclear physicists in occupied Denmark.[40]

Therefore, in the summer of 1941, when British intelligence discovered that the Norsk-Hydro plant was in the process of increasing its heavy water production ten-fold, it became clear that the Germans were actively involved in atomic weapon research.[41] Planners realized that the heavy water could be the weak link in the German program. Not surprisingly, the Norsk-Hydro facility, which was located in inhospitable terrain nestled between two mountains, became a priority target. The first attempt, Operation Freshman, in November 1942, was a failure. The two gliders carrying commandos crashed. The few survivors were captured by the Gestapo and subsequently executed. The second attempt, Operation Gunnerside, in February 1943, was more successful. A small team that totalled eleven SOE men operating in Norway temporarily knocked out the Norsk-Hydro's production capacity. However, production was re-established to full capacity by mid-August. Frustrated, the Allies attempted to bomb the plant, despite protest by the Norwegian government. Of 828 bombs dropped, reportedly only two hit the electric plant. Nonetheless, the persistent Allied attempts convinced the Germans that they should transfer the heavy water and equipment to Germany. This move gave the SOE its final opportunity. On February 20, 1944, as the Germans were in the process of transferring the equipment and remaining stocks of heavy water to Germany, SOE saboteurs blew up and sank the ferry that was being used to cross Lake Tinnsjo for the first leg of the journey.[42]

The narrative to date has provided only some examples of what the SOE accomplished. As noted earlier, the cumulative total of activities clearly had a disruptive impact on the German war effort. It is undeniable that a force of 750,000 SOE supported partisans operating in Europe and the Balkans alone created a substantive military problem for the Germans.[43]

Although SOE operations are not synonymous with resistance movements, an official report rightly assessed, "SOE provided organization, communications, materials, training and leadership without which 'resistance' would have been of no military value."[44] It is for this reason that a SHAEF report to the Combined Chiefs of Staff on July 18, 1945, acknowledged, "It can be fairly concluded, therefore, that SOE activity forced the Germans to retain considerable forces in areas of no immediate military value to us. The forces could have been usefully employed elsewhere and were contained by an economical expenditure of effort."[45] Major-General Colin Gubbins, the last director of the SOE, concurred. He wrote:

> Admittedly there were all over France from the moment
> of German conquest individual Frenchmen and French
> women determined to resist, but I think to be quite
> fair, that it was primarily the British who slowly gave
> to the Nation a will to resist. It sounds a hard criticism

of the French to say this, but without the parachuting into France of British leaders, instructors, Wireless Operators, Couriers, etc., and the example they set (even though many fell into Gestapo hands through ladle of security, and so on) which gave the necessary rallying point or focus, little would have happened.[46]

The SHAEF report also commented on the morale factor. "The part which SOE played in the organisation of passive resistance," attested the committee, "had not only very valuable direct effects, such as the Dutch railway strike and the action of the French railwaymen, but greatly bolstered the morale of the people generally."[47]

In the end, despite the virulent criticisms and sniping against the SOE that carried on into the postwar era, the general assessment by the Allied Supreme Commander and many other senior leaders was that the SOE was of immense strategic value. In fact, one official report actually acknowledged that "SOE's reputation lags behind its performance."[48] Nonetheless, in total the Supreme Commander's staff assessed, the SOE assisted Allied operations by:

1. sapping enemy morale;
2. diverting troops to internal security;
3. causing delay to movement of enemy troops;
4. disrupting telecommunications / lines of communications;
5. furnishing military intelligence; and
6. providing organization to groups of men in liberated areas to undertake guard duties prevention of demolitions — counter scorched earth.[49]

In fact, their report conclusively stated, "SOE operations made a substantial contribution to the victory of the Allied Expeditionary Force."[50]

General Dwight D. "Ike" Eisenhower himself noted in his memoir, "without their great assistance the liberation of France and the defeat of the enemy in western Europe would have consumed a much longer time and meant greater losses to ourselves."[51] Eisenhower also wrote to Major-General Gubbins and Colonel David Bruce, head of OSS European Theatre, at the end of the war and commented:

> In no previous war and in no other theater during this war, have resistance forces been so closely harnessed to the main military effort. While no final assessment of the operational value of resistance action has yet been completed, I consider that the disruption of enemy rail communications, the harassing of German road moves and the continual and increasing strain placed on the German war economy and internal security services through-out occupied Europe by the organized forces of resistance, played a very considerable part in our complete and final victory.[52]

Eisenhower went so far as to say, "the Resistance in France shortened the war by nine months."[53]

The SHAEF report for the Chiefs of Staff Committee further outlined the impact of SOE operations. It explained:

> In Denmark and Holland, indeed, there might have been no resistance at all but for the work of SOE. In considering the value of SOE operations in the occupied countries, therefore, it is fair to consider the value of organised resistance as a whole.
>
> Resistance assisted the Supreme Commander's operations in two broad fields; political and military. Politically, the existence of organised resistance fulfilled a primary aim of subversion by setting the oppressed peoples at loggerheads with the occupying power. On the one hand, the Germans so far from being able to relax, were continually on the "qui vive" and were unable to exploit their conquest to the full; on the other hand, the national will to resist was given a focus and an aim.

This morale factor was, of course, greatly enhanced by the feeling of support from and contact with the Allies, without which hope would have died. Acts of repression served to increase the tension. As resistance met with success, national self-respect and confidence were restored, and the desire and ability to resume responsibilities after liberation revived.[54]

In sum, General Eisenhower and his SHAEF headquarters were clear supporters of the SOE. They assessed that "SOE operations made a substantial contribution to the victory of the Allied Expeditionary Force. Widespread and continuous sabotage against railways and telecommunications supplemented the air effort and completed the confusion of the enemy." They went on to state that there were four types of activity that paid impressive military dividends, specifically, attacks on railways, diversion of enemy forces through guerrilla activities, prevention of demolitions, and the provision of supplementary manpower for the Allied Expeditionary Force.[55] Moreover, Colonel Donovan, the director of the OSS, observed that the value of the SOE and OSS was not just "in its role in hastening military victory, but also in the development of the concept of unorthodox warfare which alone constitutes a major contribution."[56]

Similarly, esteemed SOE historian, Professor M.R.D. Foot, calculated that the total strength of the SOE in personnel, at its peak, was approximately that of a weak division. As such, he concluded, "no single division in any army exercised a tenth of SOE's influence on the course of the war."[57]

Regardless of the achievements of the SOE, its perceived value was still a contentious issue at the end of the war and into the postwar period. Not surprisingly, its fate would hinge on the ability, as well as the desire, of its supporters to protect it in the heady days following the defeat of the Axis powers.

11

SETTLING ACCOUNTS: THE SOE AT WAR'S END

From its creation, the SOE had many detractors, critics, and outright opponents. The reasons for the opposition stemmed from a wide range of factors including differences in the philosophy of fighting war, the lack of SOE transparency, the general distrust of secretive organizations, the "selective club" mentality associated with SOE recruiting, organizational rivalry and competition for influence and resources, and the fear of uncontrolled SOE operations impacting ongoing political and military activities.[1] Churchill's personal support protected the SOE to a large extent, which also most likely created animosity with others. Not surprisingly when one considers the deep distrust in democratic societies for secret organizations, despite the SOE's many achievements during the war, its success failed to gain it the support of its detractors. As a result, before the war was even over, the struggle over what would become of the SOE had begun.

The struggle over control of SOE activities had begun relatively early. In fact, the "harnessing" of SOE energy started in September 1943. The British War Cabinet recognized that SOE activities were assuming "an increasingly military character and are progressively widening in scope and quickening in tempo."[2] At the same time, the Allied juggernaut had begun to push the Axis forces back on a number of fronts. In essence, the Allies began to rely heavily on conventional operations favouring overwhelming firepower and mass. As such, SOF operations had started to wane, transitioning from direct action raids to unconventional warfare and strategic reconnaissance.

Predictably, SOE operations were not spared. The British Chief of Staff Committee took steps "to bring SOE activities under operational control of the respective Allied Commanders-in-Chief in Europe and in South-East Asia."[3] The intent was to align all activities with the planned conventional operations and campaigns. In fact, the Chiefs of Staffs issued specific direction:

> It is intended to attach Allied Missions to the Supreme Allied Commander on the opening of operations. This will go some way to rectify the difficulties at present experienced; and in the meantime Allied Commanders-in-Chief are assuming a greater degree of control over SOE policy, which will bring SOE activities into closer relation to projected operations.[4]

At the same time, the British Chiefs of Staff Committee also dealt with the ongoing irritant of control over SOE special operations and the Foreign Office SIS activities. They believed the integration of SOE and SIS was clearly essential. Therefore, a concerted effort was made to pool the resources of the two organizations. By December 1943, the Supreme Allied Commander, South East Asia Command had organized both under one officer.[5]

Furthermore, to make their case for "coordination of SOE" the British Chiefs of Staff Committee examined reports from the Joint Intelligence Committee (JIC) and made a number of deductions. They found:

a. Lack of co-ordination facilities between SOE and SIS exists in overseas theatres except APHQ [Allied Powers Headquarters]and South East Asia Command;

b. Allied Commanders-in-Chief exert a varying degree of operational control;

c. Certain countries, e.g. Poland and Czechoslovakia, are not within the sphere of responsibility of any commander-in-chief;

d. Arrangements for co-ordination with OSS are generally satisfactory though the procedure for political co-ordination in the Balkans between the United States State Department and the Foreign Office remains to be evolved;

e. The only National Secret Army under some measure of operational control by a British or American commander-in-chief is the Polish Secret Army;

f. Certain activities in connection with Economic Warfare such as the buying and selling of currency, are not vetted by the Chief of Staff or Commanders-in-Chief.[6]

More importantly, the main points that they drew from the JIC report spoke to their attitudes regarding SOE operations:

a. The Minister of Defence, Chiefs of Staff and Commanders-in-Chief are less informed about SOE operations than about military operations;

b. SOE activities have conflicted with the policy of His Majesty's Government and are liable to continue to do so under the present organisation;

c. Conflict between particular SOE operations, operations of regular forces and of SIS are in general avoided;

d. A certain lack of confidence, however, exists between SIS and SOE;

e. Subversive activities controlled by Allied Governments, e.g. by Polish Ministry of the Interior, or by French National Committee, must be suspect as they are vulnerable to penetration;

f. Excessive expansion of SOE communication channels and duplication with SIS endanger both SIS and SOE;

g. The larger the subversive organization the more vulnerable it becomes;

h. The Germans are fully appraised of SOE activities and are taking increasingly energetic measure for protection.[7]

Not surprisingly, by November 1944, the tug-of-war over who would control — or what was to become of — the SOE in the postwar world was well under way. One general staff officer wrote, "The post-war organization of SOE and SIS requires considerable study, and we are far from sure that we would agree to the Foreign Secretary's statement that 'the only sound plan in the ultimate future will be to place SOE and the SIS under the same controlling head.'"[8] The Chiefs of Staff Committee agreed. They asserted, "[the Chiefs of Staff] wish to place on record their emphatic disagreement with the opinion of the Foreign Secretary that S.O.E. and S.I.S. should eventually be brought under a single executive, as opposed to Ministerial lead."[9]

The British Chiefs of Staff Committee, although not always supportive of the SOE, were against allowing the Foreign Office to control the SOE as the power struggle began near the end of the war. Committee minutes reveal the dire consequences the British Chiefs of Staff envisioned should this occur. The committee minutes stated, "this would mean accepting the danger of the strangulation of SOE and would undoubtedly make it more difficult to remove either SIS or SOE from Foreign Office control at a later stage should it be expedient to do so."[10]

Another high-level staff assessment spelled out the necessity for the SOE. It asserted:

a. It is concluded that SOE should continue in peace-time in connection [with] the United States in OSS, the Russians in NKVD [People's Commissariat for Internal Affairs], & how the French in the new Division General d'Etude et Recerche have made provision for permanent organizations covering SO work;

b. It is essential that SO work should be kept separate from SI anyhow in the field or otherwise loyalties could clash. The set-up of the other parallel bodies all keeps SO separate from SI although they may be coordinated at the top under one head (e.g. General Donovan of OSS with both OS & SI separately under him);

c. SOE is necessary in peacetime so that unacknowledgeable work can be carried out (e.g. keeping in touch with elements hostile to the government of a country with which HMG is ostensibly on friendly terms); and

d. It is also desirable that the framework of the organization with its training schools & research stations should be maintained so that they can be rapidly expanded if the need should ever arise.[11]

By the end of the year, the Chiefs of Staff Committee proposed that they accept the Foreign Office proposals, with the following caveats:

a. That it is only a temporary measure and that it in no way prejudices the future control of either SOE or SIS;

b. That the Chief of Staff would prefer to see SOE and SIS under the control of the Ministry of Defence; and

c. That SOE should continue to work under their own head and should not be placed under the Head SIS.[12]

However, the British government gave the entire issue of the future status of the intelligence services to a committee, headed by Sir Findlater Stewart, a senior public servant who left his position in India as the permanent under-secretary of state for India to take up an executive appointment in Home Defence in London. Under Stewart, the committee laid out clear directives:

i.   Agreed that S.O.E. and S.I.S. should, for the present, be placed under a common executive head;

ii.   Instructed the Joint Planning Staff to prepare a revised directive to S.O.E. accordingly;

iii.   Agree that arrangements should be made to appoint an Executive Head of the Secret Service having separate Special Operations and Secret Intelligence branches with common services; and

iv.   Invited "C" [Head of SIS] and "CD" [Head of SOE] to effect such measures of co-ordination as were practicable.[13]

Lord Selborne, the minister of economic warfare, under whose jurisdiction SOE officially rested, also provided his recommendation to the government on May 25, 1945. Selborne believed that the SOE was "a war-time experiment which may be said to have proved successful." He rated the main tasks of importance as:

a.   The creation, maintenance and operation of resistance forces in enemy-occupied countries;

b.   The organization and execution of sabotage in enemy and enemy-occupied territory;

c.   The dissemination of subversive propaganda in enemy and enemy-occupied territory;

d.   Certain specialized financial operations of a clandestine character as required by His Majesty's Treasury; and

e.   Procurement of information, passed to the interested Departments of HMG through, or by arrangement with SIS, or by direction of Theatre Commanders.

Despite the professed success, Selborne conceded that the SOE, a product of "wartime improvisation," suffered under "serious handicaps that could have been avoided had S.O.E. had a more clearly defined status within the official war-running machine." He summarized these as:

a. The inherent distrust of Departments for any new organisation whose functions and composition they do not fully understand;

b. Overlapping with other organizations, particularly those whose work is of a clandestine nature;

c. Growing pains, leading to frequent re-organisation with consequent temporary loss of efficiency and duplication of effort;

d. Owing to the circumstance that in the past there has been nothing in the nature of the "S.O.E. Courses" which Service officers and diplomats could take as part of their professional education, S.O.E. has been handicapped by the fact that any senior officer coming into the organisation was entirely ignorant of the technique of the organisation;

e. A general failure in Government circles to understand that S.O.E.'s activities are both world-wide and, in the clandestine sphere, unacknowledgedable [sic]; and

f. A tendency on the part of H.M. Representatives abroad, including Commanders in the field, to use S.O.E. for tasks not strictly within its charter and to some extent their private agency.[14]

Selborne astutely opined, "I have noted the above mentioned handicaps in order that the lessons of the past five years should not be over-looked. In particular, the relationship of S.O.E. to other clandestine and para-military organizations and government departments, and the scope of its future activities must be clearly defined in the light of these lessons." The minister of economic warfare also cautioned:

Despite the end of the war with Germany, Europe is in a dangerously unsettled state and the British Empire must consequently be prepared for a major or minor war in any part of the world. If Germany's return to power and aggression is to be avoided over the next twenty years there are immediate and continuing commitments for S.O.E. on the continent of Europe. There are also other and perhaps more immediate dangers in the combating of which S.O.E. is in a position to assist. It is noteworthy that the parallel organisations in both France and Belgium have already approached S.O.E. with a view to enlisting not only its guidance and support but its active co-operation. It is important, too, to note that Sir Edward Appleton has stated that the present trend of science and technical development in all departments of modern industry and national life make it certain that subversive operations will play an even greater part in any future war than they have in the present war.

If it is agreed that we must be prepared for war in any part of the world, we must ensure that the nucleus of the necessary organisation exists and that we do not have to resort to improvisation owing to lack of foresight. This war has shown that clandestine work cannot ever be effective without careful planning and patient preparation. There are no short cuts to success in this art. It is not surprising that Russia, the United States and France are continuing to nourish their own clandestine organisation.

The traditional policy of Great Britain is to maintain the integrity of small European powers, but is already clear that their integrity is likely to be threatened, and that it will be no easy task to pursue our policy with success. S.O.E. can prove a valuable instrument in furthering H.M.G.'s policy in peace, and one without which the prospects of making that policy effective would be diminished. It is no doubt a national characteristic of the British to dislike and distrust secret organizations working in peace-time, but nevertheless I believe that the existence of S.O.E. in peace is essential to the national interest and that the not uncommon comparison with the Comintern is a false one since H.M.G.'s policy is defensive and not aggressive, and since S.O.E. is merely an instrument and does not attempt to shape policy.[15]

As the debate on the future of the SOE continued to percolate, most of the key stakeholders agreed on the necessity to maintain its existence until at least the end of the war with Japan. The central issue was ownership. With the disbandment of the Ministry of Economic Warfare after the defeat of Germany, a new reporting relationship was required. Selborne (as the outgoing minister) explained:

> The Foreign Secretary and I have recommended to the Prime Minister that S.O.E. should not be wound up on the cessation of hostilities. Moreover, the Chiefs of Staff, while agreeing that the S.O.E. should be under the Foreign Secretary as long as the war with Japan lasts, have reserved the right to reconsider the position of the S.O.E. (and of the S.I.S.) at the end of the war; thus implying that they are concerned in the continuance of Special Operations in some form after that date.... If this is not done there is a great danger that the valuable experience of the last few years will be lost beyond hope of recovery. Already extensive cuts in man-power are being imposed and the question of the disposal of specialized equipment and personnel has arisen.[16]

Selborne then reiterated that SOE was a secret organization whose role he defined as "to further the policy of H.M.G. by unacknoweldgeable [sic] action in all parts of the world." In addition, he clearly articulated its functions as:

a. To collate, examine and assess all information bearing on future clandestine operations and to study and develop the art of underground warfare. To provide lecturers for the Imperial Defence College and the Staff Colleges, and to participate in the planning of future military operations in peace time and in the preparation for Staff talks with friendly Powers;

b. To train persons to carry out all forms of clandestine activity, e.g. covert propaganda, rumours, influencing public persons and minorities, and the study of objectives for sabotage;

c. To study, to devise and to maintain small reserves of all material required for sabotage and clandestine operational activities of all types, including communications; and

d. With the concurrence of the Foreign Office and under their general direction to serve the clandestine needs of H.M.G. abroad in any or all of the following ways:

  i.   to give covert support of a foreign government or organisation by counteracting discontent and special unrest, and by subsidies, if necessary,

  ii. to maintain contact with elements of a foreign country with whom H.M.G.'s official representatives may not establish relations,

  iii. to influence prominent individuals, political, commercial, industrial, etc., and to counter the activities of recalcitrant individuals,

  iv. to give covert support to British interest and to create and foster clandestine opposition to foreign interests hostile to the British Empire,

  v.   to undertake clandestine financial transactions required by H.M. Treasury, and

  vi. to establish the nucleus of organizations in foreign countries capable of fostering partisan activities should the need arise and to do so in the suitable cases in co-operation with the appropriate agency of the Government of the foreign country concerned. In certain cases this will involve the setting-up of a net-work of clandestine communications.[17]

The outgoing minister of economic warfare provided further clarification of his views with regard to the postwar makeup of the SOE. Selborne believed it should be organized on a civilian basis and that "the best results from the country's clandestine services would be obtained by keeping them as separate operational entities, but merging them into a single Service under one executive head." Selborne advocated that under such a system, SIS, PWE, MI5, and SOE together would form a clandestine service, in essence, as a fourth arm to the three fighting services. He believed SOE would be the operational arm of this "fourth service." He argued that under such a system, there would be greater coordination, closer liaison, and economy in personnel and resources because the administrative, research, and material equipment would be common to all elements of the clandestine organizations. Lastly, Selborne recommended that the "unified Secret Service" would best serve the country if "it were to come directly under the Minister of Defence." In this manner, he believed, the "unified Secret Service would be employed to the greatest advantage and that a balance would be struck between the political and military considerations which are always present in connection with this type of work."[18]

In the end, Selborne recommended that, in addition to maintaining the SOE to carry on its work against Japan until the war ended, the Government issue an immediate directive defining the scope of SOE postwar activities and authorizing the retention of a nucleus organization to provide for those activities. He went so far as to assert that the nucleus must comprise:

a. a small staff charged with the study and development of subversive activities, adequately served by

a training branch, a small technical research station, and a communications development branch to
ensure that our equipment for this type of activity
(at present the best in the world) keeps abreast of
developments; and

b.   An organisation controlling small out-stations in all
parts of the worlds which would assist in counteracting elements hostile to H.M.G. in the countries
in which such elements are located.[19]

On July 26, 1945, Clement Attlee, leading the British Labour
Party, won the British election. Attlee replaced Winston Churchill as
the new British prime minister and the SOE found themselves without their champion to protect them. The new prime minister and his
foreign secretary, Ernest Bevin, agreed that the SOE should be disbanded. The decision was made final in January 1946, when Sir Alan
Brooke, the chief of the Imperial General Staff, and Stewart Menzies,
head of the SIS, concurred.[20]

In reality, however, the SOE was not actually disbanded. Rather, it
was subsumed by the SIS. The amalgamation that the SOE fought off
for the entire war now occurred. It became the new Special Operations
Branch of the SIS.

The new organization was quickly engulfed in scandal. The files of
BSC, which were in New York, were burned at Camp X over several days.
Then, in February 1946, a fire broke out on the top floor of 64 Baker Street
that gutted the entire top level and destroyed nearly all the wartime SOE
records. Whether it was intentional to destroy sensitive information or
an accident remained a heated debate for an extended period of time.

For Canada, the decision on the fate of special operations was far
simpler. Canadian commanders and politicians were never big supporters of special, particularly secret, organizations. Although they supported
the "loan" of Canadians to the SOE, especially since it represented such
low numbers, it was more a question of supporting Allies, particularly in
the early years of the war when manpower was not an issue, rather than
a philosophical statement of endorsement. For instance, by September

1945, they had disbanded all of the organizations (Viking Force, Naval Beach Commando "W," First Special Service Force, 1 Canadian Parachute Battalion) that could be considered special operation forces. And all of these units owed their establishment to political expediency, rather than a belief in operational utility or importance.[21] In the end, when the war came to a close, the Canadian SOE volunteers were either unceremoniously returned to their units or demobilized.

Despite the lack of philosophical sponsorship, the Canadian commitment and contribution to the SOE were significant. Although the SOE was a British organization, the Canadian nexus proved extremely valuable. First, Canada provided agents of ethnic, linguistic, and cultural background that allowed the SOE to have a core of reliable, well-trained individuals to conduct the necessary operations for recruiting, organizing, arming, and leading subversive and sabotage activities, as well as information gathering.

Second, William Stephenson and his BSC were incredibly important to the British war effort. The relationships he forged with Bill Donovan and J. Edgar Hoover, directors of the OSS and FBI respectively, were critical to developing, nurturing, and solidifying American involvement, co-operation, and support to the Allied war cause, particularly prior to the entry of the US in to the war after the attack on Pearl Harbor. The co-operative relationship was also essential in paving the way for the British to acquire war material from the Americans, and attain security in their ports. Additionally, through Stephenson's efforts at turning US opinion away from isolationism and/or sympathetic attitudes towards the Hitler regime, by way of aggressive "marketing" and counter-espionage that uncovered Nazi activities in the US, Stephenson and the BSC were able to increase American support to the Allied cause.

Moreover, in the early years, the BSC became the conduit of intelligence for Donovon's fledgling Coordinator of Intelligence office and later the OSS, allowing Donovan to provide information to the president and the armed services even before he and his organizations were fully running. Moreover, Stephenson facilitated the creation and growth of American special operations by providing instruction, lesson plans, publications, and special devices that the US had access to until they could "grow" their own clandestine organization, namely the OSS, which became the Central Intelligence Agency (CIA) after the war.

Furthermore, Stephenson and his BSC, which was largely staffed by Canadians, were able to ensure the security of British war materials in South American ports, as well as uncover Axis intrigue and espionage in several South American countries. As a result of BSC actions, the Allies maintained a steady stream of war supplies pumping out of South America and they were able to thwart Axis penetration of that continent.

The third significant Canadian contribution was Camp X. Important for the selection and training of Canadian agents for overseas duty with the SOE, it was also significant for its importance in providing training, publications, technical know-how, and equipment for the neophyte OSS, as well as other US agencies (such as the FBI and OWI), which allowed them to gain a giant leap forward as they created their special operations and intelligence capabilities. It also facilitated closer co-operation with the Americans, particularly before they entered the war. Camp X, particularly Hydra, was also critical as a communication hub for encrypted message traffic for the British government, SIS, and SOE.

The cumulative effect of the Canadian contribution makes a strong case for the statement that the Canadian nexus to the SOE was substantial. In the end, the "ungentlemanly way of war" may not be Canadian doctrine. Nonetheless, although Canada is not a warlike nation, Canada has always proven to be a nation of warriors. Throughout the war, approximately 227 Canadians served in the SOE in the various theatres of the conflict. In addition, Royal Canadian Air Force personnel and those posted to RAF units also served in the Special Duty Squadrons used to drop weapons and insert and extract SOE personnel.[22] As such, the accomplishments and sacrifices of these intrepid individuals helped in diminishing the abilities of the German and Japanese war machines and assisted in the destruction of their regimes, made Canada proud, and set a distinguished legacy for Canada's special operations forces to follow.

ACKNOWLEDGEMENTS

As always there are a myriad of individuals who directly or indirectly assisted in the completion of a project of this nature. I wish to thank three people who were instrumental in moving this volume forward. First, I need to thank Lynn Philip Hodgson, the Camp X amateur historian who has spent decades advancing the cause of the Canadian participation in the SOE during the Second World War. In fact, he suggested I undertake writing this history to capture the Canadian involvement. He also generously wrote the foreword and provided photographs for the use in the volume. Second, I must thank Dr. Emily Spencer for her assistance in research, as well as her precision and professional eye in providing an edit on the raw manuscript. Her experience and expertise were instrumental in completing this book. Third, I am also indebted to Cathy Sheppard, whose enthusiasm for research and assisting others went a long way to lessening the workload of this project. Her contribution in sourcing materials and photographs was of substantive assistance.

I would be remiss if I did not also thank Katherine Taylor for allowing me to use her artwork as part of the illustrations, and I am also indebted to Holly Picard for her patience and selfless efforts to sort out my administrative arrangements to undertake all of the necessary travel for research.

Furthermore, I wish to thank Kirk Howard, the publisher at Dundurn Press, as well as the entire Dundurn team for their assistance in bringing the work to its final form.

Finally, but certainly not least, I must thank my spouse, Kim, for her eternal patience, forbearance, and immense tolerance in allowing me to continue my endless historical quest. Without her support and encouragement none of my endeavours or projects would ever see the light of day.

LIST OF ABBREVIATIONS

AFHQ	Army Force Headquarters
AO	Area of Operation
ASDIC	Anti-Submarine Detection Investigation Committee
BBC	British Broadcasting Corporation
B&E	Break and Enter
BEF	British Expeditionary Force
BNA	Burmese Nationalist Army
BSC	British Security Coordination
CBC	Canadian Broadcasting Corporation
CE	Counter Espionage
CGS	Chief of the General Staff
CIA	Central Intelligence Agency
CIGS	Chief of the Imperial General Staff
CMHQ	Canadian Military Headquarters
CO	Commanding Officer
COI	Coordinator of Information
COSSAC	Chief of Staff to the Supreme Allied Commander
CSO	Consular Security Officers

D/F	Direction Finding
DFC	Distinguished Flying Cross
EH	Electra House
ES6(WD)	Experimental Station 6 (War Department)
FBI	Federal Bureau of Investigation
FFI	French Forces of the Interior
FO	Foreign Office
FSSF	First Special Service Force
GS(R)	General Staff (Research)
HMG	His Majesty's Government
JCS	Joint Chiefs of Staff
JIC	Joint Intelligence Committee
LRDG	Long Range Desert Group
MC	Military Cross
M.D. No. 2	Military District No. 2
MI5	(Security Service)
MI6	Secret Intelligence Service
MID	Military Intelligence Division
MI(R)	Military Intelligence (Research)
NA	National Archives (formerly PRO)
Nazi	National Socialist German Workers Party
NKVD	Narodnyy Komissariat Vnutrennikh Del (People's Commissariat for Internal Affairs)
ONI	Office of Naval Intelligence
OSS	Office of Strategic Services
OWI	Office of War Information

PCO	Passport Control Officer
PRO	Public Record Office (now British National Archives)
PW	Political Warfare
PWE	Political Warfare Executive
RAF	Royal Air Force
RDX	Research Department Explosive
RCMP	Royal Canadian Mounted Police
RU	Research Units
RUSI	Royal United Services Institute
SAS	Special Air Service
SAB	Student Assessment Board
SBS	Special Boat Service
SD	Sicherheitsdienst (Security Service)
SHAEF	Supreme Headquarters Allied Expeditionary Force
SI	Secret Intelligence
SIS	Secret Intelligence Service (MI6)
SO	Special Operations
SO 1	(SOE) Propaganda
SO 2	(SOE) Operations
SO 3	(SOE) Planning & Intelligence
SOE	Special Operations Executive
SOU	Ship Observer Unit
SS	*Schutzstaffel*
STS	Special Training School
UK	United Kingdom
US	United States
VCIGS	Vice Chief of the Imperial General Staff

NOTES

1: WITH BACKS TO THE WALL: TAKING BACK THE INITIATIVE

1. The Dyle Plan refers to the Allied plan to halt the Germans in Belgium, as the country's borders presented a far narrower front to contain the Axis advance. As such, the Allies planned to advance to the Dyle River in Belgium once the Germans had violated Belgian or Dutch neutrality. The plan was then to entrench and halt the German thrust much like in the previous war. The BEF commander reported right up until the German invasion, "The development of the successive defensive positions and switch lines behind the Belgian frontier was continued steadily till 10th May. By this date over 400 concrete 'pill-boxes' of varying size had been completed with over 100 more under construction, while work on the improvement of field defences, wire and other obstacles proceeded continuously on the original front and in the sector north of Armentières recently taken over from the French." General Viscount Gort, "First Dispatch" (covering the period Septembers 3, 1939 to January 31, 1940), April 25, 1940; *Supplement to The London Gazette*, March 1941, 40; National Archives (NA) [previously Public Records Office (PRO)] CAB 66/17, Memoranda, W.P. (41) 128-W.P. (41) 177, vol XVII.

2. For a detailed account of the Battle for France see: Matthew Cooper, *The German Army 1933–1945* (Landham, MD: Scarborough House, 1978); Len Deighton, *Blood, Tears and Folly: An Objective Look at World War II* (New York: Castle, 1999); Len Deighton, *Blitzkrieg: From the Rise of Hitler to the Fall of Dunkirk* (Edison, NJ: Castle, 2000); Karl-Heinz Frieser, *The Blitzkrieg Legend: The 1940 Campaign in the West* (Annapolis, MD: Naval Institute Press, 2005); and Philip Warner, *The Battle of France* (London: Simon and Shuster, 1990).

3. Major General F.W. von Mellenthin, *Panzer Battles* (New York: Ballantine Books, 1956), 14.

4. Ibid., 14. Army Group A was commanded by Colonel General von Rundstedt, Army Group B by Colonel General von Bock, and Army Group C by Colonel General von Leeb.

5. Heinz Guderian, *Panzer Leader* (London: Arrow Books, 1990 ed.), 91. Guderian noted that a war game based on the Manstein Plan conducted on February 7, 1940, in Koblenz, Germany, demonstrated the plan to be potentially highly successful.

6. The German High Command assigned Army Group A forty-five divisions, seven of which were panzer divisions, to cut through the Ardennes Forest. Army Group B received thirty divisions, three of which were armoured, and Army Group C had nineteen divisions. Although numbers always vary to a degree between sources based on methodology and definition, as a comparison of strength between opposing forces, in May 1940, the Germans had 2,439 tanks, mainly light tanks, against the Allied 4,204 tanks; the Germans had available 135 infantry divisions to the Allied 151; and the Germans had 7,378 artillery pieces to the Allied 14,000. Frieser, *The Blitzkrieg Legend*, 38, 56.

7. Field Marshal Erich von Manstein, *Lost Victories* (Novato, CA: Presidio, 1982), 104. Major-General von Mellenthin explained, "But the decisive factor was for that for the breakthrough between Sedan and Namur we had massed seven of our ten panzer divisions, of which five were concentrated in the Sedan sector. The Allied military leaders, particularly the French, still thought in terms of the linear tactics of World War I and split their armor among their infantry divisions." He was convinced that "the whole campaign hinged on the employment of armor, and was essentially a clash of principles between two rival schools."

8. Ibid., 28, 30.

9. Gort, "First Dispatch," 25. Gort's assessment was not entirely accurate. The Allies outnumbered the Germans in both manpower and armoured vehicles. Most scholars would also argue the Allied tanks were superior in quality. See Cooper, *The German Army*, 217–36.

10. The German victory was somewhat deceptive. Its success owed as much to their innovative doctrine and tactics as it did to the Allied unpreparedness. Quite simply, the modern German mechanized spearhead was largely a facade. Nearly 80 percent of the German Army for both the French and Russian campaigns remained a foot and horse-drawn army. See Williamson Murray and Allan R. Millett, eds., *Military Innovation in the Interwar Period* (New York: Cambridge University Press, 1996); John A. English, *On Infantry* (Westport: Praeger, 1984), 47–85; Deighton, *Blood, Tears, and Folly*, 160–204; and Deighton, *Blitzkrieg*.

11. Fifty-three thousand French troops were evacuated between June 3 and 4, 1940, after the withdrawal of the British forces was complete on June 2. The British Admiralty estimated that approximately 338,226 men were evacuated between May 26 and June 3. Though accounts of exact numbers vary, the British likely left behind approximately 2,000 guns, 60,000 trucks, 76,000 tons of ammunition, and 600,000 tons of fuel and supplies. Cesare Salmaggi and Alfredo Pallavisini, *2194 Days of War* (New York: Gallery Books, 1988); and I.C.R. Dear, ed., *The Oxford*

Companion to World War II (Oxford: Oxford University Press, 1995), 312–13.

12. Murray and Millett, *Military Innovation*, chapter 3. The emphasis on strategic bombing was such that little importance was placed on fighter aircraft. Fortunately, in 1937 the Chamberlain government supported Fighter Command and provided funds, at the expense of Bomber Command, to build up its fighter aircraft inventory. This proved to be a key decision as it allowed Britain to have Spitfire and Hurricane fighters that were able to repel the Luftwaffe during the Battle of Britain.

13. Cecil Aspinall-Oglander, *Roger Keyes: Being the Biography of Admiral of the Fleet Lord Keyes of Zeebrugge and Dover* (London: Hogarth Press, 1951), 380.

14. Ibid., 380.

15. Quoted in John Terraine, *The Life and Times of Lord Mountbatten* (London: Arrow Books, 1980), 83.

16. *Combined Operations: The Official Story of the Commandos* (New York: The Macmillan Company, 1943), v. He added "it can be won only when our armies have taken physical possession."

17. Winston S. Churchill, *The Second World War: Their Finest Hour* (Boston, MA: Houghton Mifflin Company, 1949), 246–47. See also Colonel J.W. Hackett, "The Employment of Special Forces," *Royal United Services Institute* (henceforth RUSI), vol. 97, no. 585, February 1952, 28.

18. Colonel D.W. Clarke, "The Start of the Commandos," October 30, 1942, 1, NA, DEFE 2/4, Records of the Ministry of Defence, Military Operations Records, Combined Operations Headquarters, War Diary Combined Operations Command (COC), 1937–1963.

19. Ibid. Clarke noted that: "Arab armed bands [did] much the same [as the Boers] against a whole Army Corps from Aldershot aided by thousands of auxiliaries." He saw guerrilla warfare as "the answer of the ill-equipped patriot in the face of a vaster though ponderous military machine."

20. Ibid. The word *commando* is Afrikaans meaning a "quasi-military party called out for military purposes against the natives." Hugh McManners, *Commando: Winning the Green Beret* (London: Network Books, 1994), 7. See also "Commandos," *Canadian Army Training Memorandum (CATM)*, no. 20, November 1942, 20.

21. Patrick Cosgrove, *Churchill at War — Alone 1939–1940* (London: William Collins Sons & Co. Ltd., 1974), 95.

22. See Eliot A. Cohen, *Commandos and Politicians* (Cambridge: Center for International Affairs, Harvard University, 1978), 37–40; Maxwell Schoenfeld, *The War Ministry of Winston Churchill* (Ames, IA: Iowa State University Press, 1972), 124; and Cosgrove, *Churchill at War*, 95. Winston Churchill has been quoted as stating that there is nothing more exhilarating than being shot at and not being hit. See George MacDonald Fraser, *Quartered Safe Out Here* (London: Harper Collins, 2000 ed.), 55.

23. Quoted in William Stevenson, *A Man Called Intrepid* (Guilford, Connecticut: The Lyons Press, 2000), 131.

24. David Jablonsky, *Churchill: The Making of a Grand Strategist* (Carlisle Barracks: Strategic Studies Institute, U.S. Army War College, 1990), 125.

Notes

25. Ibid., 92.
26. By June 6, 1940, Churchill had also directed that Britain develop an airborne capability. "Let there be at least 5,000 parachute troops," wrote Churchill in a minute to his military staff, "Pray let me know what is being done. Action this day." Several weeks later he sent a memorandum to the Chiefs of Staff urging them to establish a corps "of parachute troops on a scale of equal to five thousand." Churchill, *Their Finest Hour*, 246–47, 466; and Air Marshall Sir John C. Slessor, "Some Reflection of Airborne Forces," *Army Quarterly 1948*, Department of National Defence (DND) Directorate of History and Heritage (henceforth DHH).
27. *Combined Operations*, 16; and Aspinall-Oglander, *Being the Biography of Admiral of the Fleet*, 381.
28. Gort, "First Dispatch,"
29. Keith Jeffery, *The Secret History of MI6* (New York: Penguin Press, 2010), 320–22. See also, W.J.M. Mackenzie, *The Secret History of SOE: The Special Operations Executive 1940–1945* (London: St. Ermin's Press, 2000), 12–37.
30. Ibid., 12–37.
31. Ibid., 38-55.
32. Colonel Bill Donovan, a close advisor to the president of the United States, wrote in March 1942, "Now that we are at war, foreign propaganda must be employed as a weapon of war. It must march with events. It is primarily an attack weapon." Kermit Roosevelt, *War Report of the OSS* (New York: Walker and Company, 1976), 21. This reference was Donovan's approved official history of the OSS.
33. A British report noted, "What made the secret war possible in the first instance to exploit national resistance as a weapon against the enemy, both in Europe and in Asia, was that the enemy found himself over-extended by his early triumphs. It was possible for the Germans to over-run Europe from Finisterre to the Volga and from the Pyrenees to the North Cape but it was not possible to maintain such an area in complete subjugation. Not many months after the disaster at Dunkirk it was appreciated by British strategists that some of the nations were ready to begin the task of freeing themselves." Colonel F. H. Walter, "Cloak and Dagger," Historical Section (GS), June 29, 1946. This secret study was prepared for the Historical Section of the Army General Staff. A more detailed classified version was prepared for the CGS, however, the whereabouts of that version is unknown.

2: "SETTING EUROPE ABLAZE": THE CREATION OF THE SOE

1. See Mackenzie, *The Secret History of SOE*, for an excellent detailed account of the creation of SOE.
2. The Inter-Service Projects Board membership consisted of representatives of the Service and Intelligence Departments, the Ministry of Economic Warfare, and Electra House.
3. Quoted in David Stafford, "The Detonator Concept: British Strategy, SOE and

European Resistance After the Fall of France," *Journal of Military History*, vol. 10, no. 2, April 1975, 192.

4.   Quoted in Mackenzie, *The Secret History of SOE*, 60.

5.   Quoted in Charles Cruickshank, *SOE In The Far East* (Oxford: Oxford University Press, 1983), 2. The term Nazi was a commonly used word to refer to Hitler's ruling National Socialist German Workers' Party (NSDAP).

6.   Quoted in William Manchester and Paul Reid, *The Last Lion: Winston Spencer Churchill: Defender of the Realm 1940–1965* (New York: Little Brown and Company, 2012), 273. White propaganda refers to largely truthful information.

7.   Hugh Dalton, *The Fateful Years: Memoirs 1931–1945* (London: Frederick Muller Ltd, 1957), 368.

8.   Quoted in Manchester and Reid, *The Last Lion*, 273. Churchill formally wrote Dalton on July 16, 1940, laying out the task and offering him the position as head of the SOE.

9.   War Cabinet Memorandum by Lord President of the Council, Neville Chamberlain, July 19, 1940. Imperial War Museum (IWM) display, January 15, 2012.

10. Jeffery, *The Secret History of MI6*, 353. Rivalry and distrust would exist throughout the war. The initial control of communications, as well as provision of forged documents by SIS, were means by which SIS was able to control, to a degree, the activities of the new SOE. However, in April 1942, the SOE took over control of its own communications.

11. "The Reconquest of Norway. SOE's Role," April 6, 1942, NA, HS 2/218, File SOE/Norway 68.

12. "Memorandum on the Functions and Responsibilities of SOE and the Relationship with the Army," September 4, 1942, 1, NA, WO 201/2714, SOE.

13. "SO 2 Programme," June 9, 1941, NA, HS 2/79, File Policy and Planning of SOE Activities in Denmark.

14. Mackenzie, *The Secret History of SOE*, 99.

15. Kenneth Macksey, *The Partisans of Europe In The Second World War* (New York: Stein and Day, 1975), 173.

16. OSS Syllabus, lesson plans, ND. Author collection.

17. Memorandum for War Cabinet, "Future of the Ministry of Information," June 24, 1941, NA, CAB 66/17, Memoranda, W.P. (41) 128–W.P. (41) 177, vol. XVII; and Ian Dear, *Sabotage and Subversion: The SOE and OSS at War* (London: Cassell, 1996), 11, 84–85.

18. Operation Savanna was conducted on March 15, 1941. It entailed the dropping of SOE trained French paratroopers into occupied France to ambush and kill German pilots of the Kampfgeschwader 100 pathfinder formation who spearheaded Luftwaffe bombing raids on Britain. They operated out of Meucon airfield. On landing in France, the assault force discovered that the pilots no longer transited to the airfield from their billets by bus but rather each made his own way to the hanger. As such, the raid was called off.

19. "Organization and Method of Working of S.O.2," NA, WO 193/626, SOE Organization and Policy March 1940–August 1941. The policy further explained, "To carry out the

first of these activities, it is necessary to search for targets of immediate importance which cannot be successful or conveniently engaged by normal military measures. These are targets situated within enemy or enemy occupied territory that can be attacked by nationals of the country concerned, who are either already in the territory or can be transported there by air or sea after special training. The essence of this type of attack is that in its ultimate phase, it is overt in character and easily carried out by force. Indirect action is carried out by underground attack against the enemy in his home country and in the countries he has occupied. The employment of countermeasures in countries he has not occupied but where his influence is being exerted to afford him material or moral support for his conduct of the war, or in countries which he may intend to occupy in the near future."

20. "Outline Plan of SO 2 Operations From September 1st, 1941 to October 1st 1942," n.d., NA, HS2/79, File Policy and Planning of SOE Activities in Denmark. See also Bernd Horn and Bill Knarr, "By, With, Through: A Historical Success Story," in Dr. Emily Spencer, ed., "*By With, Through*": *A SOF Global Engagement Strategy* (Kingston, ON: CDA Press, 2014), 1–37. This work takes the concept of using guerrilla and indigenous forces beyond the SOE example and looks at their success through history.

21. "Organization and Method of Working of S.O.2," NA, WO 193/626, SOE Organization and Policy, March 1940–August 1941.

22. In April 1940, Gubbins had commanded the ten Independent Companies that were raised earlier in the year to harass the advancing Germans in Norway. The ten Independent Companies, each consisting of approximately twenty officers and 270 men, were raised largely from second-line Territorial Army divisions in April 1940. There was practically no training for the militia soldiers or leaders of the Independent Companies before they were deployed to Norway. Although eager and keen, they had little skill or equipment and no transport. Under the overall command of Lieutenant-Colonel Colin Gubbins, they were ordered "not to offer any prolonged resistance but should endeavour to maintain themselves on the flanks of the German forces and continue harrying tactics against their lines of communications." However, the German advance was too rapid and the five Independent Companies that actually made it to Norway in time were withdrawn by early June. See Peter Wilkinson and Joan Bright Astley, *Gubbins and the SOE* (London: Leo Cooper, 1997), 50–68; and Patrick Howarth, *Undercover: The Men and Women of the SOE* (London: Phoenix Press, 1980), 21.

23. "War Cabinet — Future Strategy — Appreciation by the Chiefs of Staff Committee," September 4, 1940, 46. War Cabinet Weekly Resume (no. 53), NA, CAB 66/11, Memoranda, W.P. (40) 321-W.P. (40) 370, vol. XI.

24. Memorandum, "Note on SOE's Relations with Revolutionary Movements in Europe," November 2, 1942, NA, SOE Files, Poland 9, April 1942–February 1943.

25. SOE policy did allow for secret army personnel, in the interim, to "be usefully employed on minor sabotage not requiring technical skill, and in fostering similar action and passive resistance amongst the general populace. They might also provide armed covering parties for raids by saboteurs. SOE planners also realized that no uniform system could

be adopted throughout the occupied countries." Therefore, they attempted to lay out some common characteristics that should be followed when organizing saboteurs and secret armies:

a. Groups of saboteurs and secret armed forces should be kept small, 6 or 7 men in the case of saboteurs, and not exceeding 10-12 for armed forces. The latter should have a higher organisation of companies consisting of 3 or 4 groups.

b. Not more than 10 such groups or companies should be controlled by a district organiser.

c. Not more than 10 districts should be controlled by an area organiser.

d. Both district and area organisers should have deputies as well as a small staff and area organisers should have their own wireless communications, couriers and dumps of arms and sabotage materials.

e. Where a single organisation has been decided upon the area organiser will direct the activities of both the saboteurs and the armed forces. On the lower levels they will invariably be separate.

See "SO 2 Programme," June 9, 1941, NA, HS 2/79, File Policy and Planning of SOE Activities in Denmark; and "Outline Plan of SO 2 Operations From September 1st, 1941 to October 1st 1942," ND, NA, HS2/79, File Policy and Planning of SOE Activities in Denmark.

26. Macksey, *The Partisans of Europe In The Second World War*, 165. There was another motive for their desire not to push the Germans too hard early on. As one report assessed, "The most likely revolutionary situation in almost every country in Europe is precisely that which SOE wishes above all to avoid, that is, that by some act of unprecedented beastliness the Germans may drive their victims to a point beyond which any change inevitably becomes a change for the better. This desperation will result in a spontaneous rising which may not accord at all with Allied strategy or SOE plans, and which it may be impossible to exploit." Memorandum, "Note on SOE's Relations with Revolutionary Movements in Europe," November 2, 1942, NA, SOE Files, Poland 9, April 1942–February 1943.

27. Letter, "Following from Chiefs of Staff No. C.O.S. (M.E.) 271," General A.F. Brooke, Chairman, Chiefs of Staff Committee to Commanders-in-Chief, June 2, 1942, NA, WO 193/633, SOE Series, SOE Organisation, 30 Apr 1942–28 May 1945.

28. Ivor Porter, *Operation Autonomous: With SOE in Wartime Romania* (London: Chatto & Windus, 1989), 67.

29. Memorandum, "SOE and Revolutionary Movements in Europe," MPX to MX, December 7, 1942, NA, SOE Files, Poland 9, April 1942–February 1943.

30. Dear, *Sabotage and Subversion*, 134.

Notes

31. Letter, to Brigadier G.M.G. Davey, from MO4, GHQ, January 9, 1943, NA, HS5/584, File Greece No. 585A.
32. Dear, *Sabotage and Subversion*, 21.
33. Ibid., 149.
34. Letter, Moyne to Bullard, June 26, 1943, NA, KV4/171, General Policy on Liaison with SOE. He added, "SOE believe that many of their contacts would not be prepared to have any relations with Intelligence organisations or overt British Government Departments."
35. OSS Syllabus, Captain William G. Tharp, September 2, 1944, 1, NA, File: Wash-OSS-Ops-97.
36. Ibid., 97.
37. One report noted, "While it is true that mass murder acts as a deterrent to revolutionary action, on the other hand it also acts as an incitement to it out of feelings of personal hatred and revenge, and our only answer is to threaten similar reprisals; if possible to carry them out. It is well within the bounds of possibility that this question of reprisals is one of those which General Sikorski is discussing with Roosevelt, as he has been subjected to extreme pressure, both from Poland and from émigré circles, either to prevent the continuation of mass executions or if this is not possible, to apply similar methods to the *Auslands-deutsch* of North and South America." Memorandum, "SOE and Revolutionary Movements in Europe," MPX to MX, December 7, 1942, NA, SOE Files, Poland 9, April 1942–February 1943.
38. Ibid.
39. "Guerilla Warfare. Notes on Discussion with Brigadier Myers," October 1, 1943, NA, HS 5/425, SOE Files, Greece, no. 190, vol 2.
40. Dear, *Sabotage and Subversion*, 156–57.
41. Memorandum, "SOE and Revolutionary Movements in Europe," December 7, 1942.
42. The philosophical approach to war was a big issue for many. Bert Levy, a Canadian, was an SOE instructor on guerrilla warfare. After one lecture, a Brigadier remarked, "Your lesson was very interesting, Mr Levy. Very interesting but you know, don't you, that our country believes in a gentlemanly manner of fighting." Quoted in Andy Durovecz, *My Secret Mission* (New York: Luqus Publications, 1996), 36.
43. M.R.D. Foot, "What use was SOE?," RUSI, February 2003, 76.
44. Ibid. Foot explains that Dalton was a Labour minister who was given SOE as a sop by Churchill to allow the opposition party to control one of the secret services. Dalton was later relieved when he used SOE's telephone tapping facilities to spy on his colleagues on the Labour Party's national executive.
45. Quoted in David Stafford, *Britain and European Resistance 1940–1945: A Survey of the Special Operations Executive, with Documents* (London: The MacMillan Press Ltd., 1980), 4.
46. Quoted in Manchester and Reid, *The Last Lion*, 274.
47. Quoted in Jonathan F. Vance, *Unlikely Soldiers: How Two Canadians Fought the Secret War against Nazi Occupation* (Toronto: HarperCollins, 2008), 116.

48. Ibid., 274.
49. Macksey, *The Partisans of Europe In The Second World War,* 52.
50. Ibid., 53.
51. Ibid. Colin Gubbins stated the Foreign Office regarded SOE personnel as "nasty people who run around with explosives." Quoted in Vance, *Unlikely Soldiers,* 117.
52. Jeffery, *The Secret History of MI6,* 356. Apparently this was due to the belief by many that SOE was the more effective and efficient organization.
53. Leo Marks, *Between Silk and Cyanide: A Codemaker's War 1941-1945* (New York: The Free Press, 1998), 147.
54. Jeffery, *The Secret History of MI6,* 354.
55. Foot, "What use was SOE?", 76.

3: A MAN CALLED INTREPID: THE BEGINNING OF THE CANADIAN CONNECTION

1. For a full, detailed biography of Sir William Stephenson, see Bill Macdonald, *The True Intrepid: Sir William Stephenson and the Unknown Agents* (Surrey, BC: Timberholme Books Ltd., 1998). There are other biographies as well, particularly Harford Montgomery Hyde, *Room 3603* (Toronto: Ballantine Books, 1962); and William Stevenson, *A Man Called Intrepid* (Guilford, CT: Lyons Press, 2000). However, both are criticized for their inaccuracies. In fact, the Stevenson book has been called fiction by some.
2. Howarth, *Undercover,* 26.
3. Macdonald, *True Intrepid,* 54.
4. Ibid., 58.
5. British Security Coordination (henceforth BSC), *The Secret History of British Intelligence in the Americas, 1940-1945* (New York: Fromm International, 1999), xxvii.
6. The US Congress passed a series of Neutrality Acts in the 1930s as a result of the increasing conflict in Europe and Asia. Their genesis was spawned by a growing sentiment of isolationism and non-interventionism in the US following its involvement in the First World War. There was a popular belief, supported by the Nye Committee hearings (1934-36) and a number of books, that American participation in the First World War was orchestrated by bankers and arms dealers for financial gain. As a result, powerful lobbies in Congress pushed for non-interventionism. Importantly, Democratic President F.D. Roosevelt and his secretary of state, Cordell Hull, were critical of the Neutrality Acts.
7. *BSC,* xxvi.
8. Macdonald, *True Intrepid,* 5, 71.
9. Quoted in Ibid., 72.
10. For example, a simple ad was placed in the *Toronto Telegram:* "Wanted women for specialized military work, Apply; Mr. Bill Simpson, 25 King St. W. Toronto." Simpson's real name was Eric Curwain, who acted as Stephenson's chief recruiting officer. See Lynn Philip Hodgson, *Inside Camp X,* (Port Perry, ON: Blake Books, 2002), 65.

Hodgson asserts that this one ad alone resulted in the recruitment of fifteen hundred women from mainly Toronto but also other parts of Canada.

11. Macdonald, *True Intrepid*, 80.
12. *BSC*, xxx.
13. The relationship would eventually sour as the FBI's exclusive relationship with BSC deteriorated once Stephenson became involved with Bill Donovan as Coordinator of Information and later as head of the Office of Strategic Services. In addition, when the US entered the war, the BSC began to deal with a multitude of other security organizations.
14. David Stafford, *Camp X* (Toronto: Lester & Orpen Dennys Publishers, 1986), 13.
15. "British Offices in Washington," March 24, 1943, NA, HS7/76, File History 43, Notes on American Organisations and Personnel.
16. *BSC*, 104.
17. Ibid., xxxv. Stephenson and the BSC integrated SIS, SOE, censorship, codes and ciphers, security, and communications, and controlled all these functions in the Western Hemisphere.
18. "British Offices in Washington," March 24, 1943, NA, HS7/76, File History 43, Notes on American Organisations and Personnel.
19. *BSC*, xxviii.
20. Stafford, *Camp X* , 28.
21. Donovan earned the title "Wild Bill" as a result of aggressive command of the "Fighting 69th." Although a Republican, he was also close friends with Secretary of State Cordell Hull, Secretary of War Henry Stimson, and Secretary of the Navy, Frank Knox. *BSC*, 39.
22. The fact-finding mission in July 1940 apparently paid huge dividends for Britain. Donovan returned with four clear convictions: 1. the British would fight to the last ditch; 2. they could not hope to hold the last ditch unless they got supplies at least from America; 3. supplies were of no avail unless they were delivered to the fighting front — the protection of the lines of communication was a *sine qua non*; and 4. that fifth column activity was an important factor (later to be proven wrong). As a result, on his return to the US Donovan wrote articles, delivered radio broadcasts, and actively lobbied to support Britain. He was also influential in the destroyer for bases deal that was signed on September 3, 1940, which provided fifty aging destroyers for convoy escort in exchange for the rights to air and naval bases in Bermuda, Newfoundland, the Caribbean, and British Guinea.
23. Stafford, *Camp X*, 27.
24. *BSC*, 16–17.
25. Foot, "What use was SOE?," 79.
26. *BSC*, 11, 31–32.
27. Ibid., xxi.
28. Quoted in Howarth, *Undercover*, 312.
29. Quoted in Macdonald, *True Intrepid*, 92–93. Gubbins also stated that Stephenson's liaison role was vital. Gubbins explained, "[Stephenson] played in the very highest

quarters — at the top level in fact — Downing Street / White House 'affaire' which led to such splendid results."

30. *BSC*, xxxvi.

4: OUT OF EUROPE: BSC AND SOE OPERATIONS IN THE AMERICAS

1. *BSC*, xxxii, 55. The senior hierarchy of the SOE viewed their operations outside of Europe as immensely important. The Political Warfare section responsible for the US, working through the BSC, had specific objectives:

   1. Political warfare campaign to European, African, and Middle Eastern theatres, through ostensibly American shortwave broadcasts in 15 languages over most powerful American stations.

   2. Political warfare within USA forming and directing interventionist societies, holding meetings, planting material in newspapers (especially through Overseas News Agency, controlled by SO), distributing pamphlets (ten million copies of one pamphlet alone), spreading rumours.

   3. Campaign against America First and other isolationist societies: collections of material for US newspapers to publish and US government agencies to use; organized opposition; exposure of isolationist propaganda machine, ending in prosecution of George Hill and the German agent George Sylvester Viereck.

   4. Analysis of anti-British and isolationist feeling after Pearl Harbour, used by President in his speech of February 1942, and by US government in introducing new restrictions on anti-Roosevelt and anti-Allied propaganda, leading to prosecutions for treason.

   5. Guidance of the propaganda activities of COI and OSS along lines favourable to British policy throughout the world.

See "SOE/New York — Activities of GP, GO1, and GO3 Sections," November 22, 1944, NA, HS7/79, File SOE History 46, SOE Activities in USA and Latin America, 1940–1944.

In January 1941, the SOE also implemented a plan to:

   1. Appoint a representative in each Latin American Republic with a view to establishing an SO organisation to cover Latin America.

   2. Recruit in the Americas citizens of enemy or enemy occupied countries who would return to their countries of origin to contact already existing subversive elements and to form new subversive cells.

3. Take any warrantable notion likely to influence the entry of the US into the war and to discredit the enemies of the Allies in the US.
4. Make contact with all the various groups of dissatisfied European refugees and free movements in the USA.
5. Arrange lines of communications from the Western Hemisphere into enemy and enemy occupied countries.

See "A Short History of SOE Activities in the USA and Latin America," NA, HS7/79, File SOE History 46, SOE Activities in USA and Latin America, 1940–1944.
2. *BSC*, 241.
3. Ibid., xxvi, 239.
4. Ibid., 243–52. Similarly, the Americans developed a program called Ship Observer Unit (SOU) in December 1942 to "secure strategic information about military, naval, economic, and political conditions in enemy-occupied and neutral territory." Seamen's organizations, ship operators, and other maritime channels were accessed by American agents to gather information. The OSS official history noted that the SOU was far more successful at getting information from seamen than army, navy, or FBI agents, since seamen tended to have a mistrust of the official agencies, seeing them akin to police. Roosevelt, *War Report of the OSS*, xiii.
5. *BSC*, 163–65.
6. Ibid., 20, 59–65.
7. Macdonald, *True Intrepid*, 82.
8. *BSC*, 66–87; and Macdonald, *True Intrepid*, 83.
9. Macdonald, *True Intrepid*, 82. This ploy backfired. The rally was poorly attended so those who arrived with the phoney tickets hoping to create a ruckus were simply shown to their seats. Their presence simply filled seats that would have gone empty, giving the appearance of a larger body of supporters than actually existed.
10. *BSC*, 193–98, 204–8, 214–16; and Macdonald, *True Intrepid*, 183–84.
11. "A Short History of SOE Activities in the USA and Latin America," NA, HS7/79, File SOE History 46, SOE Activities in USA and Latin America, 1940–1944. See also *BSC*, 407–16.
12. "A Short History of SOE Activities in the USA and Latin America."
13. Ibid. See also *BSC*, 59–60.
14. *BSC*, 153–55.
15. "A Short History of SOE Activities in the USA and Latin America." See also *BSC*, 55–57, 143–51.
16. The German declaration of war was based on the American violation of its neutrality. There was some merit to their accusation. On September 11, 1941, the president had publicly ordered the US Navy and US Air Force to shoot on sight any German war vessel. He reiterated this policy publicly once again on October 27, 1941. "German Declaration of War with the United States, 11 December 1941." http://avalon.law.yale.edu/wwii/gerdec41.asp, accessed January 3, 2014.

17. Quoted in Macdonald, *True Intrepid,* 101.
18. "South America," May 15, 1942, NA, FO 371/30501, File — 1942, General File No. 56.
19. *BSC,* 253.
20. "Extract from the Minutes of a Meeting of the Chiefs of Staff on 16th June, 1942," COS (42) 180th Meeting, NA, FO 371/30501, File — 1942, General File No. 56. On June 9, 1942, the Chiefs of Staff in London sent a telegram to their Joint Staff Mission in Washington that stated:

> We are anxious to see an end of Axis machinations in Latin America which constitute serious potential threat to Allied supplies.... Our policy in regard to secret anti-Axis activity has been one of laissez faire to avoid risk of upsetting Latin American states.... Although overt security measures to prevent sabotage to ships and cargoes have been organized in all major ports by British Security Coordination ... except for this Axis have virtually had a free run.... It is therefore highly important that secret work should start quickly.... We have recommended to Ministers concerned that resources of both SIS and SOE should be made available.... We have also recommended that British Security Coordination should extend their overt security measures.

Quoted in *BSC,* 257.
21. "Interview with the American ambassador," 5th May 1942, NA, FO 371, File 1942 — General — File No. 56.
22. "SOE/New York — Activities of GP, GO1, and GO3 Sections," November 22, 1944; and "Outline of SOE Activities in USA and Latin America," NA, HS7/79, File SOE History 46, SOE Activities in USA and Latin America, 1940–1944; and *BSC,* 276.
23. "Memorandum by SOE on Axis Penetration in South and Central America," April 1, 1942, NA, FO 371/30501, File - 1942, General File No. 56, NA.
24. "COS (42) 180th Meeting, Extract from the Minutes of a Meeting of the Chiefs of Staff on 16th June 1942 — Meeting with Colonel Donovan," NA, FO 371/30501, File — 1942, General File No. 56. For example, in early 1940, the Uruguayan government uncovered a plot by Arnulf Fuhrmann and his accomplices, just five days prior to their intended launch date, to overthrow the government and subsequently mobilize all German residents of Argentina. *BSC,* 276.
25. "Memorandum," March 27, 1942, NA, FO 371/30501, File — 1942, General File No. 56.
26. "South America," May 27, 1942, NA, FO 371/30501, File — 1942, General File No. 56.
27. "From Washington to Foreign Office," Viscount Halifax No. 1881, March 31, 1942, NA, FO 371/30501, File — 1942, General File No. 56.

28. Report, "SOE in S. America," April 16, 1942, NA, FO 371/30501, File — 1942, General File No. 56.

29. Ibid.

30. "Memorandum by SOE on Axis Penetration in South and Central America — Annex A," April 1, 1942, NA, FO 371/30501, File — 1942, General File No. 56. Lord Halifax summarized of Bolivia, "I cannot disguise from myself that Anglo-American co-operation in Bolivia is not what I would wish it to be.... The Americans seem to think that daily browbeating of the Minister of Foreign Affairs with economic pressure in the background will get what is wanted.... In short, I approve of SOE activities here: I doubt if the United States legation would approve of them: I doubt whether Anglo-American co-operation of this kind would work, particularly as the United States authorities here do not seem able to keep anything secret; but I should of course take every possible precaution against our SOE activities developing in a way to which the United States Government might legitimately object." Telegraph, Viscount Halifax, No. 1736, "From Washington to Foreign Office," March 25, 1942, NA, FO 371/30501, File — 1942, General File No. 56.

31. Telegraph, Sir N. Charles, No. 326, "From Rio De Janeiro to Foreign Office," March 21, 1942, NA, FO 371/30501, File — 1942, General File No. 56.

32. "South America — Appendix," May 15, 1942, NA, FO 371/30501, File — 1942, General File No. 56; and "Memorandum by SOE on Axis Penetration in South and Central America — Annex A," April 1, 1942, NA, FO 371/30501, File — 1942, General File No. 56.

33. "Memorandum by SOE on Axis Penetration in South and Central America — Annex A," April 1, 1942, NA, FO 371/30501, File — 1942, General File No. 56.

34. "South America — Appendix," May 15, 1942, NA, FO 371/30501, File — 1942, General File No. 56.

35. "Memorandum by SOE on Axis Penetration in South and Central America — Annex A," April 1, 1942, NA, FO 371/30501, File — 1942, General File No. 56.

36. Telegraph, Mr. Bateman, No. 104, "From Mexico to Foreign Office," March 23, 1942, NA, FO 371/30501, File — 1942, General File No. 56.

37. Telegraph, Mr. Brickell, No. 11, "From Asuncion to Foreign Office," March 28, 1942, NA, FO 371/30501, File — 1942, General File No. 56.

38. Telegraph, Mr. Forbes, No. 71, "From Lima to Foreign Office," March 26, 1942, NA, FO 371/30501, File — 1942, General File No. 56.

39. "Memorandum by SOE on Axis Penetration in South and Central America — Annex A," April 1, 1942, NA, FO 371/30501, File — 1942, General File No. 56.

40. "Memorandum by SOE on Axis Penetration in South and Central America," April 1, 1942, NA, FO 371/30501, File — 1942, General File No. 56.

41. "SOE/New York — Activities of GP, GO1, and GO3 Sections," November 22, 1944; and "Outline of SOE Activities in USA and Latin America," NA, HS7/79, File SOE History 46, SOE Activities in USA and Latin America, 1940–1944. See also BSC, 288–342.

42. "SOE/New York — Activities of GP, GO1, and GO3 Sections," November 22, 1944; and "Outline of SOE Activities in USA and Latin America," NA, HS7/79, File SOE History 46, SOE Activities in USA and Latin America, 1940–1944.

43. Ibid.

44. Ibid.

45. Report, "SOE in S. America," April 16, 1942, NA, FO 371/30501, File — 1942, General File No. 56.

46. Minute, "Mr. O Scott," April 25, 1942, NA, FO 371/30501, File — 1942, General File No. 56.

47. Minute, "Proposed SOE Activities in Latin America," April 24, 1942, NA, FO 371/30501, File — 1942, General File No. 56.

48. Report, "SOE in S. America," April 16, 1942, NA, FO 371/30501, File — 1942, General File No. 56.

49. Letter, "Personal and Secret," March 28, 1942, NA, FO 371/30501, File — 1942, General File No. 56.

50. "Memorandum," March 27, 1942, NA, FO 371/30501, File — 1942, General File No. 56.

51. "Special Meeting held in Board Room, 64 Baker Street at 1700 hours on 18th August 1944," NA, HS 6/260, SOE Files, Belgium No. 228.

52. Letter, CD to Cadogan, CD/3983, December 17, 1942, NA, FO 371/30501, File — 1942, General File No. 56. In the end, BSC efforts were very successful. Axis interference with shipping amounted to only six vessels damaged, none were sunk. *BSC*, 272. Interestingly, the FBI acknowledged that they received much information from South America through BSC that they could not get from their own sources. In fact, 90 percent of British high-grade intelligence emanating from South America came through BSC/SOE. *BSC*, 343.

5: KILLING TWO BIRDS WITH ONE STONE: THE CREATION OF CAMP X

1. Walter, "Cloak and Dagger," 3.

2. Roy Maclaren, *Canadians Behind Enemy Lines 1939–1945* (Vancouver: UBC Press, 2004), 14.

3. His outlook on special operations forces was captured in a letter to the Chief of the General Staff in Canada. He wrote, "I have watched with interest the organization here of such special units as Commandos, Ski Battalions and Paratroops. The cycle is always the same — initial enthusiasm which is very high, drawing good officers and men from regular units, distracting and unsettling others, and upsetting the units' organization. With a prolonged period spent in awaiting employment, the enthusiasm evaporates." Lieutenant-General A.G.L. McNaughton, August 19, 1941, Library Archives of Canada (LAC), RG 24, Vol 12260, File: 1 Para Tps / 1, Message (G.S. 1647), Lieutenant-General McNaughton to Major-General Crerar, August 19, 1941.

4. Walter, "Cloak and Dagger," 3.

5. The officer also noted:

It is true that some of these groups will probably be infiltrated by the Gestapo and will be more of a danger than assistance, but in the majority of cases we should be able to rely on the advice of one of our own men as to the potential value and possibilities of the various groups that will undoubtedly appear.

We therefore suggest that the necessary steps be taken urgently to recruit in as large numbers as possible men who have the following qualifications:

1.   Good French (but not necessarily complete bilinguality);
2.   physical courage; and
3.   sufficient intelligence combined with just enough leadership to enable them to carry out one simple and specific job.

"Future Programme," F/FR/2161 to A/DE, 29 July 1943, NA, HS 7/121, File — SOE History 86.

6.   Walter, "Cloak and Dagger," 5; and Maclaren, *Canadians Behind Enemy Lines*, 23.
7.   Public Record Office (PRO), *SOE Syllabus. Lessons in Ungentlemanly Warfare, WWII* (London: Public Records Office, 2001), 1.
8.   A three digit identifier for a STS meant it was located outside the UK. During the war over sixty SOE training establishments were created worldwide. By January 1945, a total of 1,768 SOE personnel were employed at the various special training schools. The breakdown was 149 officers and 1,619 ORs. Another 1,164 personnel were employed at research facilities. Total SOE numbers had actually decreased from 4,361 in September to 3,962 by January 1945. "Statement of SOE Activities Prepared in Consultation with MG 1 (SP), MO 1," February 15, 1945, NA, WO 193/633, SOE Series, SOE Organisation, April 30, 1942 — May 28, 1945.
9.   Stafford, *Camp X*, 17–19.
10. Ibid., 21.
11. Ibid., 22–23.
12. Letter, "207 Military Mission," October 30, 1941, NA, WO 193/631, MO1 Collation, SOE Series General SOE 9, Military Mission 207, STS Canada. The staff officer went on to request assistance from War Office to approach Major-General McNaughton to allow Lieutenant Drummond Taylor to be attached to the school as an instructor. He explained, "Apparently, Lieut. Drummond Taylor possesses certain personal qualifications which make him very suitable and we understand that his father (and other connections of his in Canada) have already helped very considerably and his appointment would therefore be a tactful method of showing appreciation and would react favourably from the political point of view."
13. Letter, Macklin to Constantine, October 25, 1941. Lynn Philip Hodgson files (hereafter LPH Files). Macklin also noted that "this avoids approach to P.C. [Parliament of Canada]."

14. *BSC*, xi. Hodgson notes that the RCMP called Camp X — S25-1-1. Hodgson, *Inside Camp X*, 18.
15. Minute Sheet, MO1/BM/1480, November 13, 1941, NA, WO 193/631, MO1 Collation, SOE Series General SOE 9, Military Mission 207, STS Canada.
16. Letter, Macklin to Constantine, October 25, 1941, LPH Files. The British indicated they would pay all expenses.
17. Ibid. He noted "the officer selected to be Adjutant and Q.M. should, therefore, be a very reliable type.... They do not need to know the purpose of the school as their work is purely administrative."
18. The school had three COs during its existence. They were Lieutenant-Colonel Arthur Terence Roper-Caldbeck, Lieutenant-Colonel R.M. Bill Brooker, and Lieutenant-Colonel Cuthbert Skilbeck.
19. David Stafford, *Secret Agent: The True Story of the Special Operations Executive* (London: BBC Worldwide Ltd., 2000), 39.
20. *SOE Syllabus,* 13. It was only after the war that the locals actually learned of the true nature of the camp. Camp X historian Lynn Philip Hodgson asserts that the name Camp X was given by the locals due to the "mysterious goings on behind the barbed wire." Hodgson, *Inside Camp X*, 178.
21. "Notes by GM 175 on STS 103 (as result of visit on 8th & 9th March, 1943)," NA, HS7/76, File History 43, Notes on American Organisations and Personnel. The FBI members trained at STS 103. An official report captured, "While it is not known to what extent they benefited by this instruction from a practical point of view, there is little doubt that the offer of STS-103's facilities has done much to help BSC's general relations with the FBI." "American Organizations in Washington with whom British Security Coordination Works," March 24, 1943, NA, HS7/76, File History 43, Notes on American Organisations and Personnel.
22. "Outline of SOE Activities in USA and Latin America," NA, HS7/79, File SOE History 46, SOE Activities in USA and Latin America, 1940–1944.
23. OSS Syllabus, Captain William G. Tharp, September 2, 1944, NA, File: Wash-OSS-Ops-97.
24. Ibid.
25. In 1936, the president directed the FBI to provide information on a regular basis on communist and fascist subversion in the US. This drove much of the focus on espionage, subversion, and sabotage by the three existing intelligence organizations. See Dennis De Brandt, "Structuring Intelligence for War," *Studies in Intelligence. Journal of the American Intelligence Professional,* OSS, 60th Anniversary Special Edition, (June 2002), 43–44.
26. Ibid., 43.
27. Ibid., 43.
28. For instance, Hoover, leveraging intelligence he gained from the BSC, was able to influence the ONI, in essence the US Navy, to deploy four destroyers into Mexican waters to monitor and report in clear the movements of sixteen German and Italian ships tied up in the Mexican ports of Veracruz and Tampico that were preparing to

run the blockade. When the Axis ships attempted to sail on the night of November 15, 1940, the US destroyers approached the ships and trained their searchlights on them. In the ensuing panic, one German ship was scuttled and the rest fled back to port where all but three were expropriated by the Mexican government the following year. The remaining three attempted to run the blockade but were quickly captured by British warships thanks to the US Navy, which shadowed the ships and continually reported their positions. BSC also passed misinformation through Hoover, who would pass on the information via one of his agents, acting as a German sympathizer to the German embassy. For example, to deter the Germans from using poison gas in England, the BSC passed a report that revealed that Britain was prepared to use its secret weapon, consisting of glass balls containing chemicals that produced a terrific heat that could not be extinguished through any known means. *BSC*, 5–7.

29. Ibid., 51. The president had already authorized the FBI to carry out counter-intelligence and security operations in Latin America.
30. Roosevelt, *War Report of the OSS*, 5, 9–27; and *BSC*, 54.
31. Roosevelt, *War Report of the OSS*, 29–92; and OSS Syllabus. Later additions included SI because intelligence was rated as inadequate from normal open services and SO because there was no other agency to conduct unorthodox operations.
32. Roosevelt, *War Report of the OSS*, 8.
33. Ibid., 8. The president and Donovan originally agreed that it was "advisable to have no directive in writing" for specific functions of the COI. Moreover, words such as "military," "strategic," "intelligence," "enemy," "warfare," "psychological," "attack," etc. were carefully avoided both in the presidential order and in the White House announcement on the subject. However, by late October 1942, the "vagueness" in the directive began to backfire, as the COI ran into "real or imagined" conflicts with other government departments. As a result, Donovan recommended writing out the directive to "avoid misunderstandings with other departments." Ibid., 9, 15.
34. *BSC*, 28.
35. Roosevelt, *War Report of the OSS*, 76. The official history of the OSS actually makes mention of the close personal relations between Stephenson and Donovan.
36. *BSC*, 25.
37. OSS Syllabus. Under the OSS construct the major divisions were: Intelligence (SI, R&A, FN, X-2); Operations (SO, MO, ON); and Services (all administrative functions).
38. Memorandum, "United States Office of Strategic Services (OSS), 9 Oct 1942," NA, WO 193/1007, File Information on Similar American Organisations. The president designated the OSS "as the JCS agency charged with the planning, development, coordination, and execution of the military program for PW [political warfare]." The PW program was limited to operations conducted in direct support of actual or planned military operations. It included:

    a.   Sabotage, guerrilla warfare (personnel limited to organizers, fomenters and operational nuclei);

b.   Espionage and counter espionage in enemy occupied or controlled territory;

c.   Contact with underground groups in enemy occupied territory; and

d.   Contact with foreign nationalities groups in the United States.

It is important to note that Intelligence functions of OSS were restricted to those
necessary for implementing the military program for PW and for preparing
assigned portions of intelligence digests. In addition to the above, additional duties
specifically assigned to OSS included:

a.   Developing PW plans and doctrine in consultation with War
and Navy Departments and other United States agencies;

b.   Developing characteristics of special weapons and equipment
for special operations;

c.   Conducting special operations not assigned to other agencies or
under direct control of the Theatre Commander and organizing,
training, and equipping individuals required therefore;

d.   Maintaining liaison with all other government agencies
engaged in PW activities; and

e.   Collecting, evaluating, and disseminating information desired
for the execution of PW.

By November 1943, the OSS was also given the task of assisting the SOE in the
provision of leadership, organization, communications, material, and training to
resistance movements. "Abstract of JCS 155/7/D, Dated 5 April, 1943," NA, WO
204/11598, Ops SOE/OSS.

39. *BSC*, xxi.
40. "A Short History of SOE Activities in the USA and Latin America," NA, HS7/79,
File SOE History 46, SOE Activities in USA and Latin America, 1940–1944. See also
Roosevelt, *War Report of the OSS*, 76.
41. Anthony Moore, "Notes on Co-Operation Between SOE and OSS," January 1945,
NA, RG 226; Entry 136, Box 158, Folder Appendix III, 1722.
42. Ibid.
43. "Abstract of JCS 155/7/D, Dated 5 April, 1943," NA, WO 204/11598, Ops SOE/OSS.

6: SHROUDED IN SECRECY: TRAINING AND THE INTRODUCTION OF HYDRA AT CAMP X

1.   Sue Ferguson, "Forgotten Truths About Camp X," *Maclean's*, April 14, 2003, 49.
2.   Minute Sheet, "Stores for special units," November 13, 1941, NA, WO 193/631,
MO1 Collation, SOE Series General SOE 9, Military Mission 207, STS Canada; and
PRO, *SOE Syllabus*, 11.

Notes

3. "A Short History of SOE Activities in the USA and Latin America," NA, HS7/79, File SOE History 46, SOE Activities in USA and Latin America, 1940–1944.
4. *BSC*, 423–24.
5. Joe Gelleny in Blake Heathcote, *Testaments of Honour* (Toronto: Doubleday Canada, 2002), 194–98.
6. Leo Marks, *Between Silk and Cyanide: A Codemaker's War 1941–1945* (New York: The Free Press, 1998), 147. Gelleny stated, "The RCMP started doing background checks on me, on my family and everybody I knew. They gave me all kinds of tests: psychological tests, personality tests, IQ tests." Gelleny in Heathcote, *Testaments of Honour*, 194–98.
7. Durovecz, *My Secret Mission*, 3.
8. Ibid., 26–27.
9. Ibid., 26–27.
10. Ibid., 28.
11. Ibid., 63.
12. Ibid., 65–66.
13. Ibid., 66.
14. Ibid., 66.
15. Quoted in Patrick K. O'Donnell, *Operatives, Spies and Saboteurs: The Unknown Story of the Men and Women of World War II's OSS* (New York: Free Press, 2004), 4.
16. Dear, *Sabotage and Subversion*, 24.
17. Quoted in O'Donnell, *Operatives, Spies and Saboteurs*, 4.
18. Durovecz, *My Secret Mission*, 3.
19. Ibid., 57–58. Durovecz insisted, "It was an unwritten law at Camp X that this sort of mischief [in this instance stealing a locomotive and narrowly escaping a collision with a passenger train] — however dangerous — should be regarded as a bold venture rather than an offence against good order and military discipline."
20. Ibid., 68–69.
21. Quoted in O'Donnell, *Operatives, Spies and Saboteurs*, 2.
22. Durovecz, *My Secret Mission*, 85.
23. "Notes by GM 175 on STS 103, (as result of visit on 8th & 9th March, 1943)," NA, HS7/76, File History 43, Notes on American Organisations and Personnel. Unfortunately, the report did not elaborate on the comment with regards to the difficulties of working with Canadian troops who were not trained in the same manner as British troops.
24. Ibid.
25. Letter, Roper-Caldbeck to Constantine, n.d., LPH Files.
26. Letter, Constantine to Roper-Caldbeck, January 8, 1942, LPH Files.
27. Hydra personnel were all civilians at first, although there was a desire to make them all military. In total, twenty-eight personnel were required to run Hydra at the front end. "Notes by GM 175 on STS 103..." The radio transmitting station in Camp X was called Hydra after the Greek mythical creature with many heads. The reason for this was that the transmitting rhombic aerials in use had a

three wire system for radiating the signal. Another reason was the fact that the transmitters in use had a special fitted multiplex unit that allowed for up to three different frequencies to be transmitted at one time. David White, "The Rockex Cypher Machine. Its History and How it was Used," unpublished manuscript, n.d., LPH Files.

28. An official report noted, "At STS 103 in Canada, there is a radio transmitting and receiving station (referred to as Hydra) through which all cables to and from London are received and sent. The Commercial Cables are only used in the event of a breakdown of Hydra. Commercial Cables are used for the purpose of communicating with Central and South America." "Notes on the Present SO Organisation in the Western Hemisphere," n.d., 10, NA, HS7/76, File History 43, Notes on American Organisations and Personnel.

29. *BSC*, 446–49. The secret network for South America was eventually dropped.

30. At this point it was renamed the "Rockex 1"after the place of its birth — Rockefeller Center, in New York. *BSC*, 457.

31. Of note, in the fall of 1945, Camp X was used by the RCMP as a secure location for interviewing Soviet embassy cypher-clerk Igor Gouzenko, who defected to Canada on September 5. He subsequently revealed the extensive Soviet espionage operation that existed in Canada.

32. See *BSC*, 447–97, for a detailed account of Hydra.

33. The Oshawa Wireless Station ceased operations in 1969.

34. *BSC*, 424.

35. "Notes by GM 175 on STS 103..."

36. *BSC*, 424.

37. *BSC*, 425; and NA, *SOE Syllabus*, 11–12.

38. Quoted in O'Donnell, *Operatives, Spies and Saboteurs*, 2.

7: DOWN TO BUSINESS: OPERATIONS IN EUROPE

1. Stafford, *Secret Agent*, 34–35.

2. OSS Syllabus. Interestingly, Captain Tharp noted, with regard to courage, that it was "not as frequently put to the test as some believed."

3. Ibid.

4. *BSC*, 417. The SOE observed that there were two types of revolutionaries. "One is the patient, intellectual conspirator, who very rarely possesses the qualities of the second type. The second type partakes of the qualities of a successful bandit chief, i.e. he must be ruthless, determined, eager to take risks and able to make very rapid decisions. Whilst it is probably not difficult to find considerable numbers of the first category the problem of finding candidates for the second is far more difficult, for his qualities are such as can usually only be discovered in actual practice. It will, I think, be found that guerrilla bands most often produce their own leaders by a process of trial and error, and of survival." Memorandum, "SOE and Revolutionary Movements in Europe," MPX to MX, December 7,1942, NA, SOE Files, Poland 9, April 1942–February 1943.

5. *BSC*, 421.

6. Gelleny in Heathcote, *Testaments of Honour*, 197.

7. SOE special training schools were almost all isolated country mansions, many quite opulent and grand, taken over for the duration of the war. This is one reason that many detractors stated SOE stood for "Stately 'omes of England."

8. Dear, *Sabotage and Subversion*, 25.

9. Gelleny in Heathcote, *Testaments of Honour*, 198.

10. Ibid., 199.

11. "Extract from the Minutes of a Meeting of the Chiefs of Staff on 16th June, 1942," COS (42) 180th Meeting, NA, FO 371/30501, File — 1942, General File No. 56. For the Americans, to ensure the coordination of PW operations with military operations, they created a Planning Group consisting of nine members within the OSS organization charged with supervising and coordinating the planning and execution of the military program for PW. As such all major for PW were to be integrated with the military and naval programs by the Planning Group and submitted after approval by the Director of OSS to the JCS for approval. "Abstract of JCS 155/7/D, Dated 5 April, 1943," NA, WO 204/11598, Ops SOE/OSS.

12. Letter, Glenconner to Leeper (Head of Mission British Embassy to Greece), May 18, 1943, NA, HS5/587, File SOE/Greece No. 586A.

13. Ibid. The author also noted, "As I had been constantly warned by Head Office not to be difficult where the Americans are concerned...."

14. Ibid.

15. Ibid. The author added, "We are in a difficult position for if we refuse to extend them the open hand of co-operation and take them into our confidence, we shall be criticised for inter-departmental jealousy. After all, the Americans and the British are in this war together etc., etc., and are brothers in arms. If, on the other hand, we do not succeed in maintaining our control, we shall be criticised for having failed to do so and for the consequences that are bound to follow. In these circumstances, I think our only course is to help them in every way that we can by assigning to them a certain role on which they can get to work. This will, I hope keep them busy and content. At the same time, we must watch them and it will be our fault if they take us unawares."

16. "S.O. Operation Instructions to Lieutenant Colonel W. A. Eddy, U.S. Marines," October 14, 1942, NA, WO 204/115, Ops SOE/OSS. Specifically, the US president ordered the OSS to carry out "certain preliminary negotiations with French Leaders in North Africa." In fact, the expected results were such that the operation order stated, "The success of these negotiations may greatly reduce, or even make unnecessary, the tasks given you in these instructions." "S.O. Operation Instructions to Lieutenant Colonel W. A. Eddy, U.S. Marines," October 14, 1942, NA, WO 204/115, Ops SOE/OSS.

17. Letter, Glenconner to Leeper.

18. Memorandum, "Coordination of SOE/OSS Operations," G-3 section to G-3, July 19, 1943, NA, WO 204/11599, File Policy SOE & SOE/OSS Combined.

19. Quoted in Mark Mazzetti, *The Way of the Knife* (New York: Penguin, 2013), 6–7.

20. "War Cabinet Chiefs of Staff Committee — SOE Anglo-American Collaboration," COS (42) 327, June 30, 1942, NA, WO 193/1007, File Information on Similar American Organisations.

21. Ibid. British spheres of influence where the Americans would be allowed a small liaison cell were listed as India, East Africa, Western Africa, the Balkans, and the Middle East. Western Europe was recognized as a major sphere for Britain but since the US was deploying a great number of troops, arrangements were made for a US mission to work alongside the British.

22. Telegram, JSM Washington to WCP London, June 5, 1943, NA, WO 193/1007, File Information on Similar American Organisations.

23. Letter, SHAEF/17515/Ops(C), December 10, 1944, NA, WO 219/5307, File SOE/OSS Activities. Due to the Allied advance and the large areas of France and the Low Countries that were liberated, a Special Force Mission was established in Brussels to deal with matters relating to operations in the Low Countries and Luxembourg.

24. The Chiefs of Staff Committee defined the basic characteristics of SOE activities as:

    a.   SOE operations are normally subversive — e.g. sabotage, and carried out in enemy occupied territory behind the line of contact with our forces;

    b.   SOE operations may however be overt on occasion. Such occasions should be limited to those when allied intervention can be expected before the enemy can quell the resistance and punish those taking part;

    c.   In either case the operations are conducted or organized by SOE agents. These agents are or pretend to be natives of the country in which they operate; and

    d.   Agents are generally civilians. In any case they operate in plain clothes, and do not pretend to or claim the rights or privileges of a member of the armed forces of their own or any allied country — e.g. to be treated as a prisoner of war.

Memorandum, "Role of SOE in Land Operations," G-3 to Chief of Staff, April 3, 1943, NA, WO 204/11599, File Policy SOE & SOE/OSS Combined.

25. "Organization and Method of Working of S.O.2," March 24, 1941, NA, WO 193/626, SOE Organization and Policy, 30 Mar 40–Aug 41.

26. Memorandum, "Subversive Activity in the Occupied Territories," NA, KV4/171, General Policy on Liaison with SOE.

27. "Organization and Method of Working of S.O.2," March 24, 1941, NA, WO 193/626, SOE Organization and Policy, 30 Mar 40-Aug 41.

28. Ibid.

29. Ibid.

30. Quoted in Dear, *Sabotage and Subversion*, 7.

31. Office of Strategic Services, *Simple Sabotage Field Manual No. 3*, n.d., 1.

32. Ibid., 2.
33. Quoted in Durovecz, *My Secret Mission,* 32. As an example of an intended campaign, a SOE document explained:

> For example, in Norway, the SOE intent in late November 1940 was two-fold. First, we aim at organising the indigenous anti-Nazi organisations which already exist into well-trained and well-equipped groups of saboteurs and guerilla fighters who would be ready at a given signal to cut communications, destroy important objectives and annihilate scattered German garrisons in many parts of Norway either as a widespread, independent operation or as an organised diversion to coincide with some important offensive movement elsewhere. Secondly, we aim at tip-and-run raids, probably from the sea, by groups of specially-trained men, combined perhaps with attacks from the air on particular objectives. We hope that a series of these independent operations, coupled with a carefully controlled policy of passive resistance and, later, also spasmodic acts of sabotage by our indigenous organisations, will keep the enemy continually in a state of alarm in Norway so that he has to maintain much larger garrisons throughout that country and generally pay a lot more attention to holding it in subjection than would otherwise be necessary.

Memorandum, "Policy," November 29, 1940, NA, HS 2/218, File SOE/Norway 68, April 1940 to December 1944.
34. SOE Lesson Plans, "Guerilla Warfare," "A" No.1, April 1943, LPH papers. The lesson plan also stated, "Surprise, surprise, surprise. Hit hard where the enemy is most vulnerable, disappear completely and reappear for another raid somewhere else." It also emphasized "only engage in an operation which promises a 75% chance of success."
35. *BSC,* 427. Station M staff obtained the items from European refugees on a replacement basis. They also raided clothes stored for prisoners of war and internees, as well as convincing individuals who had accumulated clothes to ship to Russia under a "Bundles for Russia" drive to pass over some of the garments.
36. Dear, *Sabotage and Subversion,* 37.
37. Ibid., 39.
38. Marcus Binney, *Secret Heroes: The Men of the Special Operations Executive* (London: Hodder, 2005), 94.
39. "F Section," n.d., 9, NA, HS 7/121. File — SOE History 86. The scheme had its drawbacks. As one SOE planner noted, "In February 1943, it [Blackmail Policy] was merely the germ of an idea which, owing to the risible insufficiency of parachute supplies, we could not afford to make on a large scale because we knew we had not enough stores to carry out attacks of this nature, and our contacts with the RAF had not developed

to a stage where we could feel certain that if our bluff were called the RAF would do their part."

40. OSS Syllabus, lesson plans, n.d., author's collection.
41. Memorandum, "SOE's Plan for Co-operation with the Polish Secret Army," January 2, 1942, NA, HS 5/59, File Albania — Operational Directives Foreign Office Directive to OC Allied Mission in Albania. Churchill also stated, "I feel it is right at this moment to make it clear that, while an ever-increasing bombing offensive against Germany will remain one of the principal methods by which we hope to bring the war to an end, it is by no means the only method which our growing strength now enables us to take into account."
42. "Characteristics of a Modern insurrectional Movement, Description of a Descent Region and of its Work During the Descent," 1, NA, HS4/155, SOE Files, Poland 28.
43. Memorandum, "SOE's Plan for Co-operation with the Polish Secret Army," January 2, 1942, NA, HS 5/59, File Albania — Operational Directives Foreign Office Directive to OC Allied Mission in Albania; and "SOE's Plans for Co-operation with the Polish Secret Army," January 2, 1942, NA, HS4/160, SOE Files, Poland 32.
44. "Outline Plan of SO 2 Operations from September 1st, 1941 to October 1st 1942," n.d., NA, HS2/79, File Policy and Planning of SOE Activities in Denmark.
45. Ibid. The SOE calculated that the sabotage group would number 7 to 10 personnel and the secret army group 12 personnel. Their calculations were then based on the premise that two 250 pound containers would be required by each group for initial equipment. To support their 1941–42 campaign to raise their groups and armies a total of 1,356 sorties, over a seven month period, with an average of 194 sorties a month, were required. The following six months 1,278 sorties, or an average of 213 a month, were needed. The problem that arose was the reality that in the fall of 1941, operations could only be carried out in moonlight, which restricted the flying to 10 to 14 days a month and it entailed using a large number of aircraft for a short period, which would be vetoed by the RAF because of the going belief that the aircraft would be most valuable for bombing. "Outline Plan of SO 2 Operations From September 1st, 1941 to October 1st 1942," n.d., NA, HS2/79, File Policy and Planning of SOE Activities in Denmark.
46. Memorandum, S4 to 4351, "SO 2 Policy in Denmark," June 12, 1941, NA, HS 2/79, File Policy and Planning of SOE Activities in Denmark.
47. Ibid.
48. Memorandum, "Operational Directive to SOE/SO," February 15, 1944, NA, WO 219/5284, File SOE/SO Organisation and Terms of Reference.
49. "Action by Resistance Groups in the Event of a German Voluntary Withdrawal from Occupied Europe," July 24, 1943, NA, HS4/160, SOE Files, Poland 32.
50. "Memorandum by the Chiefs of Staff — Co-ordination of SOE," December 29, 1943, NA, WO 193/633, SOE Series, SOE Organisation, 30 Apr 1942–28 May 1945.
51. Memorandum, "Memorandum to G3 AFHQ on SOE In Italy," August 16, 1943, NA, WO 204/11598, OPS SOE/OSS, File HS/AFHQ/ 2402.
52. Memorandum, "Appendix A, Memorandum to G3 AFHQ on SOE In Italy," August 16, 1943, NA, WO 204/11598, OPS SOE/OSS, File HS/AFHQ/ 2402.

53. Memorandum, "Appendix C, Memorandum to G3 AFHQ on SOE In Italy," August 16, 1943, NA, WO 204/11598, OPS SOE/OSS, File HS/AFHQ/ 2402.
54. Memorandum, "Operations, Special Force, Fifth Army, APO # 464, US Army," dated August 24, 1943, NA, WO 204/11598, OPS SOE/OSS, File HS/AFHQ/ 2402.
55. Memorandum, "OSS/SOE Resources for Operations in Italy, September–December 1943," dated September 20, 1943, NA, WO 204/11598, OPS SOE/OSS, File HS/AFHQ/2402.
56. Ibid.
57. Memorandum, "Memorandum to G3 AFHQ on SOE In Italy," August 16, 1943, NA, WO 204/11598, OPS SOE/OSS, File HS/AFHQ/ 2402. The methodology utilized by the SOE was as follows:

The SOE party would proceed to the mainland in four main sections:

    a.   Section 1 (D-day)
This team would consist of the Commanding Officer, the adjutant, a wireless operator and set, and a clandestine section consisting of two Italian speaking officers and one wireless operator, all of whom would be in mufti. Their immediate tasks would be:

       (1) To establish a small static HQ on the mainland on which future parties can concentrate.
       (2) By means of the clandestine section to contact members of our groups and other Italian sympathisers immediately on landing.
       (3) to establish contact, by means of a suitcase W/T set, with ISSU6, North Africa, the parent unit.

    b.   Section 2 (D+2)
Second-in-command
Remainder of personnel
1 light signal section
1 jeep
4 motor cycles

    c.   Section 3 (D+6)
2 clandestine sections, each consisting of 2 Italian speaking officers, 1 W/T operator, 1 Jeep (or if possible civilian car obtained locally), and 1 driver-batman, all operating in mufti.

d.   Section 4 (D+12)
Holding and Training Section, whose task would be to receive,
hold and train numbers of our groups and locally recruited agents.

Memorandum, "Memorandum to G3 AFHQ on SOE In Italy," August 16, 1943, NA,
WO 204/11598, OPS SOE / OSS, File HS/AFHQ/ 2402.

58. "Future Programme," F/FR/2161 to A/DE, July 29, 1943, NA, HS 7/121. File — SOE
History 86.

59. "Directive to French Country Sections for Planning and Operations," n.d., 3, NA,
HS 7/121, File — SOE History 86.

60. "Directive to French Country Sections for Planning and Operations," n.d., 3, NA,
HS 7/121, File — SOE History 86. SHAEF also issued a joint PWE/OWI and SOE/
OSS Political Warfare Plan. It stated:

Activities undertaken as a continuation of current black and white
propaganda themes supplemented by agents:

A.   Preliminary Phase
Occupied Territories

(1) To Injure the Enemy
To supplement the specific SOE operations built around
the Resistance groups, the unorganized masses of the
populations will be educated, trained and directed to
undertake on and before D. Day, destructive and negative
actions leading to inter alia:

(a) immobilization of enemy rail, road, telephone and
telegraph communications,
(b) undermining enemy troop morale,
(c) confusion and diversions in enemy back areas,
(d) guerilla activities, and
(e) promotion of strikes;

(2) To Secure Maximum Aid for Allied Military Operations
The population in general will be stimulated to assist the
Allied military authorities, on the following broad lines:

(a) utilization of inhabitants' local knowledge of enemy's
dispositions, defences, dumps, etc.,
(b) utilization of local labour, skilled and unskilled, to
supplement military personnel,

      (c) preservation and reconstitution of local records useful to the Allies, and

      (d) preservation of food-stuffs, livestock, fuel, vehicles, etc.; and

    (3) to secure the morale of civilian population and to guide their opinion between now and D. Day.

Germany

To assist the main Political Warfare campaign it is proposed to concentrate on two principal and potential Fifth Columns inside Germany:

    (1) Conscripted Foreign Workers - with whom some activity has already been generated by SOE, will be further trained and organized by special agents before departure from their own countries. Defeatist talk, rumours, and general nerve-war against the German civilians will be the chief weapons; and

    (2) Todt Organization - now manned chiefly by foreign workers, will also be penetrated so as to undermine the morale of German troops, the SD, the SS and Todt guards.

  B. Preparatory Phase
     Occupied Territories
     As D. day approaches, the tempo of all activities will be accelerated.

  C. Assault Phase
     Occupied Territories
     Co-incident with the D.day official white announcement that "the invasion has begun" instructions will be issued to Resistance groups and agents to put into effect all operations designed to injure the enemy and to act on or prepare to act on those operations destined to secure maximum aid for Allied Military operations.

"Joint PWE/OWI and SOE/OSS Political Warfare Plan," October 5, 1943, NA, HS4/58, File SOE Czechoslovakia, No. 56.

61. "Extract from COS (43) 249th meeting (O) Held 14th October, 1943," NA, WO

193/633, SOE Series, SOE Organisation, Apr 30, 1942–May 28, 1945.

62. "Statement of SOE Activities Prepared in Consultation with MG 1 (SP), MO 1," February 15, 1945, NA, WO 193/633, SOE Series, SOE Organisation, 30 Apr 1942–28 May 1945.

63. "Special Meeting held in Board Room, 64 Baker Street at 1700 hours on 18th August 1944," NA, HS 6/260, SOE Files, Belgium No. 228.

64. Memorandum, CD/7092, C.D. to AD/E, AD/H, DP, AD/4, D/Q, August 11, 1944, NA, HS 6/260, SOE Files, Belgium No. 228.

65. Ibid.

8: "THE SIMPLEST THINGS IN WAR ...": CLAUSEWITZIAN FRICTION

1. Memorandum, "Note on SOE's Relations with Revolutionary Movements in Europe," November 2, 1942, NA, SOE Files, Poland 9, April 1942–February 1943.

2. Ibid. The SOE also had issues dealing with many of the exiled governments and their military staffs.

3. Memorandum, "Denmark — organisation of," November 8, 1940, NA, HS 6/260, SOE Files, Belgium No. 228. An SOE assessment noted, "One difficulty with which we have to contend in Denmark is the fact that Denmark is being treated extraordinarily well as compared with other occupied countries.... But the time may come when we shall have to employ political subversion to force the Germans to put in their own administration in order that the Danes may feel the pinch and therefore become more willing tools in our hands." Memorandum, S4 to 4351, "SO 2 Policy in Denmark," June 12, 1941, NA, HS 2/79, File Policy and Planning of SOE Activities in Denmark.

4. Memorandum, "Denmark — organisation of."

5. Comment sheet on reference F/1543/130/19 of 17th January, SD to AD/E, 19 January 1944, NA, HS2/43, SOE Series, Denmark, November 1940 to October 1945. Another reported explained, "Guerilla warfare is not suited to the Danish temperament.... We have got to prepare the minds even of pro-British elements before they can be of use to us. Political assassination should be planned in such a way that they appear to be entirely inspired and carried out by Danes." Memorandum, S4 to 4351, "SO 2 Policy in Denmark," June 12, 1941, NA, HS 2/79, File Policy and Planning of SOE Activities in Denmark.

6. Comment sheet on reference F/1543/130/19 of 17th January, SD to AD/E, 19 January 1944, NA, HS2/43, SOE Series, Denmark, November 1940 to October 1945.

7. Ibid.

8. Ibid.

9. Memorandum, AD/E to SD, January 19, 1944, NA, HS2/43, SOE Files, SOE/Denmark 27, November 940 to October 1945.

10. "Report of Meeting Held at the Foreign Office 12.00 Hrs. Friday, 9th July, 1943 to Discuss Intensification of Resistance to the Enemy in Denmark," NA, HS2/43, SOE Files, SOE/Denmark 27, November 1940 to October 1945.

11. Letter, SOE HQ to SOE Stockholm, D429, November 11, 1942, HS 2/79, File Policy and Planning of SOE Activities in Denmark.

12. "F Section," n.d., 1, NA, HS 7/121. File — SOE History 86.

13. Ibid., 1.

14. Ibid., 1.

15. Maclaren, *Canadians Behind Enemy Lines*, 14.

16. "F Section," n.d., 2, NA, HS 7/121, File — SOE History 86.

17. At one point, Lord Selborne, the minister responsible for the SOE, directed his staff in relation to sharing information with General Charles de Gaulle and his staff, "I should wish you ... tell them nothing of our innermost and most confidential plans, and above all, such bases as you may establish in France must be our bases and known only to us." Quoted in Mackenzie, *The Secret History of SOE*, 230.

18. Memorandum, "SOE and Revolutionary Movements in Europe," MPX to MX, December 7, 1942, NA, SOE Files, Poland 9, April 1942–February 1943. See also E.H. Cookridge, *They Came From the Sky* (New York: Thomas Y. Crowell Company, 1965), 171.

19. Letter, 141 to B/M, May 24, 1940, NA, HS 5/60, SOE Albania, No. 55.

20. Memorandum, "Norway," September 1, 1940, NA, HS 2/218, File SOE/Norway 68, April 1940 to December 1944.

21. Dear, *Sabotage and Subversion*, 50.

22. Ibid., 11.

23. See chapter 7, note 45.

24. "Memorandum by the Chiefs of Staff — Co-ordination of SOE," December 29, 1943, NA, WO 193/633, SOE Series, SOE Organisation, 30 Apr 1942–28 May 1945.

25. OSS Syllabus.

26. Ibid.

27. Ibid.

28. Ibid.

29. SOE manual, "Training," n.d., Part 3, NA, HS 2/229. File SOE/Norway 77.

30. Ironically, a German document captured the necessity of winning "hearts and minds" in current parlance. The report noted, "The fight against partisans would be simplified if the German forces succeeded in gaining the confidence of the inhabitants through correct and prudent treatment." SOE manual, "The Agents Life as an Individual," n.d., chapter 2, NA, HS 2/229, File SOE/Norway 77.

31. OSS Syllabus.

32. Ibid.

33. O'Donnell, *Operatives, Spies and Saboteurs*, 155.

34. SOE manual, "CE Measures," n.d., NA, HS 2/229, File SOE/Norway 77.

35. Foot, "What use was SOE?," 79. Numbers vary depending on source. The discovery of the German penetration threatened the very existence of the SOE. Its critics lobbied to have the SOE absorbed by SIS/MI6. Churchill, however, gave his confidence to the new director, Major-General Gubbins, and allowed the SOE to continue to exist. See also Mackenzie, *The Secret History of SOE*, 295–308. Mackenzie asserts

that in total 56 agents were dropped into the Netherlands, 43 were dropped into German hands, 36 were later executed, 8 survived the war, and the other 12 were listed as missing or dead. The SOE also dropped 544 containers of weapons and munitions into German hands.

36. Macksey, *The Partisans of Europe In The Second World War,* 118.

37. The security checks were a means of letting London know that the sender was okay. A lack of the security check or a change to its nature would indicate to headquarters in London that the agent had been captured and was operating under duress. Amazingly, in the case of the agent and radio set in Holland that was captured, the agent consistently failed to provide the correct security check when contacting London, yet headquarters remained oblivious and continued to dispatch agents. It was not until two SOE agents escaped and returned to England and revealed that the Germans were in control of the Dutch sets that the connection was terminated. See also Stafford, *Secret Agent,* 143–44; and Howarth, *Undercover,* 226–27.

38. See Maclaren, *Canadians Behind Enemy Lines,* 57–64; Cookridge, *They Came From the* Sky, 59–63; George H. Ford, ed., *The Making of a Secret Agent* (Toronto: McClelland & Stewart, 1978); and Vance, *Unlikely Soldiers.*

39. Captured German Document Entitled "Principles of Guerilla Warfare," dated 25.10.41, NA, HS4/143, SOE Files, Poland 9.

40. "Plan for SOE Activities in Greece," November 1942, NA, HS5/584, File Greece No. 585A.

41. Memorandum, "Projects for Sabotage Work in Occupied Countries," December 18, 1942, NA, HS4/143, SOE Files, Poland 9. The directive went on to state that "Targets should be selected with a view to slowing up an entire industry in any given area." Another document explained: "Not any German is killed and only those selected by GHQ for their particular brutality or others who are of particular importance such as Kutschera and Frank are killed. This selective policy has forced down the reprisal rate from 100 Poles to one German, to a present rate of twenty to one." Memorandum, "Polish Secret Army," April 26, 1944, NA, HS 5/59, File Albania — Operational Directives Foreign Office Directive to OC Allied Mission in Albania.

42. "War Cabinet — Future Strategy — Appreciation by the Chiefs of Staff Committee," September 4, 1940, 61, War Cabinet Weekly Resume (No. 53), NA, CAB 66/11, Memoranda, W.P. (40) 321-W.P. (40) 370, vol XI.

9: TURNING THEORY TO REALITY: CANADIANS ON SOE OPERATIONS

1. Howarth, *Undercover,* 182. One SOE officer responsible for preparing agents believed:

> I strongly advocate that before proceeding abroad an agent should be put through a proper interrogation by officers in this country competent to carry out this interrogation so that

the agent's cover story can be tested out. His cover story is his life line and if this is at fault in the slightest detail one must regard the agent as being inefficiently equipped for his job. In this respect I gather that the cover stories are prepared for the agent by the Country Sections who are of course in close touch with the training school but in many cases the training school when training an agent do not know what cover story is going to be given to the man they are training. If it is at all possible to combine these two operations, I would strongly advocate that this be done.

Letter, Major Roberts, February 21, 1942, NA, KV4/171, General Policy on Liaison with SOE.

2. "Notes on the Co-Ordination of Bombing of Skoda Works with Special Operations to be carried out Simultaneously," December 16, 1942, NA, HS 4/36, SOE Files, Czechoslovakia, No. 34.

3. Cookridge, *They Came From the Sky*, 50.

4. Dear, *Sabotage and Subversion*, 155; and Howarth, *Undercover*, 298. The risks were not insubstantial. When twenty-two OSS agents were discovered in Spain, a neutral country teetering on support of the Nazis, nine were killed in a shootout and thirteen captured. To avoid a diplomatic catastrophe, the US government disavowed the agents, who were on an approved mission, stating they were a rogue element within the OSS that was no longer under governmental control. All thirteen agents were subsequently executed by the Spanish government. O'Donnell, *Operatives, Spies and Saboteurs*, 47.

5. Stafford, *Secret Agent*, 146.

6. Howarth, *Undercover*, 80.

7. "F Section," n.d., 2, NA, HS 7/121. File — SOE History 86. The Foreign Office imposed a "go slow" approach that limited SOE actions. The Foreign Office did not want any sabotage conducted that could be traced back to deliberate interference. Ibid.

8. Ibid.

9. Memorandum, S4 to 4351, "SO 2 Policy in Denmark," 12 June 1941, NA, HS 2/79, File Policy and Planning of SOE Activities in Denmark.

10. "F Section," n.d., 2, NA, HS 7/121. File — SOE History 86.

11. For instance, the SOE shipped 418,083 weapons to the French Resistance during the war, 47 percent being sub-machine guns. This is not surprising, since the Sten sub-machine gun was so inexpensive to manufacture. PRO, *SOE Syllabus*, 18.

12. "F Section," n.d., 8, NA, HS 7/121. File — SOE History 86.

13. The source documents for Canadian military personnel serving in the SOE are Memoradum, "Canadian Service Personnel SOE France," S1350-5000/00 (D Hist), June 22, 1946; "Report on Canadians Specially Employed in World War II," DMI, July 22, 1946; and Walter, "Cloak and Dagger."

14. Walter, "Cloak and Dagger," 8–9; Maclaren, *Canadians Behind Enemy Lines*, 27–43; and Vance, *Unlikely Soldiers*, 171.

15. Maclaren, *Canadians Behind Enemy Lines*, 31; Mackenzie, *The Secret History of the SOE*, 575.

16. Vance, *Unlikely Soldiers*, 186.

17. Dear, *Sabotage and Subversion*, 146; and Vance, *Unlikely Soldiers*, 231.

18. Maclaren, *Canadians Behind Enemy Lines*, 34.

19. Walter, "Cloak and Dagger," 8–9.

20. Quoted in Maclaren, *Canadians Behind Enemy Lines*, 69; and Vance, *Unlikely Soldiers*, 266.

21. Maclaren, *Canadians Behind Enemy Lines*, 70; and Mackenzie, *The Secret History of the SOE*, 579.

22. See Vance, *Unlikely Soldiers*, and Ford, *The Making of a Secret Agent* for a detailed history.

23. See Walter, "Cloak and Dagger," 10–11; and Ford, *The Making of a Secret Agent*, 246–53.

24. Ford, *The Making of a Secret Agent*, 255; and Vance, *Unlikely Soldiers*, 207–08.

25. Ford, *The Making of a Secret Agent*, 255.

26. Ford, *The Making of a Secret Agent*, 272; and Vance, *Unlikely Soldiers*, 257–59.

27. Maclaren, *Canadians Behind Enemy Lines*, 94.

28. *Maquis* were rural guerrilla bands of French Resistance fighters (*maquisards*) during the Second World War.

29. When d'Artois was in London in December 1943, he met another new SOE recruit, nineteen-year-old Sonia "Tony" Butt. While on training together in Scotland, they decided to get married, on April 15, 1944. They did not see each other for the next six months as each was sent on a separate mission. Butt, the youngest SOE operator to be deployed in the field, was dropped near Le Mans to assist the resistance movement create as much havoc as possible prior to the Normandy invasion. They reunited in Paris after the Normandy campaign.

30. The *Milice*, or French Militia, was a Vichy French paramilitary force created in cooperation with the Germans on January 30, 1943, to assist with rooting out and destroying the French Resistance during the Second World War.

31. Walter, "Cloak and Dagger," 13–14.

32. D'Artois was hardly squeamish. In a *Toronto Star* interview in December 1944, he recounted how the Germans had bludgeoned to death fifty-nine captured *maquisards*, considering them criminals and terrorists. In retaliation, d'Artois lined up fifty-two captured German prisoners and executed them one at a time. Stafford, *Camp X*, 235; and Maclaren, *Canadians Behind Enemy Lines*, 97.

33. After the war, d'Artois remained in the Canadian Armed Forces. In 1947, he led a risky rescue operation in the Arctic to save Canon J.B. Turner, who had been accidentally shot. He was awarded the George Medal for his efforts. Newly promoted, Major d'Artois was also given command of an embryonic force called the Canadian Special Air Service Company from 1948–49. See Bernd Horn, "A Military Enigma: The Canadian Special

Notes

Air Service Company, 1948–49," *Canadian Military History*, vol. 10, no. 1, Winter 2001, 21–30. He also served in the Korean War, completing an operational tour with the 1st Battalion, The Royal 22nd Regiment. D'Artois died in 1999.

34. Maclaren, *Canadians Behind Enemy Lines*, 128.

35. In reality, only eleven actually possessed Canadian citizenship. Another twelve were in Canada illegally, and the remainder were American Yugoslavs. Walter, "Cloak and Dagger," 18.

36. Gelleny in Heathcote, *Testaments of Honour*, 194.

37. Letter, DH18 to AD 3, October 27, 1942, NA, HS 4/91, SOE Hungary No. 8. This assessment was not surprising as an SOE appreciation determined that "She [Hungary] had never been actively engaged in the War. She had suffered no severe casualties, she was not a defeated nation and, above all, there was no suffering amongst the civil population. Far from her alliance with Germany leading to a deterioration of conditions of life, Hungary in the last four years, has derived nothing but benefit from her association with Germany and the standard of living has continued, if anything, to rise." "Appreciation on Special Operation in Hungary by Comd. Force 399," n.d., NA, HS4/131, SOE Files, Hungary No. 47.

38. Letter, DH18 to AD 3, October 27, 1942, NA, HS 4/91, SOE Hungary No. 8.

39. Durovecz, *My Secret Mission*, 7–8.

40. "Appreciation of Possible SOE Operations in Hungary," December 4, 1943, 2, NA, HS4/131, SOE Files, Hungary No. 47.

41. Ibid.

42. Ibid.

43. Note, VCD to CD, July 21, 1943, NA, HS 4/90, SOE Files, Hungary No. 7. He also noted that "our two year flirtation with Romania has brought us no dividends worth mentioning nor has 'John' helped forward subversion in Bulgaria."

44. Ibid. The Béla Kun Red Terror referred to violence that was committed during the four-month reign of Béla Kun and his Hungarian Soviet Republic from March to August 1919. Similar to the "Red Terror" in the Soviet Union, it was aimed at destroying political opposition.

45. The committee was careful to note that the "Bombing of Budapest is justified in any case on purely military grounds, as it is the most important railway centre East of the Reich frontiers." Report, "Hungary," November 15, 1943, NA, HS 4/91, SOE Hungary No. 8. The sentiment was widespread within the SOE. A letter a week prior affirmed, "We should do all possible to obtain the bombing of Hungary. This is more likely than anything else to convince the Hungarian Government of the necessity of immediate action. Past experience has shown that the Hungarian Government is above all concerned to spare Budapest the direct consequences of war. These people appear to think that the British are fond of them and will give them preferential treatment. Until they are shown the contrary, they will go on thinking they 'can get away with' anything." Letter, B4 to B1/COS London, "Plans for Hungary," November 8, 1943, NA, HS 4/91, SOE Hungary No. 8. And, a memorandum two days prior stated, "The 'Surrender Group' should be told in the

most categorical manner that Hungary is regarded as an enemy country and should be treated as such unless she proves by action her right to different treatment.... As soon as possible targets in Hungary should be bombed by the RAF. Such bombing would show the 'Surrender Group' that the British are serious when they say that Hungary is their enemy. It would shatter their complacency and convince them that they cannot count on any special tenderness of the British towards them in the future. It would bring home to Hungarian public opinion the desperate situation of their country and the need for speedy action." Memorandum, "Work into Hungary," November 13, 1943, NA, HS 4/90, SOE Files, Hungary No. 7.

46. Memorandum, "Hungarian Operations," December 9, 1943, NA, HS 4/90, SOE Files, Hungary No. 7.

47. Ibid.

48. Memorandum, "Conversation with Lt. Col Howie, Monday 2nd October, 1944," NA, HS 4/90, SOE Files, Hungary No. 7.

49. Memorandum, "Hungarian Operations," December 9, 1943, NA, HS 4/90, SOE Files, Hungary No. 7.

50. "Directive for Hungary — SOE Operational Policy," December 9, 1943, NA, HS 4/91, SOE Hungary No. 8.

51. Once the Germans occupied the country in March 1944, all SOE agents were either captured or under such heavy surveillance that they became inoperable.

52. The Dibbler team consisted of British Captain John Coates, who was the leader, and Canadians Lieutenant Bertram (Bodo), Lieutenant Mike Thomas (Turk), and Lieutenant Joe Gordon (Gelleny).

53. Coates was a former commando, schooled in the SOE training establishments, and spoke eight languages, including fluent German and Russian. SOE headquarters instructed him to "get in touch with the miners and industrial workers in the Pécs area and to endeavour to organise sabotage, strikes and passive resistance." He was also to examine and make plans for attacking local targets, but not to initiate attacks until ordered to do so. He was also to arrange for the infiltration of agents deeper into the country. Letter, "SOE Work in Hungary," AOC to BAF, July 17, 1944, NA, HS 4/132, SOE Files, Hungary No. 47.

54. "Brief Notes on the Activities of the Hungarian Section during the Past Six Months," September 13, 1944, NA, HS 4/132, SOE Files, Hungary No. 47.

55. Memorandum, "Hungarian Operations," December 9, 1943, NA, HS 4/90, SOE Files, Hungary No. 7.

56. Letter, MPH 2 to MHM, September 10, 1944, NA, HS 4/132, SOE Files, Hungary No. 47.

57. As usual, there are discrepancies in accounts. In fact, Gelleny's own account of events differs slightly between his book, Joseph J. Gelleny, *Almost* (Port Perry, ON: Blake Book Distribution, 2000), and his chapter "Joe Gelleny," in Heathcote, *Testaments of Honour*, 194–214. See also "Summary of Report By Capt. J.G. Coates — Dibbler Mission Covering Period From 11 Sep 44 to 11 Jan 1945," January 25, 1945, NA, WO 204/11601, AFHQ Files, Report on SOE Mission in Hungary.

58. "Summary of Report By Capt. J.G. Coates — Dibbler Mission Covering Period From 11 Sep 44 to 11 Jan 1945," January 25, 1945, NA, WO 204/11601, AFHQ Files, Report on SOE Mission in Hungary.

59. Gelleny, *Almost*, 186–90.

60. Walter, "Cloak and Dagger," 22.

61. Cruickshank, *SOE in the Far East*, 83. The title Force 136 came into effect March 17, 1944.

62. Maclaren, *Canadians Behind Enemy Lines*, 182. When STS 101 closed down due to the Japanese invasion, many of the training staff returned to India to work in the headquarters. Some melted into the jungle to train and lead indigenous forces to fight the Japanese. See F. Spencer Chapman, *The Jungle is Neutral* (Bungay, Suffolk: Triad/Granada, 1982).

63. Dear, *Sabotage and Subversion*, 207–08.

64. Kendall was a civilian who had been recruited by MI6 to organize an intelligence-gathering network along the South China Sea from Taiwan to Hainan prior to the start of the war. When the SOE later told him he was required to use a military rank, he decided to give himself the rank of major. Marjorie Wong, *The Dragon and the Maple Leaf: Chinese Canadians in World War II* (London, ON: Pirie Publishing, 1994), 120; and Maclaren, *Canadians Behind Enemy Lines*, 184–87.

65. Cruickshank, *SOE in the Far East*, 76; and Wong, *The Dragon and the Maple Leaf*, 120.

66. See Wong, *The Dragon and the Maple Leaf*, for a detailed history of Chinese Canadian involvement in the Second World War, including a comprehensive look at their involvement in the SOE.

67. Maclaren, *Canadians Behind Enemy Lines*, 185. See also Cruickshank, *SOE in the Far East*, 156–57.

68. Cruickshank, *SOE in the Far East*, 156–57.

69. Despite the original reluctance at recruiting Chinese Canadians for military service, the Canadian government appeared to change its perspective after the initial group was trained. When the SOE requested an additional twenty-five in December of 1944, the minister of national defence authorized recruitment of up to an additional 150 Chinese Canadians. See Maclaren, *Canadians Behind Enemy Lines*, 200.

70. Wong, *The Dragon and the Maple Leaf*, 124. The training camp is now a heritage site located in Okanagan Mountain Provincial Park.

71. Walter, "Cloak and Dagger," 23.

72. Ibid., 23.

73. Ibid., 24.

74. The SOE was heavily criticized by its detractors for its poor results in sabotage in the Far East. Most critics believed the SOE placed too much emphasis on guerrilla warfare activities and intelligence gathering (a departure from SOE focus in Europe). See Cruickshank, *SOE in the Far East*, 249–57.

10: RECKONING: THE VALUE OF THE SOE IN THE SECOND WORLD WAR

1. "Provision of Personnel for SOE," DMO/641/LM, February 15, 1945, NA, WO 193/633, SOE Series, SOE Organisation, 30 Apr 1942–28 May 1945.
2. "Chiefs of Staff Committee Value of SOE Operations," November 21, 1945, 4–5, NA, AIR 20/7958.
3. Minute, VCAS to CAS, "Value of SOE Operations," COS (45) 665 (o), NA, AIR 20/7958.
4. "SOE Activities in Greece, Crete and the Aegean, from June 42–Sep 44," November 8, 19 45, NA, AIR 20/7958.
5. "War Cabinet — Future Strategy — Appreciation by the Chiefs of Staff Committee," September 4, 1940, 6. War Cabinet Weekly Resume (No. 53), NA, CAB 66/11, Memoranda, W.P. (40) 321-W.P. (40) 370, vol. XI.
6. Memorandum, "Support and Employment of Secret Army in Poland," November 10, 1942, NA, HS 5/59, File Albania — Operational Directives Foreign Office Directive to OC Allied Mission in Albania.
7. Memorandum to Prime Minister, "SOE Activities — Summary for the Prime Minister — Quarter: Mar–Jun 1942," NA, REM 3/409/5.
8. "F Section," n.d., 7, NA, HS 7/121. File — SOE History 86.
9. Ibid., 10.
10. Ibid., 13–14.
11. "SOE Activities in Greece," April 8, 1943, NA, HS 5/578, File — Greece No. 578.
12. Memorandum to prime minister, "SOE Activities — Summary for the Prime Minister — Quarter: Apr–Jun 1943," NA, REM 3/409/5; and "Situation in Yugoslavia," Appendix A, NA, HS5/151, File — SOE Balkans, No. 7.
13. "S-2 Report, No. 136, Enemy Situation," April 27, 1944, LAC, RG 24, War Diary 1 CSS Bn, vol. 15,302.
14. Foot, "What use was SOE?," 80.
15. Memorandum to prime minister, "SOE Activities — Summary for the Prime Minister — Quarter: July–Sep 1943," NA, REM 3/409/5.
16. Ibid.
17. "F Section," n.d., 11, NA, HS 7/121, File — SOE History 86.
18. Ibid., 12.
19. There were also numerous individual acts that have not been captured that added to the cumulative effect. For instance, the Salesman network sunk a nine-hundred-ton minesweeper that was overhauled and repaired in Rouen. After its trials were complete and twelve million francs of Anti-Submarine Detection Investigation Committee (ASDIC) equipment, twenty tons of ammunition, and supplies for three months had been loaded, the ship was sunk by saboteurs. Another network destroyed a foundry in Leroy and a number of factories in their area of operation; disabled locomotive turntables and engines, derailed troop trains, destroyed the telephone exchange, destroyed warehouses full of German equipment and supplies, loading cranes, and a steel railway bridge. By the Allied seizure of France, SOE had fifty networks operating in France. Dear, *Sabotage and Subversion,* 145, 149.

20. Foot, "What use was SOE?," 80. FFI was the formal name given to French Resistance fighters by General Charles de Gaulle during the later stages of the war. The name change was intended to reflect the changing nature of the French Resistance, from an occupied country to one in the process of liberating itself. During the liberation of France, FFI units were more formally organized into light infantry units that served the Allied cause along with Free French Forces. By October 1944, FFI units were amalgamated into the French regular army.

21. "Chiefs of Staff Committee Value of SOE Operations," COS (45) 146, July 18, 1945, NA. The SOE network "Hugh" reported five hundred rail cuts in its area between June 6 and July 6, 1944. Nonetheless, it must also be pointed out that it has been shown that a major cause of delay to enemy troop movements was due to Allied strategic and tactical air forces.

22. Dear, *Sabotage and Subversion*, 152.

23. Ibid., 188. For detailed accounts of the Jedburgh teams see: Colin Beaven, *Operation Jedburgh: D-Day and America's First Shadow War* (London: Penguin Books, 2006); Roger Ford, *Steel from the Sky: The Jedburgh Raiders, France 1944* (London: Weidenfeld & Nicolson, 2004); Will Irwin, *The Jedburghs: The Secret History of the Allied Special Forces, France 1944* (New York: Public Affairs, 2005).

24. "F Section," n.d., 74, NA, HS 7/121. File — SOE History 86.

25. "Chiefs of Staff Committee Value of SOE Operations," COS (45) 146, July 18, 1945, NA.

26. "F Section," n.d., 15, NA, HS 7/121. File — SOE History 86.

27. "Chiefs of Staff Committee Value of SOE Operations," COS (45) 146, July 18, 1945, NA. The committee also noted that SOE actions "successfully attacked targets which had been unsuccessfully attempted in the aerial interdiction programme."

28. Quoted in Cookridge, *They Came From the Sky*, 107.

29. Ibid., 108.

30. "Chiefs of Staff Committee Value of SOE Operations," COS (45) 146, 18 July 1945, NA.

31. Ibid.

32. Irwin, *The Jedburghs*, 338.

33. Ibid., 239.

34. Ibid., 237.

35. Dear, *Sabotage and Subversion*, 17.

36. Thomas Gallagher, *Assault in Norway* (Guilford, CT: The Lyons Press, 2002 ed.), 3.

37. Ibid., 3.

38. Heavy water, or deuterium oxide, was vital to early experimentation since it has twice as many hydrogen atoms as ordinary water and is 10 percent heavier. The heavier weight acts as a slowing mechanism "moderating the speed of the neutrons set free in an atomic reactor and permitting these elementary atomic particles to achieve a chain reaction that could split the nuclei of a fissionable element and cause an explosive release of atomic power." The focus on heavy water was somewhat overblown. Allied scientists later discovered that graphite would also moderate the

speed and was in fact more effective. See Dan Kurzman, "Sabotaging Hitler's Bomb," *Military History Quarterly,* vol. 9, no. 2 (Winter 1997), 38; Gallagher, 8; and Nigel West, "SOE's Achievements: Operation Gunnerside Reconsidered," *Royal United Services Institute (RUSI),* vol. 148, no. 2, April 2003, 77.

39. A cyclotron is an apparatus in which charged atomic and subatomic particles are accelerated by an alternating electric field while following an outward spiral or circular path in a magnetic field. Katherine Barber, ed., *The Canadian Oxford Dictionary* (New York: Oxford University Press, 1998).

40. Dear, *Sabotage and Subversion,* 119; and Stevenson, *A Man Called Intrepid,* 113. Bohr had already split the uranium atom, with a release of energy a million times more powerful than the same quantity of high explosives." Stevenson, *A Man Called Intrepid,* 55.

41. See Stevenson, *A Man Called Intrepid,* 55–62, 78, 416–41; Jonathan F. Keiler, "The Prospect of a Nazi atomic bomb is sobering but German scientists themselves doomed the project to failure," *Military Heritage WWII History,* July 2004, 28–31; and Dan Kurzman, "Sabotaging Hitler's Bomb," *Military History Quarterly,* vol. 9, no. 2 (Winter 1997), 38–47.

42. Bombing was in fact the first option the British considered. However, British Air Command felt that the difficult location of the plant made it near impossible to hit with the technology available at that time. Furthermore, the Norwegian government was reluctant to expose its civilian population to the possible collateral damage. Therefore, sabotage operations under the control of the SOE were undertaken. See Thomas Gallagher, *Assault in Norway* (Guilford, CT: Lyons Press, 2002 ed.); Janusz Pielkalkiewicz, *Secret Agents, Spies and Saboteurs* (London: William Morrow, 1973), 264–79; Nigel West, "SOE's Achievements: Operation Gunnerside Reconsidered," *Royal United Services Institute (RUSI),* vol. 148, no. 2 (April 2003), 77; and Dear, *Sabotage and Subversion,* 119–30. The Allies had finally succeeded in destroying the heavy water capability of Norsk-Hydro. However, the effort was not entirely required. German scientists had concluded that a bomb building project was impractical and that nuclear energy would be useful mainly to power submarines. Similarly, Albert Speer, the Reich's armaments minister, concluded that the German atomic scientists could make little contribution to the war effort, and thus concentrated German experimental resources and energies on the more promising rocket and jet projects. See also Keiler, "The Prospect of a Nazi atomic bomb," 32–33; and Kurzman, "Sabotaging Hitler's Bomb," 47.

43. "Chiefs of Staff Committee Value of SOE Operations," November 21, 1945, 2, NA, AIR 20/7958.

44. "Annex — The Value of SOE Operations in the Supreme Commander's Sphere," 1, NA, AIR 20/7958.

45. "Chiefs of Staff Committee Value of SOE Operations," November 21, 1945, 3, NA, AIR 20/7958.

46. Cited in Foot, "What use was SOE?," 83.

47. "Chiefs of Staff Committee Value of SOE Operations," COS (45) 146, July 18, 1945, NA, AIR 20/7958.
48. Foot, "What use was SOE?", 79.
49. "Annex —The Value of SOE Operations in the Supreme Commander's Sphere," 2–7, NA, AIR 20/7958.
50. Ibid., 7.
51. Dwight D. Eisenhower, *Crusade in Europe* (Garden City, NY: Doubleday, 1948), 296.
52. Quoted in Irwin, *The Jedburghs*, 241.
53. Cookridge, *They Came From the Sky*, vi.
54. "Chiefs of Staff Committee Value of SOE Operations," COS (45) 146, July 18, 1945, NA, AIR 20/7958. SHAEF Headquarters also sent a specific message with regard to the American OSS. It stated:

> When the Office of Strategic Services was first established, the military services were not any better prepared to utilize services than it was to render the type of service ultimately required. However, its value in this theater has been so great that there should be no thought of its elimination as an activity.
>
> Future value of the Office of Strategic Services in the European Theater appears to be high but is subject to certain contingencies. Valuable assistance in the prosecution of the war was effected by OSS by successful short range operations on the entire front where they obtained tactical intelligence and accomplished local sabotage. Strategic operations had the same objects as the tactical but were executed deeper within enemy territory. They were not consistently effective but had some sporadic successes of great importance. Also OSS performed admirably in helping to organize resistance groups in France, Belgium, Holland, Denmark and Norway and in assisting to supply them.
>
> In the future OSS will function as an intelligence information gathering agency and as a counter-espionage organization. It is expected that a net utilizing high grade personnel will feed back a wide range of intelligence and information to the Theater Commander through the tight control of the intelligence staff. Complete control by the Theater Commander of OSS activities within his theater or based on his theater is regarded as an essential prerequisite of efficient and smooth operations.

Message to AGWAR for Joint Chiefs of Staff, from SHAEF Forward, May 23, 1945, NA, WO 219/5307, File SOE/OSS Activities.
55. Ibid.
56. Roosevelt, *War Report of the OSS*, v.
57. Howarth, *Undercover*, 298.

11: SETTLING ACCOUNTS: THE SOE AT WAR'S END

1. The pragmatic political stance that SOE took, namely to support any group that was willing to fight the Axis, did not sit well with many who feared the postwar consequences of arming and training groups hostile to democratic ideals. For instance, the head of the SOE himself acknowledged, "In planning this resistance, it can therefore be said that SOE are not concerned with either political issues or the politics of the day: they are solely concerned in harnessing the maximum amount of available resistance to the one common end — the harassing and defeat of the Axis, and therefore of making them war conscious as opposed to being politically conscious." "SOE — PWE Policy Committee — SOE Activities in Greece — Memorandum by Head of SOE," April 8, 1943, NA, HS 5/579, SOE/Greece, No. 579.

2. War Cabinet, "Meeting to be held on 14 Sept 43," NA, WO 193/633, SOE Series, SOE Organisation, 30 Apr 1942–28 May 1945. This is not surprising, since, as Lord Selborne explained, "It is important to realize that the activities of S.O.E. in enemy-occupied countries cover all stages of subversive activity. It is usually necessary in the first instance to create a spirit of resistance amongst the population and then to begin the formation of the necessary cells and groups and the establishment of firm communications between them and the base from which the work is being directed. The early stages are therefore purely clandestine but the work, as it continues, acquires more and more a para-military character until it culminates in open guerilla activity in support of Allied military operations." Cabinet Defence Committee, "Extract from the Minutes of DO(45) 4th Meeting held on 31 August, 1945," NA, WO 193/622, SOE Files.

3. The Chief of Staff to the Supreme Allied Commander (COSSAC) controlled the SOE Western European Group in London and Allied Commander-in-Chief, Mediterranean Theatre, controlled the SOE Middle East and Balkans Group, as well as Northern Italy in Cairo. The rationale was to create closer relations between subversive activities and projected operations; facilitate closer liaison with the exiled government military staffs; and closer integration of SOE and OSS activities through the British-American staff of the Supreme Allied commander. "Draft Memorandum Chiefs of Staff SOE Operations," December 29, 1943, NA, WO 193/633, SOE Series, SOE Organisation, 30 Apr 1942–28 May 1945.

4. "Memorandum by the Chiefs of Staff — Co-ordination of SOE," December 29, 1943, NA, WO 193/633, SOE Series, SOE Organisation, 30 Apr 1942–28 May 1945.

5. "Draft Memorandum Chiefs of Staff SOE Operations," December 29, 1943, NA, WO 193/633, SOE Series, SOE Organisation, 30 Apr 1942–28 May 1945.

6. "Memorandum by the Chiefs of Staff — Co-ordination of SOE," December 29, 1943, NA, WO 193/633, SOE Series, SOE Organisation, 30 Apr 1942–28 May 1945.

7. Ibid.

8. "PM/44/716 dated 23 Nov 44 — Memo from Foreign Secretary to Prime Minister regarding his assumption of Ministerial responsibility for SOE on Disbandment of MEW," November 26, 1944, NA, WO 193/633, SOE Series, SOE Organisation, 30 Apr 1942–28 May 1945.

Notes

9. Annex, "Draft Minute Chiefs of Staff Committee to the Prime Minister," December 4, 1944, NA, WO 193/633, SOE Series, SOE Organisation, 30 Apr 1942–28 May 1945.
10. "Chiefs of Staff Committee Meeting to be held on 27th November, 1944," NA, WO 193/633, SOE Series, SOE Organisation, 30 Apr 1942–28 May 1945.
11. Hand-written memo, "Future of SOE," drafted by MO1 Colonel, November 25, 1944, NA, WO 193/633, SOE Series, SOE Organisation, 30 Apr 1942–28 May 1945.
12. "Chiefs of Staff Committee Meeting to be held on 27th November, 1944," NA, WO 193/633, SOE Series, SOE Organisation, 30 Apr 1942–28 May 1945.
13. Cabinet Defence Committee, Extract from the Minutes of DO(45) 4th Meeting held on August 31, 1945, NA, WO 193/622, SOE Files.
14. Ibid.
15. Ibid.
16. Ibid. Donovan, argued that the formulation of national policy is "influenced and determined by knowledge (or ignorance) of aims, capabilities, intentions and policies of other nations." Roosevelt, *War Report of the OSS*, 117.
17. Cabinet Defence Committee, "Extract from the Minutes of DO(45) 4th Meeting held on 31 August, 1945," NA, WO 193/622, SOE Files.
18. Ibid.
19. Ibid. Similarly, OSS director, Bill Donovan argued, "It is not easy to set up a modern intelligence system. It is more difficult to do so in a time of peace than in a time of war." He insisted that it was critical to create the new organization before the war ended and before the organization was dismantled and its personnel disappear "so that profit may be made of its experience and 'know-how' in deciding how the new agency may best be conducted." Roosevelt, *War Report of the OSS*, xi.
20. Stafford, *Secret Agent,* 229.
21. See Colonel Bernd Horn, "The Canadian SOF Legacy," in Dr. Emily Spencer, ed., *Special Operations Forces: A National Capability* (Kingston, ON: CDA Press, November 2011), 8–28.
22. Maclaren, *Canadians Behind Enemy Lines,* 150, 172, 199–200. Approximately 3,226 personnel, including all services and civilian employees, were employed in the SOE by 1942. By April 30, 1944, the total strength rose to 11,752. Mackenzie, *The Secret History of SOE* , 717–19.

INDEX

3rd Infantry Division, 162

21 Army Group, 102

207 Military Mission (*see also* Special Training School 103), 76

Abaliget, 146

Abwehr, 129

Africa, 62, 68, 81, 100, 109

agents

air staff, 154

aircraft

    Halifax bomber, 138, 145

    JU 87 Stuka, 15

    Mosquito Bomber, 118

    Whitley Bomber, 9, 98, 136

Albanians, 122

Allies

America First [Party], 54

American isolationist groups, 54

Arab Rebellion, 21

Archambeault, Captain J.P., 152

Ardennes, 15, 17–18, 189n6

Argentina, 61, 65, 200n24

Arisaig, 74–75, 97–98

Army Force Headquarters (AFHQ), 111–12

atomic weapon program (German), 163–64

Attlee, Clement, 179

Auchinleck, General Sir Claude, 40

Balkans, 73, 75, 109, 124, 130, 164, 170

Bari, 147

Bayly, Benjamin (Pat) Deforest, 93

Beaulieu, 77, 95

Bégué, Commandant Georges (*see also* George Noble), 133

Belgium, 108, 109, 113, 129, 158, 159

Benoit, Captain Joseph Henri Adelard, 152, 153, 139–40

Bertram, Gus (*see also* Gustave Bodo), 144–45, 222n52

Bertrand (*see also* Frank Pickersgill), 130

Bevin, Ernest, 179

Bieler, Captain Gustave Daniel Alfred, 135–37

"black" propaganda, 27, 116

Bletchley Park, 23, 93

Blitzkrieg, 15–16

Bodo, Gustave (*see also* Gus Bertram), 144–45, 222n52

Bohr, Niels, 163, 226

Bolivia, 61, 62, 65, 201n30

Boston, 54

Bourne, Lieutenant-General Sir Alan, 22

Brazil, 60, 61–62, 65

Brickendonbury, 75

Britain (*see also* England), 11–12, 13, 15, 16, 19, 21, 26, 33, 39, 42, 44, 45, 46, 47, 49–50, 51, 53, 69, 77, 84, 93, 175, 190n12, 191n26, 192n18, 197n22, 204n28, 210n21

Index

British Broadcasting Corporation
(BBC), 31, 159
British Expeditionary Force (BEF), 16,
18, 22, 188n1
British Purchasing Commission, 53
British Security Coordination (BSC),
45, 46–50, 51–58, 64–77, 81–83,
91–93, 97, 99, 105, 150, 179–181,
197n13, 197n17, 198n1, 200n20,
202n25, 204n21, 204n28
British Supply Council, 75
Brooke, Field Marshal Sir Alan, 22, 99,
179
Brooker, Lieutenant-Colonel R.M.
Bill, 204n18
Bruce, Colonel David, 166
Budapest, 143–44, 146–47, 221n45
Bulgaria, 12, 73, 78, 221n43
Burma, 148, 152
Burmese Nationalist Army (BNA), 152

Camp X (STS 103), 13, 72–83, 84–94,
95, 97–98, 140, 179, 181, 204n20,
2014n21, 207n19, 207n27,
208n28, 208n31
Canadian Army, 74, 77, 151, 152
Canadian Broadcasting Corporation
(CBC), 47
Canadian government, 73, 74, 76, 150,
223n69
Canadian Military Headquarters
(CMHQ), 73, 74, 137
Canadian National Research Council,
105
Canadian Pacific Railroad, 90
Caribbean Sea, 60
Central Intelligence Agency (CIA),
180–81
Chamberlain, Neville, 28, 190n12
Chicago, 54

Chief of Staff to the Supreme Allied
Commander (COSSAC), 228n3
Chief of the General Staff (CGS), 76,
77, 202n3
Chiefs of Staff Committee, 26–27, 30,
31, 110, 115, 123–25, 130–31,
143–44, 160, 166, 169–172, 10n24
Chile, 60–61, 62, 65
China, 27, 149–150, 151, 153, 223n64
Chinese Canadians, 12, 73, 149–51,
223n66, 223n69
Churchill, Prime Minister Winston,
12, 13, 19–22, 24, 28, 40, 41, 42,
43–48, 51–52, 72, 100, 107–108,
163, 168, 179, 190n22, 191n26,
192n8, 195n44, 212n41, 217n35
Clarke, Lieutenant-Colonel Dudley
W., 21, 190n19
Coates, Captain John, 145–47, 222n52,
222n53
Colombia, 60, 62, 65
Comintern, 176
Commando Bay, 151
commandos, 21, 22, 25, 64, 74–75, 97,
163, 180, 190n20, 202n3, 222n53
Communications Division, 47
Communists, 36, 40, 149
Constantine, Major-General Charles,
76–77, 92
Consular Security Officers (CSO), 53
Coordinator of Information (COI),
80–82, 197n13, 198n1, 205n33
Copenhagen, 118, 119, 162
Counter-Intelligence (CE), 74,
125–29, 136
Cuba, 62–63
Cynthia, 54–55
Czechoslovakia, 15, 108, 163, 170

Daily Mail, 43

231

Dalton, Hugh, 27–30, 33–34, 35, 36, 37, 40, 103, 192n8, 195n44

Danish resistance, 120

D'Artois, Captain Guy, 140–41, 220n29, 220n32, 220n33

Davies, Tommy, 75–76

D-Day, 113–15, 140, 141, 159, 160–61, 213n57

de Gaulle, General Charles, 122–23, 141, 217n17, 225n20

Debenham-Taylor, John, 95–96

Dehler, Lieutenant John, 141

Delmer, Sefton, 31

Denmark, 16, 108, 118–20, 162–63, 166–67, 216n3, 227n54

Department of Justice, 55

Devlin, Frank, 90

Dibbler Mission, 145–48, 222n52

Dill, General Sir John, 21, 22

Director of Security Coordination, 47

Dittmar, Wilhelm, 65

Dolly, Lieutenant C.C., 152–53

Donovan, Colonel William "Wild Bill," 13, 48, 54, 59, 68, 70, 71, 72, 80, 81–82, 84, 99, 167, 172, 180, 191n32, 197n13, 197n21, 197n22, 205n33, 205n35, 229n16, 229n19

Drava River 145

Drew-Brook, Tommy, 45

Dunkirk, 11, 19, 191n33

Durovecz, Andy, 87–88, 90–91, 207n19

Dyle Plan, 16, 188n1

Eastern Front, 155, 157, 160

Ecuador, 61, 65

Eden, Anthony, 40

Eisenhower, General Dwight D. "Ike," 165–67

Electra House (EH), 23, 27, 28, 30, 191n2

England (see also Britain), 19, 20, 33, 42, 46, 48, 72

England Game, The, 129

Enigma, 25

Europe, 21, 25, 26, 28, 31, 34, 35, 39, 43, 46, 48, 52, 74, 78, 81, 84, 99, 100, 102, 113, 115–18, 121, 131, 132, 138, 142, 148, 149, 150, 154, 155, 159, 163, 164, 165, 166, 169, 174–75, 191n33, 194n26, 198n1, 210n21, 227n54, 228n3

F Section, 121–22, 129–30, 133–34, 135, 137, 139, 158

Fairbairn, Major William Ewart, 89

Far East, 52, 68, 73, 81, 109, 148–151, 154, 223n74

Farben (see also I.G. Farbenindustrie), 56

Federal Bureau of Investigation (FBI), 13, 44, 45, 56, 59, 70, 71, 78, 79–80, 92, 94, 180, 181, 197n13, 199n4, 202n52, 204n21, 204n25, 204n29

Fifth Army, 112

fifth columnists, 61

finishing school, 75, 77, 84, 95–96, 98

First World War, 16–17, 19, 45, 48, 56, 196n6

Flossenbürg, 137

Foot, M.R.D., 39–40, 41, 48–49, 167, 195n44

Foreign Office (FO), 23, 30, 40, 57, 59–60, 66–68, 120, 123–24, 144, 155–56, 169, 170, 171, 172, 177, 196n51, 219n7

France, 9, 11, 15, 16–17, 18, 19, 31, 32, 34, 39, 46, 73, 108, 109, 113, 121–22, 129–30, 133–41, 152, 156–57, 158, 159, 161–62, 164–66, 175,

192n18, 210n23, 217n17, 224n19, 225n20, 227n54

French ciphers, 55

French Forces of the Interior (FFI), 141, 159, 162, 225n20

French Resistance. *See under* resistance

Funkspiel, 129, 139, 139

Gelleny, Lieutenant Joe, 85–86, 97–98, 142, 145–48, 207n6, 222n52

General Motors, 90

General Staff (Research) (GS(R)), 23

German Army, 15, 144, 189n10
    2nd SS Panzer Division (*Das Reich*), 159
    11th Division, 160
    166 Infantry Division, 163
    223 Panzer Division. 162–63

Germany, 11–12, 15–19, 20–24, 26, 31, 32, 33, 34, 35, 37–39, 46, 51, 54, 56, 58, 61, 63, 74, 80, 102, 103–04, 108, 112–14, 115–16, 118–20, 125–30, 135, 138–39, 140, 143–44, 146, 155, 156–57, 160, 162, 163–64, 174, 176, 188n1, 189n6, 189n10, 192n5, 193n22, 194n26, 199n16, 204n28, 214n60, 217n35, 220n30, 220n32, 222n51, 226n42

Gestapo, 11, 119, 127–28, 130, 139–37, 138, 140, 156, 163, 165, 202n5

Goebbels, Joseph, 65

Goose Bay, 151

Gordon, Lieutenant Joe. *See* Joe Gelleny

Gort, General, the Viscount, 18, 189n9

Gouzenko, Igor, 208n31

Grasett, General, Sir A.E., 149

Greece, 123, 157, 158

Group A Schools, 84, 98

Group B Schools (*see also* Finishing Schools), 84, 98

GSI(k), 148

Gubbins, Major-General Colin, 33, 40, 50, 164–65, 166, 193n22, 196n51, 197n29, 217n35

guerrilla warfare, 12, 21–23, 33–35, 38, 73, 75, 104–05, 148–49, 150, 152, 158, 167, 190n19, 195n42, 205n38, 216n5, 220n28, 223n74

guerrillas, 23, 27, 33, 37–38, 75, 105, 127–28, 148–49, 150, 151, 152, 158, 160, 208n4, 211n33, 220n28,

Guter, Erich, 65

Hadik, 146–47

Hahn, Otto, 163

Hambro, Sir Charles, 58, 99–100

heavy water (deuterium oxide), 163–64, 225n38, 226n42

Heydrich, SS-*Obergruppenführer* Reinhard, 163

Himmler, *Reichsführer* Heinrich, 163

Hitler, Adolf, 12, 15, 16, 17, 25, 31, 43, 180, 192n5

Holland, 16, 17, 22, 102, 108, 109, 113, 129, 158, 166, 217n35, 218n37, 227n54

Home Defence (Security) Executive (*see also* Security Executive), 46

Hong Kong, 149–150

Hoover, J. Edgar, 13, 44, 45, 48, 54, 180, 204n28

Horthy, Admiral Miklós, 147

Hungary, 73, 87, 142–44, 147, 221n37, 221n45

Hydra, 92–93, 181, 207n27, 208n28

Indo-China, 148, 152

Industrial Intelligence Centre, 43

interrogation, 98, 127–29, 137,
    146–47, 218n1
Inter-Service Projects Board, 26, 191n2
irregular warfare, 25–28, 34, 39, 73,
    83, 105, 155
Ismay, General Hastings, 20
Italy, 23, 31, 34, 38, 55, 111–13, 147,
    156, 157, 228n3

Japan, 12, 27, 37, 51, 56, 58, 59, 61–64,
    65, 75, 79, 148–50, 151, 152–53,
    176, 178, 181, 223n62
Jedburghs, 160
Joint Chiefs of Staff (JCS), 20, 47,
    69–70, 82, 205n38, 209n11
Joint Intelligence Committee (JIC),
    26, 47, 169–70

Kai-Shek, Chiang, 150, 151
Karen guerrillas, 152
Kendall, Major Francis Woodley,
    149–51, 223n64

Lais, Alberto, 55
Lake Okanagan, 151
Lake Tinnsjo, 164
LATI airline, 65
Latin America, 47, 48, 51–52, 53,
    57–61, 65, 66–71, 72, 78, 198n1,
    200n20, 205n29,
Levy, Bert "Yank," 104–05, 195n42
London, 13, 19, 43, 48, 49, 73, 74,
    75, 76, 91–93, 99, 102, 124, 129,
    139, 150, 172, 200n20, 208n28,
    218n37, 228n3
Long Range Desert Group (LRDG), 22
Lord Halifax, 60–61, 201n30
Los Angeles, 54, 62
Luftwaffe, 9, 17, 18, 113, 190n12,
    192n18

Macalister, John, 130, 137–39
Macklin, Colonel W.H.S., 76–77,
    303n13
Malaya, 58, 148, 153
Malayan Peoples' Anti-Japanese
    Army, 148
Manstein, Major-General Erich von,
    17–18
Manstein Plan, 17–18, 189n5
maquis, 140, 157, 220n28
McKellar, Senator Kenneth, 57
McNaughton, Major-General Andrew,
    73–74, 203n12
Mediterranean, 161, 162, 228n3
Mellenthin, Major-General F. W. von,
    17, 18, 189n7
Menzies, Stewart, 40, 42, 44, 179
Meuse River, 15, 17
Mexico, 61, 62–64, 104–05
MI6 (*see also* Secret Intelligence
    Service [SIS]), 22, 93, 217n35,
    223n64
Middle East, 49, 75, 198n1, 210n21,
    228n3
Milice, 141, 220n30
Military District No. 2 (M.D. No. 2),
    76, 77
Military Intelligence (Research)
    (MI(R)), 23, 26, 27, 28, 33, 75
Military Intelligence Division (MID),
    79–80
Military Research Centre No. 2, 77
minister of economic warfare,
    173–75, 178
Ministry of Economic Warfare, 27, 30,
    31, 176, 191n2
Ministry of Information, 31
Morin, Guy (*see also* Gustave Daniel
    Alfred Bieler), 136
Mounier, Captain P.C. 152

Index

Mountbatten, Vice-Admiral Lord
Louis, 20, 49, 58
Musician circuit, 136

Nazis/Nazism, 19, 27, 49, 53, 54, 55,
60–65, 93, 113, 115, 129, 163,
180, 192n5, 219n4, 226n41,
Nelson, Sir Frank, 45
Netherlands. *See* Holland
Neutrality Acts, 44, 46, 79, 196n6
New York, 44–45, 47, 48, 54, 55, 56,
76, 77, 78, 91–93, 150, 179
NKVD. *See Varodnyy Komissariat
Vnutrennickh Del*
Noble, George (*see also* Commandant
Georges Bégué), 133
Normandy, 140, 160, 161–62
Normandy campaign, 140, 159,
161–62, 220n29
Norsk-Hydro, 163–64, 226n42
North Africa, 100, 209n16, 213n57
Norway, 33, 108, 109, 122, 157, 158,
162–64
Nye, Senator Gerald, 54, 196n6

occupied Europe, 11, 21, 31, 39, 74,
84, 113, 116, 117–18, 121, 131,
132, 138, 149, 159, 166
Office of Naval Intelligence (ONI), 53,
79, 80, 94, 204n28
Office of Strategic Services (OSS), 13,
47, 78, 81–83, 94, 97, 99–107,
111, 112, 166, 167, 170–72,
180–81, 197n13, 198n1, 205n38,
209n11, 209n16, 219n4, 227n54,
228n3, 229n19
Office of War Information (OWI), 78,
81, 94, 181
operations
Dragoon, 162

Freshman, 163–64
Gunnerside, 164
Oblivion, 150–51
Savanna, 32, 192n18
Tideway Green, 153
Torch, 100
Orfü, 146
Oshawa, 89, 90, 94, 33n208
Oshawa Wireless Station, 94, 33n208

parachute training, 97–98, 140
Paraguay, 64
Paris, 11, 135, 136, 138–39, 141,
155–56, 163
partisans, 38, 130, 145, 155, 157, 164,
217n30
Passport Control Officer (PCO),
44–46, 47
Pearl Harbor, 51–52, 56, 79, 81, 180
Pécs, 145–46, 222n53
Peru, 61, 64
Petawawa, 142
Phoney War, 16, 73
Pickersgill, Frank, 130, 137–39
Placke, Josef, 139
Poland, 15–16, 38–39. 108, 139, 157,
158, 170, 195n37
political warfare (PW), 31, 198n1,
205n38, 209n11, 214n60
Political Warfare Executive (PWE),
31, 178, 214n60
Portal, Air Chief Marshal Charles, 40,
123
propaganda, 23, 27–28, 29, 30–32, 52,
54, 56, 65, 66, 81, 84, 116, 119,
173, 177, 191n32, 192n6, 198n1,
214n60
Prosper circuit, 138

Ramat David, 75

Rawicz, 139
Reconnaissance Unit, the, 149
recruiting, 12–13, 35–37, 42–43, 45,
    48, 52, 53–55, 72–75, 78, 84,
    95–97, 111, 113, 116, 118, 124,
    127, 134, 140, 141, 142, 149,
    150–51, 168, 196n10, 198n1,
    202n5, 223n69
Reichssicherheitshauptamt (Reich
    Security Main Office), 163
Reims, 140
Research Department Explosive
    (RDX), 106
Research Units (RU), 31
resistance, 23, 29, 35, 52, 74, 102–03,
    109–13, 115, 116, 124–25, 126,
    130, 133, 164, 165, 166–67, 173,
    191n33, 193n25, 205n38, 210n24,
    227n54, 228n1, 228n2
    Albanian, 122
    Danish, 120
    Far East, 148
    French, 9–11, 121–22, 130, 133–
        35, 136, 138–39, 140–41, 158,
        159–61, 162, 214n60, 219n11,
        220n28, 220n30, 225n20
    Hungarian, 143–45, 22n53
    Latin America, 66
    Norwegian, 122–23, 193n22,
        211n33
    South America, 93
Rhodes, 36
Rieth, Dr. Kent, 56
Ringway, 98
Rockefeller Center, 46
Romania, 73, 78, 221n43
Roosevelt, Franklin D., 21, 48, 49,
    79–81, 195n37, 196n6
Roper-Caldbeck, Lieutenant-Colonel
    Arthur Terence, 92, 204n18

Royal Air Force (RAF), 49, 57, 107,
    118–19, 123, 132–33, 136, 140,
    181, 211n39, 212n45, 221n45
Royal Canadian Air Force, 181
Royal Canadian Mounted Police
    (RCMP), 47, 94, 150, 207n6,
    208n31
Royal Corps of Signals, 93
Royal Flying Corps, 42
Royal Navy, 19, 57
Rural Realty Company Ltd., 76

sabotage, 11, 12–13, 22–23, 28, 29–30,
    32–35, 39, 41, 58–59, 60, 61, 64,
    67, 68, 74, 78, 79, 85, 102–07, 108
    –09, 110, 111, 114, 116, 118–20,
    126, 130, 133, 135, 136, 142, 145,
    148, 151, 155–59, 161–62, 167,
    173, 177, 180, 193n25, 200n20,
    204n25, 205n38, 201n24, 211n33,
    212n45, 219n7, 222n53, 223n74,
    226n42, 227n54
San Francisco, 54
Saône Valley, 139
Schlieffen Plan, 17
Schutzstaffel (SS), 139, 159, 163, 214n60
Seattle, 54
secret armies, 12, 23, 29, 31, 33, 35,
    102, 103, 107–09, 110, 115, 116,
    158, 193n25
Secret Intelligence Service (SIS) (*see
    also* MI6), 22, 27, 28–29, 40–41,
    42, 44–45, 46, 56, 60, 69, 72, 92, 93,
    97, 123–24, 169–73, 178, 179, 181,
    192n10, 197n17, 200n20, 217n35
Section D, 23, 26–28, 30
Security Executive, 46, 70
Selborne, Lord, 173–79, 217n17, 228n2
Sherwood, Robert, 48,
Ship Observer Unit (SOU), 199n4

Index

Shwebo, 152
Siam, 148
Sicherheitsdienst (SD), 146
Singapore, 75, 148
Skilbeck, Lieutenant-Colonel
　Cuthbert, 204n18
Skogen, 127–28
SO 1, 30–31
SO 2, 30–32, 34
SO 3, 30–31
Société National de Chemin de Fer, 162
Sound City Films, 43
South America, 13, 28, 53, 57–59,
　63–64, 67, 69–70, 78, 93, 109,
　181, 202n52, 208n29
South American Security Scheme, 78
Special Air Service (SAS), 22
Special Boat Service (SBS), 22
Special Training School (STS), 75, 76,
　203n8, 209n7
　STS 101, 75, 148, 149, 223n62
　STS 102, 75
　STS 103, *see* Camp X
St. Quentin, 136
Standard Oil, 56
State Department, 44, 57, 59, 67,
　68–69, 70, 79, 170
Station IX, 105
Station XII , 106
Station M, 46–47, 105, 211n35
Stephenson, Sir William, 13, 42–52,
　54, 56–57, 59, 66, 68, 71–72, 75,
　76, 80, 81, 84, 91, 93, 94, 95, 99,
　150, 180–81, 197n13, 197n17,
　197n29, 205n35
Stewart, Sir Findlater, 172
Stoltz espionage group, 65
Student Assessment Board (SAB), 95
submarines, 59, 60–61, 62, 63, 64,
　226n42

subversion, 11, 12, 13, 28, 32, 34,
　45, 39, 53, 74, 79, 102–03, 105,
　115–16, 117, 134, 142, 148, 156,
　158, 166, 204n25, 216n3, 221n43
Supreme Headquarters Allied
　Expeditionary Force (SHAEF),
　101, 113–14, 115, 161, 164–165,
　166–67, 214n60, 227n54.
Surrender Group, 143–44, 221–22
Szent-Györgyi, Albert, 142–43

Tanjung Balai, 148
Taschereau, Captain R.J., 152
Taylor, Alfred James, 75–76,
Telekrypton, 93
Thomas, Mike (*see also* Mike Turk),
　145, 222n52
Tito, Josip Broz, 145
Toronto, 45, 76, 85, 86, 89, 90, 93,
　142
torture, 12, 73, 90–91, 98, 127–29,
　137, 138–39
Tse-Tung, Mao, 150
Turk, Mike (*see also* Mike Thomas),
　145–47, 222n52
Turkey, 36, 109, 142
Typex, 93

United Nations, 57, 59, 120

V1 rocket, 140
*Varodnyy Komissariat Vnutrennickh
　Del* (People's Commissariat for
　Internal Affairs) (NKVD), 171
Vemork, 163
Venezuela, 57, 60, 61, 62, 64, 66
Vichy French Embassy, 55

War Cabinet, 26, 28, 30, 31, 33, 34,
　155, 168

War Office, 22, 23, 27, 33, 73–74, 112,
    135, 203n12
Washington DC, 47, 54–55, 56, 68, 75,
    92–93, 150, 200n20
Wavell, General Archibald, 21–22
Wehrmacht, 18, 162
Welwyn Experimental Laboratory. *See*
    Station IX
Western Union, 92
Whitby, 75, 76, 93
White House, 47
Wilson, General Sir Henry Maitland,
    162
Winnipeg, 42
wireless operators, 73–74, 96, 109, 165
WRUL (radio station), 54, 55

Yugoslavs, 12, 55, 73, 78, 97, 124, 141,
    145, 158, 221n35

Z Force, 149
Zugliget, 147

ABOUT THE AUTHOR

Colonel Bernd Horn, OMM, MSM, CD, Ph.D., is a retired Regular Force infantry officer who has held key command and staff appointments in the Canadian Armed Forces, including Deputy Commander of Canadian Special Operations Forces Command; Commanding Officer of the 1st Battalion, the Royal Canadian Regiment; and Officer Commanding 3 Commando, the Canadian Airborne Regiment. He is currently the Director of the Canadian Special Operations Forces Command Professional Development Centre, an appointment he fills as a reservist. Dr. Horn is also an adjunct professor of the Centre for Military and Strategic Studies, University of Calgary, as well as an adjunct professor of history at the Royal Military College of Canada. He is also a Fellow at the Canadian Defence and Foreign Affairs Institute. He has authored, co-authored, edited, or co-edited forty books and well over a hundred monographs/chapters/articles on military history, Special Operations Forces, leadership, and military affairs.

VISIT US AT

Dundurn.com
@dundurnpress
Facebook.com/dundurnpress
Pinterest.com/dundurnpress